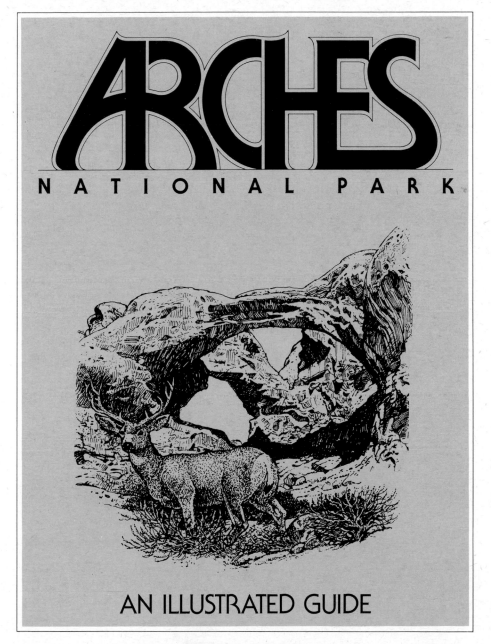

ARCHES

NATIONAL PARK

AN ILLUSTRATED GUIDE

By John F. Hoffman

Foreword by David D. May

Photography by **Frank L. Mendonca** Drawings by **John D. Dawson**

**WESTERN
RECREATIONAL
PUBLICATIONS**

SAN DIEGO, CALIFORNIA

Dedicated gratefully to my parents
Ralph and **Floy Hoffman**
who awakened my interest in the outdoors.
Without their enduring generosity and
encouragement, this book could never
have been written.

*Unnamed Arch on East
side of Eagle Park*

Western Recreational Publications
P.O. Box 12645
San Diego, California 92112-3645

Library of Congress Catalog Card Number:
85-50727

International Standard Book Number:
0-934148-02-3 (softcover)
0-934148-03-1 (hardcover)

Production

Art direction   John Odam
Cover design   Tom Gould
Editorial services   Clement David Hellyer
Maps   Andy Lucas, John Odam, and John Dawson
Typesetting   Thompson Type
Color separation   American Color Corporation
Printing   Arts & Crafts Press

Manufactured in the United States of America

Revised, Enlarged Edition

Current printing (last digit):
10 9 8 7 6 5 4 3 2 1

Morton Wesley Huber
May 1989

CONTENTS

Cover Photographs
Outside front cover: **Delicate Arch**
Inside front cover: **Ring Arch**
Inside back cover: **Turret Arch**

FOREWORD

This book contains new and fully authenticated information about Arches National Park. Some of it contradicts the traditional stories and conventional impressions about the Park's origin and early development.

The book's author, John F. Hoffman, is not just **interested** in the Canyon Country of southeastern Utah, he is **in love** with it — especially with Arches.

The Canyonlands Natural History Association is pleased to have played a role in the production of this book. The Association is a private, nonprofit group organized for the purpose of complementing the educational and interpretive goals of the National Park Service. The Association becomes involved in many educational projects, but participation in a commercial publishing venture is exceedingly uncommon. However, the opportunity to help disseminate John Hoffman's comprehensive knowledge of the Park was seen to have such public value that the Association's Board of Directors was pleased to approve the suggestion of Peter L. Parry, superintendent of Arches National Park, that the Association involve itself in this project. As a participant in the Board's decision, and as an individual whose profession it is to help develop publicly available information about national parks, I am delighted to see this book become a reality.

John Hoffman's interest in Arches and the red-rock country of southeastern Utah dates back to the 1950s. When he walked into my office in 1973 and announced his plan to conduct extensive field research on the region's history and geography, I was glad to arrange for some minor administrative assistance to facilitate his work. John settled down to his self-imposed task, which he at first estimated would require a year. He discovered very quickly that his time schedule was unrealistic, given the depth of the investigation he planned to

pursue. He found also that neither the history nor the geography of Arches stopped at the Park's boundary, and that his interests were equally unconfined. As John's knowledge grew, the horizons of his interests expanded just a little bit faster. Those horizons continue to expand today, and I suspect that they always will. John periodically announces that he is finished here now, and is ready to move on to another project. I doubt it; I just don't believe it. I feel confident that, as this page soars through the printing press, John is telephoning one more old-timer in search of information, or puzzling over some discrepancy in the historical record.

John and I do not always see things alike; to be frank, there have been times when we have disagreed intensely. But there never has been a moment when I have failed to be impressed by his encyclopedic knowledge of and love for the Canyon Country. Those attributes of his are, I believe, responsible for the fact that this is not just another book about Arches National Park. This is, in fact, **the** book that future authors will quote or "restate" when they want to be accurate.

David D. May
Executive Secretary
Canyonlands Natural History Association

[Opposite] Arches National Park is more than just arches. It is also the site of many other types of dramatic landforms. **The Three Gossips**, in Courthouse Towers, is but one example of such spectacular non-arch features. The monolith's towering "gossips" were sculptured by weathering and erosional processes from the reddish Slick Rock Member of the Entrada Sandstone. They stand majestically on the beige Dewey Bridge Member of the Entrada. The Three Gossips have also been called The Three Graces—certainly a more dignified title for this distinctive landform, but one that lacks the humorous connotations which the present name evokes.

[Right] The **Parade of Elephants** is one of many Park landforms with imaginative titles. This fanciful herd of larger-than-life pachyderms plods along in rocky silence immediately south of Double Arch, in The Windows section.

This photograph may be the first ever taken of **Delicate Arch,** now probably the best-known natural arch in the world, and widely recognized as the insignia landform of Arches National Park. The photographer is unknown, as is the date the photo was made, although it was taken sometime between 1907 and 1910. Seen standing beneath the span are Flora Stanley and two of her children:

Ferol (left) and Esther. Mrs. Stanley's father, John Wesley Wolfe, crippled in the Civil War while serving as a Union soldier, came to southeastern Utah's red-rock country from Ohio. In 1898, with his son Fred, Wolfe established a small cattle ranch, the "Bar DX" (brand $\overline{DX}$), in the vicinity of Delicate Arch. In 1910, the Wolfe family moved back to Ohio. The ranch's headquarters were close to the west bank of Salt Wash, near today's parking lot at the start of the foot trail to Delicate Arch. Wolfe Cabin, a rustic, one-room log structure, still stands at that spot. It has been restored by the National Park Service.

INTRODUCTION

To many visitors, Arches National Park is a preposterous land. It is a seemingly chaotic terrain dominated by strange — even freakish — features: streaked sandstone arches, balanced rocks, hundreds of jutting and weirdly shaped stone spires, gigantic red-rock monuments, colossal cliffs, abysmal canyons, and expansive sworls of slickrock. An altogether surrealistic scene: fantastic and incongruous. Much of this bizarre landscape looks like the tortured product of Salvador Dali's brush.

It is harsh country, a land stripped bare by the relentless hand of erosion. Still, though it is haphazard in appearance, this terrain is not an aberration, nor a trick of nature. The geology of Arches is the direct — and predictable — result of systematic processes.

Though the barren Parkland appears nearly devoid of wildlife, it is not. Many animal species inhabit the area, but because of the adaptations they have developed to survive in this arid environment their presence, especially that of the larger animals, is not readily apparent to Park visitors.

In summer, sun-drenched days with scorching temperatures commonly prevail, while in winter, dark, fiercely cold, and snowy days are not at all rare. Intrusive and irritating winds often rake the country, particularly in the spring.

Although rugged, Arches is also fragile. Weathered sandstone ledges may crumble easily when stepped upon. The delicate crust of cryptogamic soil common throughout the Park — and vital to its ecology — instantly breaks apart when trodden upon, exposing the underlying sandy ground to erosion.

The land now known as Arches was long generally shunned by man. Indians used it only occasionally, going there to quarry chert for arrow points and stone implements, and to hunt and gather foodstuffs. Early whites in the region used today's Parkland to graze cattle and sheep, prospected its broken surface for precious metals, and explored for oil. Not until Arches became part of the national park system — and then only after paved roads were constructed — did substantial numbers of people venture into the rocky realm.

Fins at Sand Dune Arch

To some visitors, Arches is nothing but a wasteland. For them, the Park is a dry, dusty, damnable place — a hell hole: the domain of rattlesnakes and scorpions and cacti. To these onlookers, Arches is not "civilized"; it is raw and inhospitable. The starkness, the primitiveness of the area shock those who are too removed from the reality of nature, or too urbanized, to appreciate or understand this land. It seems to them forbidding and painfully primordial. Seeing no value in it — and, in some cases, fearing it — they are impatient to be gone from what, to them, is a grim, desolate, and Godforsaken spot.

To the perceptive, Arches is a desert paradise, a land of rare qualities, a land offering much more than spectacular topography. For those who will take the time to look, not just at the intriguing natural arches, but also at the grains of sand, a realization will come — subtly for some, dramatically for others — that man shares a oneness with nature. His well-being, indeed his survival, depend upon the physical environment — tamed and wild. For those who will live in harmony with nature, not in confrontation with it, life will be more tranquil and satisfying.

There is also at the Parkland an affirmation of a stark reality: no landforms, including natural arches, are eternal. Like man himself, these sandstone spans are transitory, enduring a mere millisecond on the clock of geologic time.

True, there is a harshness to Arches. Yet there is also a freshness that infuses cleanliness and renewal — and even hope.

GEOGRAPHICAL SETTING

ARCHES NATIONAL PARK is located in the spectacular red-rock country of southeastern Utah, just north of the small, Mormon-founded town of Moab. It covers some 73,234 acres, or about 114 square miles, of semidesert terrain. Hundreds of natural arches, among them scores of significant spans, are found in this rugged locale, perhaps the greatest concentration of these unusual landforms in any area of equal size in the world. The Parkland has also numerous spires and pinnacles, many of them eroded into fantastic shapes, with some of them bearing an uncanny resemblance to animals and humans.

COLORADO PLATEAU— LAND OF PARKS

Arches lies on the Colorado Plateau, a vast and semiarid highland of strikingly colorful and rugged country. An almost hypnotically beautiful part of the American West, the Colorado Plateau is noted for its many spectacular erosional landforms, rich deposits of fossilized plants and animals, ancient Indian ruins, and historic sites, some dating from the Spanish Period. These outstanding features have led to the establishment of eight national parks and twenty-one national monuments on the plateau-land, several of them among the most famous in the national park system. Here are the majestic vistas of the incomparable Grand Canyon, the brilliantly colored and delicately carved spires of Bryce Canyon, the massive-walled canyon of Zion, the great soaring arc of Rainbow Bridge, the stone logs of Petrified Forest, the prehistoric Anasazi Indian cliff dwellings at Mesa Verde, and the old Mormon fort—Winsor Castle—at Pipe Spring on the Arizona Strip.

Location and Size

The Colorado Plateau extends from the western slope of the high Southern Rocky Mountains of Colorado and New Mexico to the desert basins and mountain ranges of Utah, Arizona, and New Mexico. This great upland spreads over approximately 150,000 square miles—most of western Colorado and northwestern New Mexico, almost all of northern Arizona, and virtually the full sweep of eastern and southern Utah. The plateau straddles the Four Corners, the only point in the country where the boundaries of four states meet, those of Colorado, New Mexico, Arizona, and Utah. Although a seemingly enormous region, the Colorado Plateau actually accounts for slightly less than 5 per cent of the area of the forty-eight contiguous states.

The plateau's outline is roughly similar to that of a pear. A broad curved base extends east to west, from northwestern New Mexico across most of northern Arizona, with a neck tapering northward into western Colorado and eastern and southern Utah. The greatest width of the Colorado Plateau, about 400 miles, is near the northern boundaries of New Mexico and Arizona, while its extreme length of more than 450 miles stretches from northeastern Utah to about the midpoint of the New Mexico-Arizona boundary.

[Opposite page] The soaring arcs of **Double Arch**, suggestive of great flying buttresses of cathedrals, adjoin the southwest side of Elephant Butte in The Windows section of the Park. The larger arch, with a span of 160 feet and a height of 105 feet, is the second largest in the Park. The smaller arch is 60 feet wide and 61 feet high. The Slick Rock Member of the Entrada Sandstone, stained by streaks of desert varnish, forms the spans and abutments. Wavy strata of the Dewey Bridge Member floor the openings. In past years, Double Arch was also called Double Windows, Twinbow Bridge, and The Jug Handles.

[Right] Illuminated by the golden glow of an autumn afternoon, **Duck-on-the-Rock**, a tapering spire of Entrada Sandstone, rises southwest of Turret Arch in The Windows section. Its imaginative name is credited to Harry Reed, custodian of Arches in the late 1930s when the area was a national monument. On the skyline are the snowcapped La Sal Mountains, southeast of the Park.

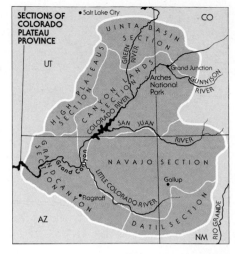

Colorado Plateau Physiographic Province

The Colorado Plateau is one of thirty-four natural regions constituting the United States. These regions, called *physiographic provinces* by geographers, are primarily defined by geologic structure. Each province has distinctive physical features which give it a unique character. Major John Wesley Powell, a distinguished nineteenth-century American scientist and explorer, made the first division of the United States into physiographic provinces in 1895. The Colorado Plateau Physiographic Province is distinguished by having:

☐ Vast areas of relatively horizontal layers of sedimentary rocks, deposited in layer-cake fashion. At many places in Arches National Park, exposures of nearly horizontal rock bedding may be observed.

☐ High altitudes, generally more than a mile above sea level, with some peaks reaching almost 13,000 feet. Altitudes in the Park range from 3,960 feet—the lowest point—near the U.S. Highway 191 bridge over the Colorado River, to 5,653 feet at the summit of Elephant Butte in The Windows section. Lofty Mount Peale, twenty miles southeast of the Park,

in the La Sal Mountains, attains an elevation of 12,721 feet.

☐ Pronounced, angular topography, accentuated by bold and steep escarpments and massive cliffs. The vertical walls of Park Avenue, the cliffs of the Colorado River canyon, and The Great Wall west of the Petrified Sand Dunes exemplify such topography at Arches.

☐ Conspicuous areas of nearly barren and bald rock aptly called *slickrock*. The Petrified Sand Dunes, lying between Courthouse Towers and The Windows, is a particularly broad tract of slickrock in the Park.

☐ Many dramatic erosional landforms, including natural arches and bridges, slender spires and towering monuments, buttes, and numerous deep, steep-walled gorges and canyons. All of these features can be seen at Arches.

☐ Brilliantly colorful scenery, presenting a veritable rainbow of rock colors. Red predominates at Arches; among the other rock and soil colors are orange, yellow, green, purple, brown, gray, black, and white.

☐ Dome or *laccolithic* mountains, formed by molten rock slowly intruding between layers of sedimentary rock, causing the overlying rocks to bulge upward. Three groups of laccolithic mountains can be seen from Arches: the La Sal Mountains, southeast of the Park; the Abajo Mountains, to the south; and the Henry Mountains, to the west.

☐ A few large, dead volcanoes and many cinder cones, volcanic necks, and lava flows. None of these features, however, are present at Arches.

☐ A generally semiarid climate, with hot summers and cold winters, an average annual precipitation of less than 10 inches, and a high evaporation potential. At Arches, the yearly precipitation is about 8.5 inches.

☐ Predominantly sparse vegetation, with

heavier growths at springs, along banks of streams and rivers, and with forests on the higher slopes of isolated mountains and the tops of high plateaus. More than 25 per cent of the Parkland is covered by desert scrub, and nearly 45 per cent by an open "pygmy forest" of junipers and piñons.

Canyon Lands Section

The Colorado Plateau Physiographic Province is subdivided into six sections: the Uinta Basin, Canyon Lands, High Plateaus, Navajo, Datil, and Grand Canyon. Much of the northern half of the province contains the Canyon Lands Section, a large, barren, and irregularly shaped tract centered approximately on The Confluence—the junction of the Colorado River with its principal tributary, the Green River.

The Canyon Lands Section is the most rugged and least accessible part of the Colorado Plateau. Although numerous and extensive canyons characterize the province, they predominate in the Canyon Lands Section. Locally the area is referred to as "Canyon Country." Here are also great expanses of slickrock. Probably a quarter of the terrain is exposed stone.

Four of the eight national parks on the Colorado Plateau are entirely or partially within the Canyon Lands Section. Arches National Park lies near its northern edge. Nearby, astride the spectacularly broken country surrounding The Confluence, is the epitome of the Canyon Lands Section, Canyonlands National Park. Capitol Reef National Park stretches along the western boundary, and the upper reach of Grand Canyon—the narrow corridor of Marble Gorge—cuts deeply through the extreme southwestern part of the Canyon Lands Section.

WEATHER AND CLIMATE

During the summer months, when most tourists visit Arches National Park, the

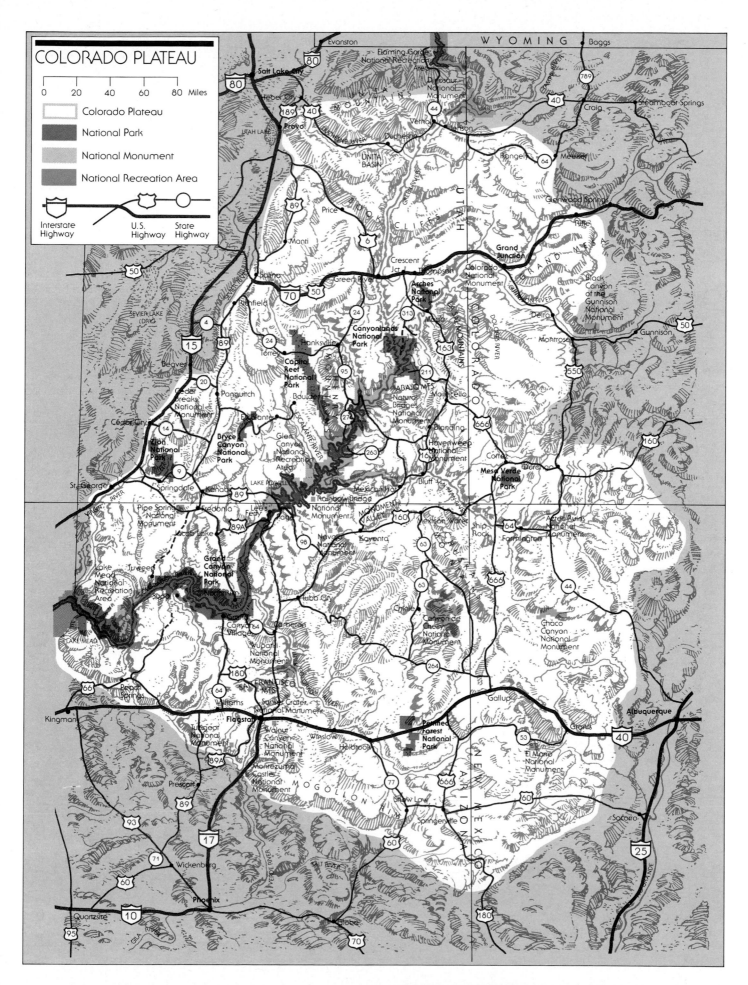

[Right] A **pothole**, like this one in the Petrified Sand Dunes, is a depression eroded into rock. After rains, it fills with water, becoming a natural—although temporary—cistern, providing a watering hole for animal life. A very large pothole is called a *tank*.

[Below] Resembling a tawny, billowing sea, the **Petrified Sand Dunes** sweep across the area between Courthouse Towers and The Windows. In Early Jurassic time, about 180 million years ago, winds from the northwest blew into the region that is now the Colorado Plateau, and deposited fine-grained sand, creating a vast sand-dune desert. These dunes were later covered by layers of marine and continental deposits. The buried dunes were compacted and cemented to form Navajo Sandstone. Eventually, erosion removed the overlying strata and exposed the crossbedding of the ancient dunes.

weather is usually hot and dry. To them, the starkly barren land seems forever arid. But year-round residents of the surrounding area will testify that scattered, heavy thunderstorms can at times be devastating, and the winter months cold and snowy. The weather at Arches, an early ranger observed, "is certainly consistent. When it is dry and hot, it is really dry and hot; and when it rains it doesn't put out any half-portions."

Climate is defined as the average or characteristic weather conditions that prevail in a particular area. *Weather* is the day-to-day condition of the atmosphere, that is, all of the short-term changes of temperature, moisture, and air movement. The average person may not recognize the immense importance of climate to his world. Climate plays a decisive role in determining the landforms, soils, flora and fauna, and cultural features of every region.

A weather station is located at the Park's Visitors Center. However, its readings are representative of only a small area of the Parkland. Situated in Moab Canyon, and close to the Park's western boundary, the station has an altitude of about 4,000 feet above sea level, a lower elevation than most of Arches. A more typical climatic estimate for the Park can be obtained by averaging weather data from Moab and Thompson. Both have meteorological records which date back much longer than at Arches. Moab is about three miles south of the Park's boundary while Thompson is some nine miles north. Theoretically, the climatic characteristics of Arches should lie between these two stations.

Steppe Climate

Climatologists classify the climate of the Parkland as *steppe*, meaning that it is a dry climate, but has greater precipitation than a desert. It is semiarid, that is, the steppe climate is transitional between desert and humid climates.

Temperature

The yearly temperature spread at Arches is great, with the extremes ranging from below 0°F in winter to a maximum of about 110°F in summer. Fluctuations can be dramatically sudden, with temperatures dropping from the low fifties to below zero in a few hours.

The average annual temperature in the Park is about 54°F. July is the hottest month, with maximum readings averaging almost 80°F. While daily highs during the summer often exceed 100°F, the heat is less oppressive than in more humid regions because of lower humidity. Nevertheless, a ranger once complained during the super-heat of July, "I find that I can absorb just so much of this Utah sunshine and after about the second trip of the day through The Windows section I begin to wish for a cool shady spot for a siesta."

The mean temperature of the coldest month, January, is approximately 28°F. Winter temperatures are cold enough that the Colorado River, which flows along the east and south boundaries of the Park, will freeze over.

The *frost-free season*—the number of days the temperature is continuously above 32°F—runs from the last frost in spring to the first in fall, or about 177 days for Arches.

Sunny skies and clear nights prevail most of the year at the Park. These atmos-pheric conditions create wide *diurnal temperature ranges*—broad contrasts in the air temperature between day and night. During the long, typically cloudless daylight hours of summer, the Parkland receives considerable radiant energy from the sun—*insolation*—that rapidly heats the rocky terrain and raises the air temperature, often to a torrid reading by mid-afternoon. But once the sun sets, the ground cools and the temperature drops, usually to a pleasant, refreshing level, providing relief for inhabitants and visitors of the Arches region.

Precipitation

Precipitation—rain, drizzle, snow, sleet, and hail—is meager and highly variable at Arches. The mean yearly precipitation for the Park is approximately 8.5 inches. The wettest month, October, receives about one inch of moisture. May, June, and July have historically been the driest months, receiving for this quarter-year period only about 1.6 inches. June, the driest month, has approximately one-half inch of precipitation.

Locally heavy rainfall comes from summer thunderstorms at Arches. These often violent storms develop from towering, anvil-shaped cumulonimbus clouds, usually in moisture-laden air masses from the Gulf of Mexico. Accompanied by sharp gusts of wind, thunderstorms appear very

The Marching Men, a line of towering pinnacles, parade along the southern edge of Klondike Bluffs, a raw jumble of rock west of Salt Valley, in the remote northwest corner of the Park. The large figures were carved from Late Jurassic-age Entrada Sandstone, their reddish shafts formed in the Slick Rock Member, and the white capping layer—where present—in the Moab Member. The Marching Men were once called The Fingers. In early 1938, Harry Reed, the second custodian of Arches, visited Klondike Bluffs, which were then outside the boundary of Arches but proposed for inclusion. Reed was enthusiastic about what he saw, calling it "one of the most scenic sections of the area," and noting that The Fingers were well named, and among the section's outstanding attractions. On November 25, 1938, President Franklin D. Roosevelt signed a proclamation which added about fifty-three square miles to Arches, including the Klondike Bluffs. In the lower right foreground of the photograph is a blackbrush, a ubiquitous Parkland plant. A member of the rose family, this spiny, drought-resistant plant dominates about 90 per cent of the Park's desert-scrub biotic community. Behind it lies a weathered juniper log, while beyond, dotting the sandy soil stretching to the base of the pinnacles, are bushy evergreen junipers.

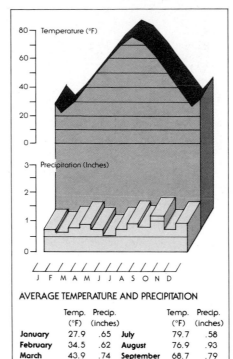

AVERAGE TEMPERATURE AND PRECIPITATION

	Temp. (°F)	Precip. (inches)		Temp. (°F)	Precip. (inches)
January	27.9	.65	July	79.7	.58
February	34.5	.62	August	76.9	.93
March	43.9	.74	September	68.7	.79
April	54.5	.77	October	56.1	1.03
May	63.5	.56	November	40.6	.57
June	72.4	.50	December	31.5	.76
			ANNUAL	**54.2**	**8.50**

rapidly, producing lightning and thunder, dropping rain in near-cloudburst proportions, and noticeably cooling the countryside. The resulting rapid runoff can be very destructive. In 1941, rainstorms repeatedly washed out the old dirt road leading to The Windows section. The harassed custodian, Henry Schmidt, lamented, "The rains came, the winds stayed with us and much of the road is now somewhere between Arches and Boulder Dam. I don't like to 'cry' about the road to The Windows, but now and then, after filling the same washout three times in six days, I sort of 'holler' at myself, often producing a fair-sized echo that re-echoes until it dwindles down to a sigh."

Dry spells seem to persist with unrelenting vengeance. In 1934, a record-breaking drought reduced the mighty Colorado River to mere creek-size at Arches.

At Arches National Park, aridity is definitely an asset. Without the arid climate, few of the fantastic landforms which characterize the Parkland would exist. In humid climates, sedimentary rocks—sandstones, shales, mudstones, limestones, and conglomerates, the types of rocks found in the Park—are less resistant to erosion, and form a rounded, subdued landscape rather than the angular topography seen in the Parkland.

Snow is common at Arches in the winter months. The mean annual snowfall is about 10.65 inches. Snowfall may accumulate to a depth of several feet at higher Parkland elevations.

Potential evaporation exceeds precipitation in arid and semiarid regions. Although the capacity for evaporation is high at Arches, the water supply is so small that actual evaporation is quite low.

Wind

Strong winds are frequent in the spring, rushing over the flats and whistling through the arches and around cliffs, in-tensifying the raw, barren character of the Parkland. These wind-harried days can be irritating, making both people and wildlife uncomfortable. Arthur Winslow, in his 1898 report on what is now called Landscape Arch, noted the area's winds, commenting that "strong and prolonged winds are frequent here, as anyone who has sojourned in that country can testify to his misery."

Occasionally, gale-force winds produce veritable sandstorms that sweep menacingly across the land. Such sandstorms are among the most spectacular features of arid lands, where the loose, dry soil—unprotected by a nearly continuous mantle of vegetation—can be carried easily into the air by strong winds.

Storm Tracks

Arches National Park is situated on storm tracks from the Pacific Ocean and Gulf of Mexico, the two principal sources of moisture for southeastern Utah. Winter and spring storm systems move east from the Pacific, crossing the Cascade Mountains of the Pacific Northwest, the high Sierra Nevada in California, and the mountain ranges of the Great Basin before reaching the Arches region. As the moist Pacific air currents rise over these great mountainous barriers, substantial precipitation occurs. This type of precipitation is called *orographic*, and occurs when moist, moving air is forced up topographical obstacles. The resulting precipitation leaves the air relatively dry. As a consequence, a *rain-shadow* (an area of low precipitation) spreads east of the mountains.

COLORADO RIVER

The Colorado River forms eleven miles of the Park's eastern and southern boundaries, from the mouth of Salt Wash on the east downstream to the U.S. Highway 191 bridge. For the entire distance, the river runs deeply entrenched in a narrow, steep-walled gorge of reddish sandstone.

All of Arches drains into the Colorado, primarily through two intermittent streams: Salt Wash and Courthouse Wash. Salt Wash has the most extensive drainage system in the Park, but measurements of its flow are not recorded. However, the flow of Courthouse Wash, which enters the Colorado a short distance downstream from the U.S. Highway 191 bridge, is gaged. Draining an area of 162 square miles, not all of which lies in Arches, Courthouse Wash has an average daily discharge of 2.12 cubic feet per second (cfs),* or 1,540 acre-feet per year.† The maximum recorded discharge, 12,300 cfs, occurred on August 5, 1957. In contrast, there is no recorded flow at times each year.

The American "Nile"

The Colorado—principal river of the Southwest—has been called the "Nile of America." Like the mighty Nile, the Colorado is classified by geographers as an *exotic river*, or one that has its headwaters in a humid area and flows into an arid region. Such rivers are literally lifestreams for the desert lands through which they flow.

---

*A cubic foot per second is equivalent to approximately 7.48 gallons of water per second or 448.8 gallons per minute.

†One acre-foot is the quantity of water required to cover an acre to the depth of one foot, or 325,829 gallons; an acre-foot of water is approximately the quantity of water needed to support five city dwellers for one year.

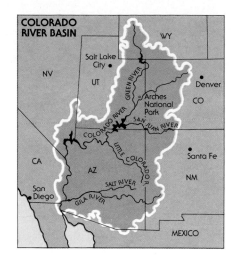

COLORADO RIVER BASIN

Length, Course, and Basin
The Colorado River is about 1,450 miles long and drains a basin of some 244,000 square miles. It is an international river: the last ninety miles of its course lie in Mexico, where it drains an area of about 1,000 square miles. In the United States, the river basin encompasses approximately 243,000 square miles, or slightly more than a twelfth of the total area of the forty-eight conterminous states, including about 90 per cent of the Colorado Plateau. The river basin spreads over parts of seven states—Wyoming, Colorado, Utah, New Mexico, Arizona, Nevada, and California.

Rising in north-central Colorado from the slopes of 12,940-foot Mount Richthofen—on the Continental Divide in Rocky Mountain National Park, about seventy-five miles from Denver—the growing river plunges southwest. It emerges onto the Colorado Plateau near the small town of Rifle, Colorado, about 100 airline miles northeast of Arches. Sixty-four river miles below the Park is The Confluence—meeting place of the Colorado with its principal tributary, the Green River. Most of the Colorado's 300-mile course across the Colorado Plateau is through deep canyons, isolating the river from much of the adjacent uplands. Leaving the plateau at the foot of the Grand Canyon, the Colorado runs southward to its mouth at the head of the Gulf of California. The flow, however, now rarely reaches tidewater because of upstream dams and diversions for irrigation and power.

Discharge, Sediment Load, and Temperature
The river gaging station nearest to Arches is about twenty miles upstream from the Park's eastern boundary, and one mile below the mouth of the Dolores River, on the east bank. Records date back to January 1895, although from 1895 to 1910 calendar-year estimates only are available. Several staff and chain gages were maintained also at the Moab bridge, from October 1, 1913 to November 10, 1914. The flow at the Moab gaging station was comparable to the discharge recorded on the gage below the mouth of the Dolores.

From its alpine headwaters to The Confluence—roughly 400 river miles, or nearly 28 per cent of its total length—the Colorado has an annual discharge of about 5,600,000 acre-feet, from a drainage basin of approximately 26,500 square miles, 84 per cent of which is in western Colorado and the remaining 16 per cent in east-central Utah.

The river flow fluctuates between the peak period in April, May, and June to low run-offs during August and September. The average daily discharge recorded at the gaging station below the Dolores River is 7,711 cfs, or 5,587,000 acre-feet per year. The maximum daily discharge recorded at the gaging station occurred on June 19, 1917 at 9 P.M., when 76,800 cfs was registered. An unofficial maximum daily flow occurred on July 4, 1884, when 125,000 cfs was observed at Fruita, Colorado (about fifty-five river miles upstream from the gage near the mouth of the Dolores). A minimum daily discharge of 558 cfs was registered on the gage below the Dolores on July 21, 1934. In reporting the low flow, the Moab newspaper, *The Times-Independent*, noted that "the river can be waded at most points and is little larger than a fair-sized creek."

Recorded sediment load of the Colorado at the gaging station below Dolores River has ranged from a maximum of 2,790,000 tons on October 14, 1941 to a minimum of 14 tons at the gage on August 22, 1960. The often extremely muddy-looking river has given rise to the expression: "Too thick to drink and too thin to plow."

The warmest water temperature recorded for the river at the gaging station below the Dolores River was 85°F on July 29, 1966. The freezing point is reached on many days in December through February. During the winter, ice may cover stretches of the river from bank to bank.

Channel Width and Gradient
Average width of the Colorado's channel at Arches is about 500 feet. The gradient or slope of the river from the mouth of Salt Wash downstream to the U.S. Highway 191 bridge is about 3.5 feet per mile.

Rapids
Most of the river's drop occurs at two minor rapids, Salt Wash and Big Bend. In most rivers, rapids are produced where water cascades over resistant bedrock that projects above the water's surface. However, the two rapids at Arches have a different origin. They have formed at the mouths of tributary streams, Salt Wash Rapid at the mouth of Salt Wash and Big Bend Rapid at the mouth of an unnamed tributary that enters the river from the east (across the river from the Park). At the mouths of these tributaries rocks—sometimes of boulder size—are washed into the river during flash floods. These rocks accumulate in the river, constricting its channel and partially damming the flow. As the river rushes across the overflow points of these dams, rapids result.

The area and configuration of these rapids vary somewhat from year to year, due to changes in the number and distribution of rocks that create the dams. There may be substantial changes in the rapids following a severe flash flood.

The presence, area, configuration, and severity of rapids are directly related to the volume of water in the river at any given time. As the water level rises in late spring—the period of maximum runoff—the rocky dams that create these rapids are increasingly submerged. Sometimes the dams are buried, causing the rapids to disappear.

GEOLOGICAL BASE

THE STARK, rocky realm of Arches National Park is a profusion of surrealistic landforms—arches, balanced rocks, weirdly shaped spires, towering pinnacles, and fins. Much of this unusual scenery was created by the erosion of sedimentary rocks.

CLASSES OF ROCKS

All rocks fall into one of three major classes: igneous, sedimentary, and metamorphic. *Igneous rocks* are created by the solidifying of *magma*, or molten rock material. *Sedimentary rocks* are formed by the accumulation and consolidation of sediments derived from existing rocks. *Metamorphic rocks* are igneous or sedimentary rocks that have been altered by extreme heat or pressure.

A BRIEF GEOLOGICAL HISTORY

Sedimentary rocks exposed in the Park range in age from 300 million to 100 million years. While this interval of 200 million years is an enormous span of time, it is less than one-twentieth of the Earth's estimated age of 4.5 billion years.

Beneath the oldest exposed rocks at Arches—the Pinkerton Trail Formation—lie about 2,000 feet of even older sedimentary rocks. Below them are ancient Precambrian-age igneous and metamorphic rocks of the *basement complex*, the crustal layer below the dominantly sedimentary rocks.

Above the youngest rocks in the Park— the Mancos Shale—there once was a covering of rocks more than a mile thick that has since been removed by erosion.

[Opposite] The orange-to-reddish shafts of fins and spires in the **Fiery Furnace** bear a fanciful resemblance to tongues of flame, especially in the warm glow of a late afternoon sun. The shafts of these towering landforms are of the Entrada Sandstone's Slick Rock Member. Some of the shafts are capped by the Entrada's white Moab Member. The Fiery Furnace lies near the southern end of Salt Valley, on its eastern rim. In a June 1959 article in *Desert Magazine*, rock-climber Cecil M. Ouellette told of a trip he had made into this rugged labyrinth of spires, fins, chutes, and arches, saying the chaotic terrain was "void, silent and almost uncanny in its solitude."

[Right] A broad tract of smooth, bare sandstone—appropriately called *slickrock*—extends toward three of the alcoves at **Cove of Caves**, north of Double Arch in The Windows section. The prominent maroon stripe across the rock, appearing much like the centerline on a highway, is natural coloration.

Precambrian

Geologists term the first major division of the Earth's geologic history the *Precambrian era*. During this lengthy era, which lasted some 4 billion years or about 90 per cent of geologic time to date, the first rocks were formed and the first life forms appeared. The Precambrian ended about 600 million years ago.

Some 2 billion years ago, during Late Precambrian time, two continental-scale fault systems developed in the basement complex: the northeast-trending Colorado Lineament, and the northwest-trending Olympic-Wichita Lineament. These two gigantic fault zones, which were created at about the same time by tremendous compressional forces within the Earth, intersect in the Arches region.

The Colorado Lineament is believed to stretch from Arizona to Minnesota, a distance of about 1,350 miles. The Colorado River follows the lineament's trend through Colorado state, Utah, and northern Arizona. That part of the lineament which passes through the Park is called the Roberts Rift. It was so named by Robert J. Hite of the U.S. Geological Survey for J. E. Roberts, who was involved in mining west of Arches.

The Olympic-Wichita Lineament is estimated to be more than double the length of the Colorado Lineament. It perhaps begins in the Pacific off Vancouver Island, British Columbia, then extends some 2,750 miles southeast across the continent, and into the Atlantic Ocean beyond Florida.

Both of these extensive lineaments are termed *wrench faults*, that is, faults on which the primary movement is horizontal, with a secondary component of vertical displacement. The infamous San Andreas Fault of California is a well-known example of a wrench fault. The direction of primary—horizontal—movement on the Colorado Lineament is *left-lateral*, meaning that the relative displacement of the

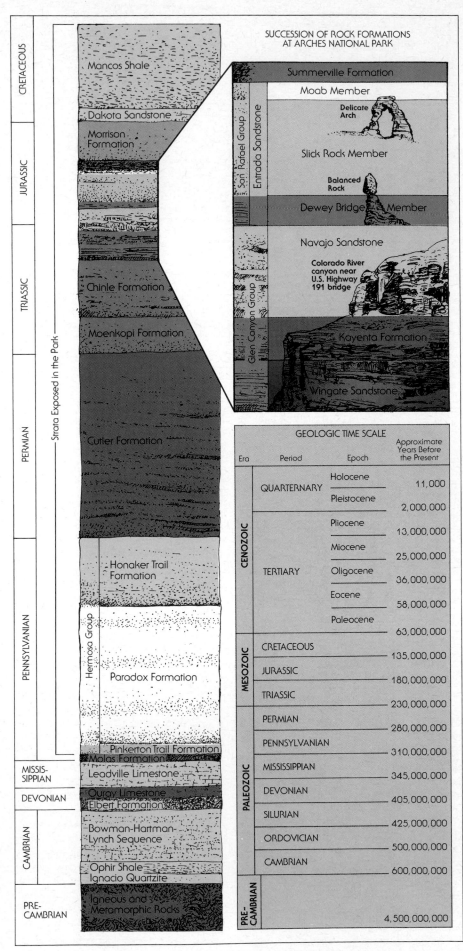

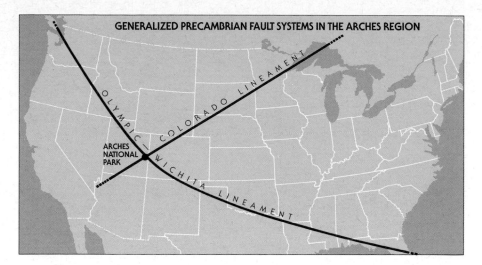

opposite sides of the fault is to the left. Along the Olympic-Wichita Lineament the direction is *right-lateral*, like the San Andreas Fault, where the relative movement of the fault's opposite sides is to the right.

On the Olympic-Wichita Lineament, the secondary—vertical—movement, or *normal faulting*, in which one block is displaced downward relative to the opposite block, created a series of troughs and ridges in what is today's Arches region. These features, of course, are not now visible—they are buried beneath several thousand feet of sedimentary rock.

Movement on the lineaments began in Late Precambrian time, about 2 billion years ago. Displacement continued intermittently for some 1.8 billion years, or until the end of the Paleozoic era about 230 million years ago.

These lineaments set the orientations of the major geologic structures seen at the surface today in the Arches region.

Paleozoic

With the end of the Precambrian, about 600 million years ago, the second major division of the Earth's geologic history began: the Paleozoic era. It lasted some 370 million years. The Paleozoic is subdivided into seven periods: Cambrian, Ordovician, Silurian, Devonian, Mississippian, Pennsylvanian, and Permian.

During the Cambrian period, from 600 million to 500 million years ago, the ancient Cordilleran Sea spread eastward from what is now Nevada and western Utah to cover the Precambrian igneous and metamorphic rocks—the basement complex—of today's Arches region with about 1,000 feet of sediments.

The first deposit laid down in the sea is called the Ignacio Quartzite. This is overlaid by the Ophir Shale, which is covered by the Bowman-Hartman-Lynch limestones and dolomites.

The Cordilleran Sea withdrew at the close of the Cambrian. What happened in the present Arches region during the next 125 million years is not known. No rocks of Ordovician, Silurian, or Early Devonian age exist in the area. Thus, there is a 1,250,000-century hiatus, or *disconformity*, in the area's geologic record!

The Arches region was again inundated by a sea in Late Devonian time and continued to receive marine sedimentation through Early Mississippian time. The Elbert Formation, primarily a dolomite unit, was deposited in the Late Devonian. On top of it was laid the Ouray Formation, a limestone dating from Late Devonian and Early Mississippian times. Deposited over the Ouray was the Leadville Formation, a limestone and dolomite unit.

Then the sea withdrew in Late Mississippian, and the Arches region lay exposed to weathering. From then into Early Pennsylvanian, a mantle of red soil, the Molas Formation, developed.

In Early Pennsylvanian time, about 300 million years ago, part of what is now the eastern Colorado Plateau, including the present Arches region, began to subside, forming an oval-shaped depression now called the Paradox Basin.

What caused this great basin to develop? Possibly it was a result of *plate tectonics*, or "continental drift." The Earth's rigid outer layer—the *lithosphere*—is broken into huge blocks or plates, including seven enormous plates, and at least a dozen smaller ones. The plates lie on, and slowly move over, the softer *asthenosphere*. The Paradox Basin may have been depressed when the North American Plate, on which the basin formed, collided with the South American Plate and the African Plate.

The Paradox Basin encompasses more than 11,000 square miles in what is today southeastern Utah and southwestern Colorado. The basin's alignment runs northwest-southeast some 200 miles from near present Green River, Utah to about the Colorado-New Mexico boundary south of Cortez, Colorado. Its maximum northeast-southeast width is about 100 miles.

Simultaneous with the subsidence of the Paradox Basin, a sea advanced into the depression and a large mountain range, the Uncompahgre Highland, rose adjacent to the basin's northeastern side. The deepest part of the Paradox Basin, the Uncompahgre Trough, lies along the southwest flank of the Uncompahgre Highland. This trough is about 100 miles long and 30 miles wide. Four smaller highlands also formed along the margins of the basin: the Peñasco on the southeast, the Defiance-Zuñi to the south, the Kaibab on the southwest, and the Emery to the northwest.

The first formation deposited in the Paradox Basin, the Pinkerton Trail—the oldest rock unit exposed by erosion in Arches—rests on top of the red Molas Formation. The Pinkerton Trail consists of limestone, shale, and sandstone. Above it lies the Paradox Formation, a cyclic unit of *evaporites*—halite (rock salt), anhydrite, and potash—and black shale and sandstone. The evaporitic sediments were

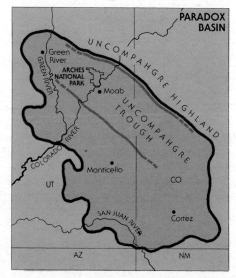

[Right] The opening of world-famous **Delicate Arch** is tall enough to accommodate a four-story building. The arch is a remnant of a fin of Entrada Sandstone. Erosion removed the rest of the fin, leaving the arch free-standing. In time, the same erosive forces will level this graceful landform. The Slick Rock Member of the Entrada comprises all the arch except the top five feet of cap rock, which are of the Entrada's Moab Member. [Below] **Devil's Garden** lies on the northeastern flank of the Salt Valley Anticline. The Slick Rock Member, seen here as deeply cut reddish rock, stands in vivid contrast to the white Moab Member. Long fractures — looking like grooves left by a giant rake — resulted when the anticline collapsed. Rock on the sides of these fractures erodes, sometimes leaving vertical fins in which arches may form.

Tower of Babel [top] and **Sheep Rock** [bottom] are two of several massive rock shafts that stand in Courthouse Towers. Both of these impressive towers are remnants of an upland that once extended between the Willow Flats plateau and the high plateau west of Park Avenue. The towers are sculpted in the Slick Rock Member of the Entrada Sandstone, and rest on the Entrada's Dewey Bridge Member. The Tower of Babel, approximately a quarter-mile east of Sheep Rock, rises about 500 feet. Sheep Rock may once have been the northern abutment of a large arch that in turn may have had another big arch adjoining, creating a feature similar to North Window and South Window of The Spectacles. If such a pair of arches did exist, they collapsed long before man arrived on the scene.

GENESIS OF COURTHOUSE TOWERS

Many of the Park's most striking non-arch landforms are found in the **Courthouse Towers** section. Among them are Sheep Rock, The Three Gossips, Tower of Babel, and The Organ. All are remnants of a large mesa [**top**] that once extended south from The Great Wall, a red-rock cliff terminating the tableland that includes Willow Flats. All land surfaces are subjected to erosional processes, and all pass through a continuous sequence of changes, or *cycle of erosion*. Streams are the greatest eroders of land. The stream now called Courthouse Wash and its tributaries slowly and relentlessly dissected the mesa, cutting it into several large buttes [**center**]. As erosion continued, some of these buttes were reduced to smaller landforms known as towers and pinnacles [**bottom**]. In time, erosion will level the picturesque Courthouse Towers area, leaving the surface almost flat.

deposited when sea water was concentrated and evaporated during intervals when the basin was cut off from the sea. Overlying the Paradox Formation is the Honaker Trail Formation, an interbedded unit of limestone, shale, and sandstone.

Sediments from surrounding highlands, principally the Uncompahgre, were deposited on the Paradox Basin margins.

In Late Pennsylvanian time, the sea withdrew from the basin. The area was then subjected to a short span of erosion.

By Permian time, the last period of the Paleozoic era, the weight of red sediments from the Uncompahgre Highland—the Cutler Formation—exerted tremendous pressure on salt in the Paradox Formation. Under such stress, salt will flow plastically, as ice flows in a glacier. The salt moved to the southwest, away from the heavy overburden adjacent to the Uncompahgre Highland. When the flowing salt came into contact with the northwest-southeast ridges of the Olympic-Wichita fault zone, the salt's course was turned upward. As it rose, the salt penetrated the overlying strata, creating great elongated salt cores. In the troughs of the fault zone, sediments continued to accumulate, forming downfolds, or *synclines*. The process began in about Middle Pennsylvanian time and lasted some 150 million years, extending approximately half-way through the next era—the Mesozoic.

Mesozoic

The Mesozoic began after the close of the Permian about 230 million years ago, and lasted some 167 million years. It is divided into three periods: Triassic, Jurassic, and Cretaceous.

During Early Triassic and possibly Middle Triassic, a sea extended over the Arches region. Sediments were deposited, primarily on tidal flats, and were compacted into the reddish-brown siltstones and sandstones of the Moenkopi Formation.

In Late Triassic time, lake and stream sediments from a source region far to the south were laid down. This rock unit, the Chinle Formation, consists of red sandstone, red mudstone, limestone, and conglomerate.

After the Chinle, but during the Late Triassic, wind-deposited sand accumulated, giving a Sahara-like appearance to what is now the Colorado Plateau. The source for this fine-grained sand was to the northwest. Compaction and cementation resulted in the Wingate Sandstone, a massive reddish-orange rock.

Next during the Late Triassic, sediments that formed sandstones, shales, and limestones were deposited by streams flowing southwest from the Uncompahgre Highland. This rock unit is called the Kayenta Formation.

At the end of the Late Triassic and possibly extending into Early Jurassic, the region again reverted to desert. Another wind-deposited or *aeolian* rock unit, the Navajo Sandstone, developed.

In Late Jurassic, a shallow sea invaded the region, entering from the west. The

Office tent at base camp of **Arches National Monument Scientific Expedition**, 1933-34, at Willow Spring. Funded by the federal Civil Works Administration, the survey was directed by the National Park Service through Zion National Park, and was the first intensive geological survey of Arches. In addition to the geologic work, the expedition also conducted an archeological survey, and compiled a map of the area. Frank A. Beckwith was expedition leader, and Joseph C. Anderson was geologist. The geological field work required parts of two eight-week periods. Anderson's work culminated in a report titled "Geological Reconnaissance in the Arches National Monument."

Entrada Sandstone formed out of sediments deposited in this marine environment and from aeolian deposition. The Entrada is divided into three members: the Dewey Bridge, the oldest; and lying above it the Slick Rock; and atop it the Moab, the youngest. Most of the natural arches, fins, and spires of the Park were to form much later in the Entrada. More than 130 million years were to pass before these distinctive landforms developed.

Overlying the Entrada is another Late Jurassic rock unit, the Summerville Formation. It consists of sandy mudstone, shale, and sandstone, and was deposited in a tidal-flat environment.

Also dating to the Late Jurassic is a floodplain-deposited formation, the Morrison. This unit is composed of shale, sandstone, and conglomerate.

In Late Cretaceous age, sediments of the Dakota Sandstone were laid down on a coastal-plain environment. This unit contains sandstone, shale, and coal.

Following the Dakota Sandstone deposition, the sea, in Late Cretaceous, advanced over the present Arches region again. Sediments for a thick marine unit, the Mancos Shale — a dark gray, fossiliferous shale — were laid down. Today, the Mancos Shale is the youngest rock exposed at Arches.

Deposited over the Mancos Shale was the Mesaverde Group, also of Late Cretaceous age. It consists of sandstone, shale, and coal. This was the final deposit of the Mesozoic era in Arches.

In Late Cretaceous time, compressive forces in the Earth's crust produced *anticlines*, or upfolds, over the Paradox salt cores. When the stresses relaxed, the anticlinal crests collapsed, forming *grabens*, or down-dropped blocks. In some places these blocks sunk several hundred feet.

At the close of the Cretaceous, the land emerged from the sea. It has remained above sea level in the Arches region throughout the present era, the Cenozoic.

Cenozoic

The fourth major division of the geologic time scale, the Cenozoic, began about 63 million years ago. It consists of two periods: the Tertiary, which lasted until about 2 million years ago, and the present period, the Quaternary.

In the Middle Tertiary, the Colorado Plateau began to be uplifted, a process that is continuing. This massive rise caused a further collapse of salt-core anticlines in the Arches region. The uplift increased ground-water circulation and stream erosion. This, in turn, dissolved and removed salt underlying the surfaces of anticlinal crests. That brought about additional slumping which resulted in collapsed anticlines. Salt Valley and Cache Valley in the Park are examples.

All of the Cenozoic rocks deposited in the Arches area have been removed by erosion, as have some of the Mesozoic units.

It was this erosion which created the dramatic landforms and landscape of Arches National Park.

"ARCHES" AND "WINDOWS" ARE SYNONYMOUS, BUT BRIDGES ARE SOMETHING ELSE

Early visitors and residents of Utah's Canyon Country generally used the terms "arch," "window," and "bridge" interchangeably to designate natural rock openings. True, all three do have certain features in common: all are created by geologic processes; and all have continuous, unbroken spans, that is, they are not mere openings formed by one rock leaning against another. But there are certain characteristics that distinguish bridges from arches and windows. *Bridges* span present or former watercourses; arches and windows do not. Bridges are cut initially by the hydraulic and abrasive action of streams, then expanded by weathering and erosion. *Arches* and *windows* are sculptured by weathering — the chemical action of air and water, and the physical effects of temperature, frost wedging, and gravity.

Geologists and geographers are by no means agreed on definitions for those landforms. Technical literature rarely makes any distinctions between an arch, a window, and a bridge. American geologist William D. Thornbury, a recognized authority on landforms, describes in his book *Principles of Geomorphology* (1969) the processes involved in the development of a natural bridge, referring alternately to the bridge as an arch. British geographer W. G. Moore, in his *A Dictionary of Geography* (1962) defines a natural bridge as "a bridge or arch of natural rock." But Moore offers no definition for "arch" in his dictionary.

The terminology can be even more confusing and imprecise in popular literature, where occasionally some very unusual definitions are given. For example, Natt D. Dodge wrote in an article for the April 1947 issue of *Arizona Highways*: "Technically, a natural bridge is a span over or a passageway across a barrier or obstruction, whereas a natural arch or window is an opening through a barrier."

In essence, arch and window are merely different terms to describe the same feature. Traditionally, when people think of a window they envision an opening in a building's wall. So, "window" frequently is used to designate a small opening high on a rock wall or fin, while "arch" generally describes large openings that rise from ground level. Unfortunately, nature does not recognize such nice but artificial distinctions, since large and small natural rock openings occur at all levels.

Then why not use size as the criterion to distinguish arches from windows? This is scarcely a practical solution, as who is to say at what dimensions an opening stops being a window and becomes an arch? North Window and South Window — The Spectacles — illustrate the dichotomy.

THE EVOLUTION OF SALT VALLEY

Salt Valley runs broadly through the northern half of Arches National Park. About eleven miles of the valley's eighteen-mile length lies in Arches. The valley's maximum width—which occurs within the Park—exceeds two miles. Although Salt Valley is one of the Parkland's prominent features, it appears generally drab by comparison to other sections. But many of the geologic processes and events that created the valley were responsible for the striking landforms found elsewhere in the Park. Salt Valley's geologic history began some 2 billion years ago, when two gigantic fault systems formed in the Precambrian-age rocks, the *basement complex.* Vertical dislocation on one of the faults, the Olympic-Wichita Lineament, created high blocks called *horsts.* One of these horsts is now buried deep beneath Salt Valley. Between 600 to 300 million years ago, the Salt Valley region was alternately above or below ancient seas. Sediments deposited over the basement complex were compacted into rocks, forming strata some 2,000 feet deep. Then about 300 million years ago, part of present southwestern Colorado and

southeastern Utah — including today's Salt Valley area — subsided, forming an oval-shaped depression — now called the Paradox Basin — 200 miles long by 100 miles wide. While the basin was forming, a large mountain range, the Uncompahgre Highland, rose along the depression's northeastern side. Four smaller highlands also formed on the basin's margins. The Paradox Basin was periodically connected to an ancient sea. When cut off, the basin's water evaporated, precipitating salt and other evaporites. The original thickness of the salt deposited was well over 3,000 feet! Meanwhile, sediments from the Uncompahgre Highland accumulated on the basin's northeastern side. Their great weight squeezed the salt slowly toward the southwest. When it encountered the horsts, the salt was deflected upward, piercing the overlying strata and forming elongated salt cores. This intrusive process lasted some 140 million years, ending in Late Jurassic time. During at least the next 150 million years, the Salt Valley region experienced several environments: marine, marginal marine,

fluvial, and continental. Then about 65 million years ago, near the end of Cretaceous time and after deposition of the Mesaverde Group, regional compressive forces created anticlines — structural upfolds — over the salt cores. One of these was the Salt Valley Anticline. When these forces were released the anticlinal crests slumped in places. For the past 63 million years, the Arches-Salt Valley region has been above sea level. Beginning in Middle Tertiary, about 30 million years ago, the present Colorado Plateau began to rise. This uplift increased ground-water flowage, dissolving salt in the crests of the anticlines, including the Salt Valley Anticline. The unsupported anticlinal summits then collapsed, creating depressions such as Salt Valley. This slumping was accompanied by faulting and jointing. Weathering and erosion along the sides of rock where they were fractured by joints often produced fins, setting the stage for the development of natural arches and spires that would give the future Parkland its strange but scenic appearance and appeal.

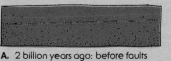

A. 2 billion years ago: before faults development in the Precambrian basement-complex rocks and overlying deposition occurred.

B. 300 million years ago: after faulting, and deposition of pre-Pennsylvanian-age rocks and the Paradox Formation.

C. 275 million years ago: deposition of Honaker Trail Formation completed, and salt-core development began.

D. 250 million years ago: Cutler Formation deposited and salt-core development continued.

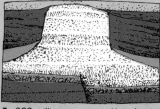

E. 200 million years ago: Moenkopi Formation laid down.

F. 60 million years ago: completion of Mesozoic rock deposition.

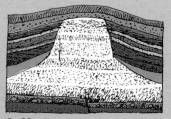

G. 50 million years ago: at end of Early Tertiary folding.

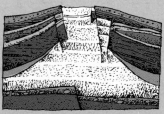

H. 25 million years ago: crestal collapse of salt anticline; Cretaceous rocks removed by erosion.

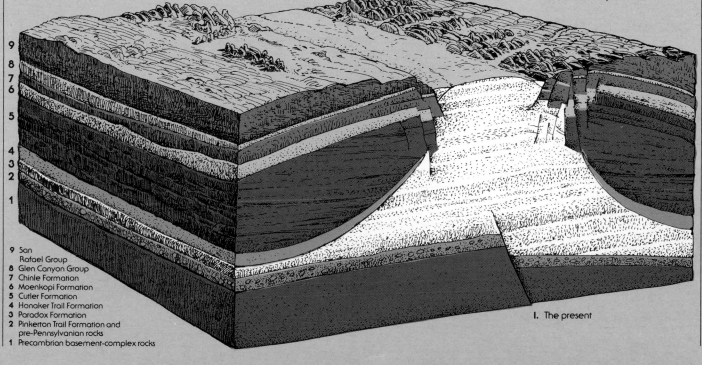

9
8
7
6
5
4
3
2
1

9 San Rafael Group
8 Glen Canyon Group
7 Chinle Formation
6 Moenkopi Formation
5 Cutler Formation
4 Honaker Trail Formation
3 Paradox Formation
2 Pinkerton Trail Formation and pre-Pennsylvanian rocks
1 Precambrian basement-complex rocks

I. The present

HOW THE ROCKS OF THE PARK GOT THEIR COLORS

The rocks of Arches are among the most colorful on earth, creating a richly hued setting for the Park's many spectacular arches, weirdly eroded spires, and precipitous cliffs. Displaying an impressive variety of colors—red, orange, yellow, green, blue, lavender, purple, pink, tan, brown, gray, black, and white—these rocks produce highly variegated and often vivid scenery—a veritable "painted desert." Their prominent colors are even more conspicuous in the stark landscape of the Park, where sparse, scanty high-desert vegetation leaves much of the rocky terrain exposed to view.

Natural lighting influences the tones and intensities of colors. Bright and direct sunlight produces strong colors, while overcast skies will mute tones. Often at sunset, many of the rocks in the Park seem ablaze with red and orange, especially the maze of spires and fins at the Fiery Furnace, which takes on a brilliant, glowing appearance as if heated by a great subterranean fire.

Red is the dominant color of the Parkland. Indeed, various shades of red, ranging from pale salmon pink through deep maroon, are so characteristic of the Park and of many other areas of the Colorado Plateau that the region is commonly called "Red Rock Country."

Compounds of iron are responsible for coloring most rocks. Depending on its chemical state—oxidized or reduced—iron can produce a wide range of colors, including red, orange, yellow, green, blue, brown, gray, and black. Other coloring agents of rocks are copper, which produces tints of green; carbon, which gives gray and black; and manganese, which imparts red, purple, brown, and black.

Rocks usually are the same color inside and out. However, their surfaces may be colored by one or more types of coatings. Occasionally, color from an overlying rock formation will wash down and coat the formation beneath. Lichens form another type of coating. These crust-like plants are common on many rocks in the Park, especially in Devil's Garden. Live lichens appear on rocks as spots and patches of orange, yellow, green, brown, or gray—or a mixture of two or more of these colors—while dead plants are black or white. Lichens frequently create fascinating patterns, often circular in design, which further enhance rock surfaces.

Many rocks in the Park are coated with glossy brown or purplish-to-black splotches and streaks of *desert varnish*. This patina, often appearing as if it were a "sun tan" on the rocks, is common in arid regions, where it may cover parts of rocks of all sizes, from loose pebbles and cobbles strewn about the ground to the sheer faces of massive cliffs. These satiny coatings enrich the surface textures of rocks, often painting beautiful patterns. Dark, irregularly tapering lines of desert varnish commonly streak the sides of arches,

[Above] Streaks of **desert varnish** stain the narrow fin pierced by Hole-in-the-Wall, a small arch in Courthouse Towers.

[Below] **Lichen** on south side of Cove of Caves.

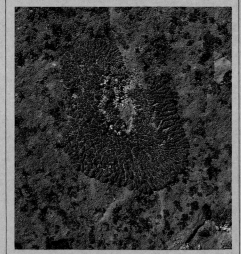

spires, fins, and monuments. They also may create giant natural "tapestries" which drape over many of the Park's red-rock cliffs.

Some desert-varnished rocks have smooth, blackboard-like surfaces. Prehistoric Indians pecked and scratched many of their mysterious petroglyphs into these flat, dark surfaces. Several of these rock-art sites exist in the Park. Explorers and pioneers also sometimes yielded to the temptation to inscribe on varnished rocks, leaving historic inscriptions to document their presence and activities. A few of these inscriptions are found at the Park.

Desert varnish was long believed to result from weathering processes that leached manganese and iron oxides from rock and deposited them on the surface. However, in 1977 two California Institute of Technology mineralogists reported results of their investigations on the origin of desert varnish showing that it is produced by external causes, primarily wind-deposited clay particles. George R. Rossman and Russell M. Potter analyzed the varnish with infrared spectroscopy, x-ray diffraction, and electron microscopy, and found it to be composed of more than 70 per cent clay, and less than 30 per cent manganese and iron oxides. Since desert varnish can also form on rocks that do not contain manganese and iron, such as quartzite, they concluded that most of the varnish came from sources outside of the rocks. Rossman and Potter found that fine, windblown particles of clay settle on the rough, porous surfaces of rocks, and when moisture—surface run-off or groundwater carrying dissolved manganese and iron—migrates into the clay and then evaporates, a fine precipitate of manganese and iron is left. These oxides cement the light, loose clay particles, forming a smooth, thin coating of lustrous desert varnish.

The **first detailed geological study** of Arches was undertaken in 1927, two years before the area became part of the national park system. Carle H. Dane of the U. S. Geological Survey headed the field party, and wrote a technical report summarizing the finding. Titled *Geology of the Salt Valley Anticline and Adjacent Areas, Grand County, Utah*, it was published in 1935 as U. S. Geological Survey Bulletin 863. Shown here in July 1927 is a member of the field party working in The Windows section under massive North Window, one of the pair of arches collectively called The Spectacles. Other early geological studies of Arches were conducted by Joseph C. Anderson of the Arches National Monument Scientific Expedition (1934), and by National Park Service geologists Vincent W. Vandiver (1936), Charles N. Gould (1938), and Ross A. Maxwell (1941).

Both of these openings, located in The Windows section, rise from ground level, and both are certainly large — North Window has a span of 93 feet and a height of 51 feet, while South Window stretches 105 feet with a height of 66 feet. Yet pioneers in the region called them both windows, not arches. Conversely, Double Arch, which has been known also as Double Windows, has openings that rise from ground level, the larger 163 feet long and 105 feet high, the smaller spanning 60 feet with a height of 61 feet. Obviously, then, the choice of terms is arbitrary: one person's arch may be another's window.

Generally, however, the smaller the opening, and the higher above the ground, the greater the likelihood it will be called a window.

There are two additional complications to clearly differentiating between arch and window. First, sometimes both of these terms have been bypassed in the naming of natural rock openings. For example, Hole-in-the-Wall, a small but significant aperture through a fin in the Park's Courthouse Towers section, fits the concept of a window, yet its namer chose another, more graphic title. Hole-in-the-Wall further exemplifies the problem of "arch vs. window" by also being called alternately Baby Arch and Archette (literally, "diminutive arch").

Second, the term "arch" is sometimes applied to arch-shaped recesses eroded into the faces of cliffs. Some of these rise more than a hundred feet and have bases of similar length. But these features are not true arches. They are only insets, which do not pierce through the host rock. They are properly identified as *alcoves*.

A HOLE, OR AN ARCH?

What is the difference between a natural rock hole and an arch? Is there some special measurement that an opening must possess to merit designation as an arch?

Since no widely accepted, comprehensive definition of "natural arch" has yet been formulated, precise answers are impossible. Often a decision to call an opening a hole instead of an arch is based simply on an observer's intuition. Again, some obviously small openings—mere holes to many people—are called arches because they are unusual landforms, or have classical arch shapes, or are rare in their areas, or because some historically important event occurred at or near them. In other words, they have significance.

To some people all openings, regardless of size, are arches. For them, even a pin-hole-sized opening may create an arch. Others may designate as arches only openings that are large and impressive. Obviously, what is large and impressive to one observer may appear small and lackluster to another.

Probably an opening is called an arch simply when it looks like one to the viewer. As former U.S. Supreme Court Associate Justice Potter Stewart commented in a 1964 opinion on a case related to the definition of hard-core pornography, the term may be "indefinable," but "I know it when I see it. . . ."

ARE SIZE AND AGE OF NATURAL ARCHES RELATED?

It would appear logical to assume that large openings in rock take longer to form than small ones, and that large arches are — therefore — older than small arches. Although this seems to be sound reasoning, it is an over simplification which does not take certain variables into account.

Two important variables in the formation of sandstone arches are (1) the strength of the natural cement which bonds the individual sand grains together and (2) the amount of weathering and erosion to which the rock is exposed. If the rock in which an arch is developing is made up of well-cemented grains, the arch will form at a slower rate than if the grains were poorly cemented. If the fin in which an arch is forming is directly exposed to the weather, the arch will develop faster than if the fin is sheltered by surrounding landforms.

Thus, a large and apparently old arch may — in fact — be much younger than a small, youthful-looking arch. With arches, as with people, appearances can sometimes be deceiving.

WHY ARE ARCHES FOUND IN SUCH ABUNDANCE IN THE PARK?

Why are there so many natural arches in the Parkland?

There are four primary reasons: (1) the type of rock, (2) the unloading of compression on the rock, (3) the geologic stability of the region, and (4) the Park's semiarid climate.

(1) The type of rock in Arches. Nearly all of the Park's arches were formed in Entrada Sandstone, a rock type that is particularly conducive to the development of such landforms. Sandstone consists predominantly of quartz grains, cemented together by silica, calcium carbonate, or one of the iron oxides. However, the percentage of this natural cement may vary from place to place within the rock. Weathering and erosion occur most rapidly where there is the least amount of cement, and at such vulnerable sites arches may develop.

(2) The release of compression, or unloading. The Entrada Sandstone was once heavily compressed by overlying strata more than a mile thick. As this immense overburden was slowly worn away by ero-

NATURAL ARCHES: CHARACTER, LIFE CYCLE, AND SELECTED TYPES

What is a Natural Arch?

The answer seems obvious, yet there is no generally accepted definition for "natural arch" that includes such attributes as size, shape, and location relative to ground level. However, the term is usually applied to natural rock openings with unbroken spans, formed by weathering processes rather than first by stream erosion, as is the case with *natural bridges*. Herdman F. Cleland, an early investigator and classifier of natural bridges, differentiated between arches and bridges in a paper presented at a meeting of the Geological Society of America in 1909. According to Cleland, a natural

bridge "spans a valley of erosion," while a natural arch is "a similar structure which, however, does not span an erosion valley." Dale J. Stevens, a professor of geography at Brigham Young University, proposed basic criteria for a natural sandstone arch. In the *Great Plains-Rocky Mountain Geographical Journal* for 1974, he specified that light must penetrate a natural opening, a rock span must exist, and that the size and shape of the aperture and span are irrelevant.

Life Cycle of Arches

Natural arches, although inanimate, have "life cycles" like living things, progressing through *youth*, *maturity*, and *old age*. Youth is characterized by a relatively small opening surrounded by considerable rock. Hole-in-the Wall exemplifies youth. In maturity the opening is greatly increased, but there is still much rock around it. Tapestry Arch typifies maturity. In old age the arch's span is slender, and the opening dominates the landform's appearance. Landscape Arch illustrates old age. Ultimately, the span will fail and fall, marking the arch's "death."

Fin Recess-type Arch

Landscape Arch—the world's longest natural span—rises in south Devil's Garden. This awe-inspiring landform is about one mile from the Devil's Garden parking lot, and is easily accessible over an improved foot trail. It exemplifies the most common type of arch in the Park, the fin recess. This type develops from a recess, or indentation, in a *fin*—a thin sandstone wall, which may exceed a hundred feet in height and several hundred feet in length. Originally, there may have been only one recess from which the arch formed. In some cases there also may have been another recess on the fin's opposite side. As time passed, weathering and erosion enlarged the recess or recesses [a], and eventually either the single recess cut through the fin, or—if there were recesses on both sides—intersected. In either case, an opening was created which then was further expanded [b]. The slender, delicate span of

Landscape Arch is dramatic evidence that this superb feature is well into the old-age stage of its life cycle [c]. Its widest light opening is 306 feet long. The span's narrowest width is 15.5 feet, and at its thinnest the span is 16 feet thick. Soon—as geology measures time—it will fall. The first published report of Landscape Arch appeared in the April 22, 1898 issue of *Science*. In the short note, Arthur Winslow described the arch—then unnamed—and incorrectly called it a bridge. And he also wrongly stated that the long span was "a monstrous product of wind erosion." Other arches have been cited as examples of wind erosion. Another erroneous origin given for arches is that they are the remnants of tunnels cut by ancient rivers. Delicate Arch has been credited with this genesis. Rather, it is an example of a fin recess-type arch.

Pothole-type Arch

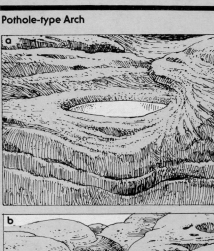

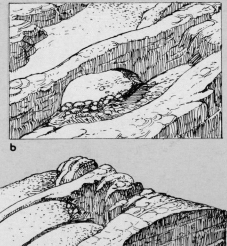

Ring Arch, in Courthouse Towers, exemplifies a class of natural arches that develop from potholes. In these, a small pothole forms near the edge of a cliff [a]. Weathering processes slowly deepen the pothole. Eventually, water from the pothole percolates to the cliff's face, where a cave forms at the point of seepage. With time, the enlarging vertical pothole and the horizontal cave meet, creating an opening [b]. Finally, this opening increases until an arch is formed [c]. Ultimately, weathering and erosion will take their toll, and the arch will collapse.

Cave-type Arch

Tapestry Arch, near the Devil's Garden Campground, illustrates a type of arch created by the intersection of a cave and a *joint*, or fracture along which no movement has occurred as opposed to a *fault*, a fracture on which slippage has taken place. As weathering and erosion attacked the rock mass [**a**] and formed a cave in it, these same geologic processes widened and deepened a joint behind and above the cave [**b**]. In time, the two met, making a hole, then a small arch [**c**]. Continued weathering and erosion enlarged the opening, forming a bigger arch [**d**]. As with all natural arches, ultimately the span will become so fragile it will fall. Tapestry Arch, now in the mature stage of its life cycle, is sculptured in the Entrada Sandstone. The white Moab Member of the Entrada caps the span, while the rest of the arch is formed from the red Slick Rock Member. The opening has a span of fifty feet and a height of thirty feet.

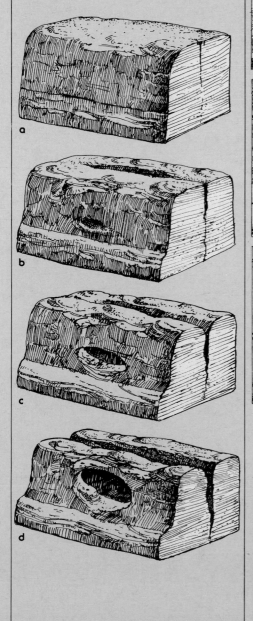

Fallen Arches

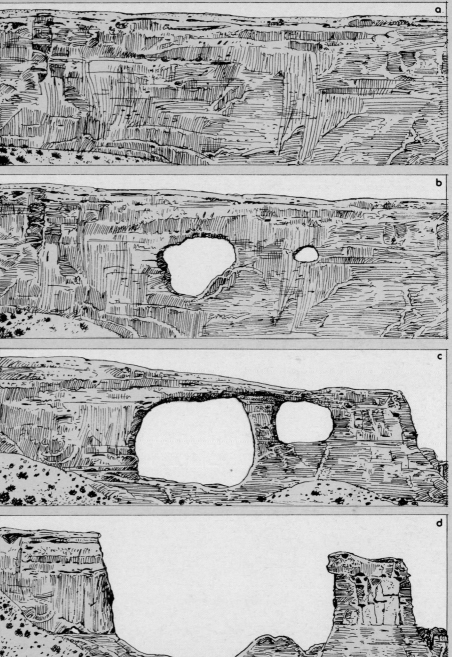

It would appear that two large arches once existed in Courthouse Towers, in the expanse between Sheep Rock and the fin containing Hole-in-the-Wall. These postulated ancient arches probably resembled in appearance The Spectacles — North Window and South Window — in The Windows section. Like The Spectacles, this arch duo presumably formed in a fin [**a**] where the sandstone was weakened either by fractures or by a reduced amount of natural cement (silica, calcium carbonate, or one of the iron oxides) holding the grains together, or both. Weathering processes attacking the rock surface eventually developed recesses. These expanded, and ultimately developed into openings [**b**]. They continued to enlarge until the openings became relatively big arches [**c**], and finally collapsed [**d**]. Sheep Rock, once the north abutment of one of these supposed large arches, today stands magnificently isolated. A small arch, Hole-in-the-Wall, has since formed near the end of the fin that once was the south abutment of the other ancient span. Also aptly called Baby Arch, it is at the beginning — youth — of its life cycle. Hole-in-the-Wall developed in the Slick Rock Member of the Entrada Sandstone. The opening probably began in the prominent bedding plane along the arch's base. The adolescent arch has a span of twenty-five feet and a height of fourteen feet. Symptomatic of its youthful stage is the impressive volume of rock surrounding the opening—the rock mass above the arch is approximately 300 feet thick!

National Park Service

sion, the tremendous compressive force exerted by its weight on the Entrada was gradually relieved. Slowly the Entrada expanded — elastically rebounding — and release fractures developed in the rock. This process is called *unloading*. Where the fractures are closest together, the intervening wedges of Entrada are relatively thin and weak, and the sandstone there is especially susceptible to weathering and erosional processes. At such sites, the Entrada's structural condition for arch formation is propitious, and development may be initiated.

(3) The geologic stability of the Arches area. Obviously, such landforms as natural arches, precariously balanced rocks, and delicately carved spires could not survive in earthquake country. The Arches region fortunately is relatively free of seismic activity of any significant magnitude. However, there have been some noticeable

tremors in the area. On April 25, 1915 a minor earthquake was felt in Moab. Another slight quake was recorded there on January 17, 1950. A report in the town's newspaper, *The Times-Independent*, two days later noted that "the tremor was of sufficient severity to rock fixtures and rattle windows." Yet neither of these shakes caused any noticeable damage to the landforms in Arches.

(4) The Parkland's semiarid climate. Such unusually shaped landforms as are found at Arches could not survive long in humid climates like those that prevail in places like Florida or Michigan, for example. Although it is true that a few arches, balanced rocks, and spires do occur in humid regions, they are rare there, and survive for much shorter periods as compared with the longevity of similar landforms in arid regions. Wet climates form rounded, subdued topography rather than

the angular, pronounced landscape typical of areas with dry climates.

THE ROLE OF WIND IN FORMING THE PARK'S LANDFORMS

Winds sweep frequently across the Park's barren, red-rock landscape. At times they seem to blow incessantly. A strong gust may hurl grit violently, sandblasting anything in its path. Because of this, many people believe that wind abrasion is commonly responsible for producing numerous landforms, particularly those in deserts. However, wind is **not** a major agent of erosion. **Water** is the principal agent of erosion in deserts, just as it is elsewhere. However, the wind's sandblasting action may aid to a limited extent in the minor shaping of some landforms. The wind's erosive power is most pronounced in deserts, where the soil is not pinned down by vegetation to the same degree as it is in humid regions. But none of the Park's arches and weird-looking *hoodoos*★ were sculpted solely by wind abrasion.

Wind abrasion, also called *corrasion*, is effective only near the ground. Even when blowing severely, wind can lift sand grains and tiny rock particles only a limited distance above ground level, seldom more than eighteen inches. Wind abrasion may polish and facet pebbles on the ground, and can cut nicks and grooves into boulders and cliffs near their bases. But since many arches are located high above ground level, it is obvious that wind abrasion could not have produced them. Furthermore, if natural arches were created by wind, it would be expected that the windward side of arches would be smooth, and free of powdered rock. Yet this is not the case: both the windward and leeward sides of arches are of equal smoothness, and their

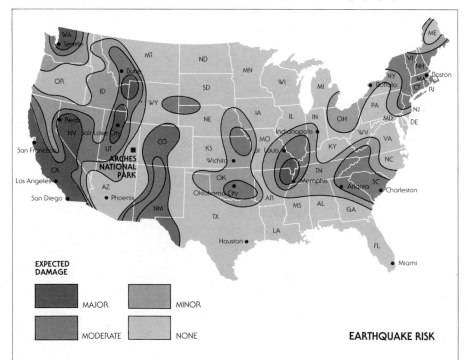

EXPECTED DAMAGE

■ MAJOR	■ MINOR
■ MODERATE	■ NONE

EARTHQUAKE RISK

★Rock pillars composed of horizontal strata of varying hardnesses that erode at different rates. Hoodoos may exhibit fancied resemblances to persons, animals, or mythical creatures.

[Opposite, circled] **Chip-off-the-Old-Block**, a neighbor and smaller version of Balanced Rock, collapsed during the winter of 1975-76.

Owl Rock [right, circled], also called Eagle Rock, perched on a prominent spire in the Garden of Eden until it fell between March 1 and 3, 1941. Though the distinctive-shaped rock has fallen, the spire is still called Owl Rock. In February 1978, skilled rock-climber "Piton Ron" Olevsky made the first recorded ascent of Owl Rock.

National Park Service

[Below] What is now **Skyline Arch**, in south Devil's Garden, was suddenly enlarged to about twice its former size in November 1940. A huge block of sandstone which previously had slumped down to form the northern half of the arch, but remained balanced in the opening, finally fell out. Until the block fell, the arch was aptly called **Arch-in-the-Making.** Henry Schmidt, custodian of Arches at the time, discovered the newly enlarged opening while on a horseback trip through Devil's Garden. One of his objectives had been to photograph the unusual arch, but—as he later noted—"from evidence at the site, we were about three to five days too late" because "Arch-in-the-Making . . . had been made." The arch now has a span of sixty-nine feet and a height of forty-five feet.

surfaces usually are coated with dust and grit.

However, wind does create landforms by *deposition*. Sand dunes are formed by *aeolian* deposition, that is, by the dropping of sand carried by the wind. Dune sand in the Park is derived from the massive sandstone formations that dominate the area. Weathering processes are constantly at work to disintegrate the stone into fine, loose grains of sand. Winds blow these grains into billowing, unconsolidated piles or dunes, some of them reaching fifty feet or more in height and hundreds of feet in length.

Sand dunes which are held in place by vegetation are termed *fixed dunes*. Those which are not so anchored are continually shifted about by wind currents. These moving dunes, called *active dunes*, may advance to cover roads, buildings, farm fields, and other features, and then march onward. In May 1940, Henry Schmidt, then custodian of Arches, commented that "high winds have made the sandy sections [on the Willow Flats road] almost impassable at times, and it is not uncommon to arrive at the dunes . . . in the morning and find [a dune] stretching its potent self across the road."

Wind also can produce a ground crust or layer called *desert pavement*. By an erosive process termed *deflation*, wind lifts and carries away fine, free bits of rock, loose soil particles, and sand to leave behind pebbles that form a mosaic-like surface which looks much like an old cobblestone road. Tracts of desert pavement occur at many places in the Parkland.

HOW FAST DO THE PARK'S LANDFORMS CHANGE?

How long before a natural arch collapses? How long until a balanced rock topples? If Denis Julien, the fur trapper who carved his name in what is now Devil's Garden in 1844, were to return, would the arches,

National Park Service

National Park Service

balanced rocks, and delicate spires look the same to him today? No doubt the main features that Julien saw a century and a half ago would appear to him unchanged now. Over the span of a man's lifetime, the Park's landforms will appear to change very little. Measured in lifetimes, or even in centuries, the rate of change is very slow.

However, change is a continuing process, and inevitable. And when change does occur, it may be spectacular. In November 1940, a huge block of rock fell from what is

now called Skyline Arch, more than doubling its opening. The next year Schmidt reported that, in early March, Owl Rock, located in the Garden of Eden, fell from its perch high atop a prominent spire.

During the winter of 1975-76, Chip-off-the-Old-Block, a small spire next to Balanced Rock, toppled. In prehistoric times, two large arches — possibly similar to The Spectacles — may have stood in Courthouse Towers. Sheep Rock, and the fin pierced by Hole-in-the-Wall, may be remnants of the abutments of such arches.

Bobcats (*Lynx rufus*), like the one illustrated here at Indian Head Arch in northern Devil's Garden, also are called wildcats, or bob-tailed cats, and are members of the same family (Felidae) to which common house cats belong. Except for an occasional house cat which has turned feral (wild), the only other member of the cat family found in Arches is the mountain lion. Bobcats, like other cats, are carnivores and hunt small mammals such as mice, rats, squirrels, cottontails, and jackrabbits. They also prey on ground-dwelling birds. Somewhat larger than big house cats, bobcats weigh fifteen to thirty pounds, and have an overall length of two-and-a-half to three feet. Their fur is yellowish-gray with the underside of the body whitish. The sides are dotted with light, reddish spots, and with black spots on the undersides. Dark, irregular stripes mark the face. The distinctive bobbed tail is about five inches long, and black on the upper surface at the tip. The cat's long, pointed ears have short, black tufts on the ends. These animals are solitary and nocturnal, and consequently seldom seen by Park visitors. Bobcats prefer broken, forested country such as occurs in Devil's Garden where piñon pines and junipers grow among sandstone fins. They den in rocky crevices, caves, or hollow logs.

PLANT AND ANIMAL LIFE

DESERT PLANTS and animals have adapted to life in a hostile environment. Many of their adaptations deal with resisting the effects of extreme dryness and intense heat, and—on high-desert terrain such as Arches—freezing winter temperatures.

ENVIRONMENTAL STRESSES ON THE PARK'S FLORA AND FAUNA

It is axiomatic that water is essential to life. Yet aridity is the mark of deserts, and life there must cope with a critical shortage of this vital substance. Annual precipitation at Arches is paltry and irregular, usually totaling about 8.5 inches, and because of the high level of evaporation, available moisture is usually less than the annual average would indicate.

Desert life must also contend with stresses produced by extremely hot summer temperatures, frequently persisting for prolonged periods. Daytime summer readings at Arches may rise above 100°F. Wide ranges in daily and annual temperatures are characteristic of desert regions. In the summer, the difference between the maximum daytime reading and the nightly low at the Park can exceed 50 degrees, and the yearly temperature spread may exceed 125 degrees.

Clear skies and low humidities prevail in deserts. With few clouds and relatively little water vapor to deflect sunlight, the ground at Arches receives a high percentage of the possible yearly total of sunshine. Ground surface temperatures in bright, summer sunlight often exceed the air temperature by twenty-five to fifty degrees. Such high surface temperatures further aggravate living conditions for desert plants and animals.

Desert flora and fauna must also survive frequent winds. Arches has been characterized by author Maurine Whipple as "the country of **wind**." Hot, dry air blowing on plants and animals evaporates precious water from their bodies. And when desiccating winds move over the desert soil, moisture is evaporated, decreasing the already limited water supply for plant life. Occasionally winds laden with dust will sweep across the desert. These swirling windstorms most often occur during spring at Arches, irritating plants and animals and coating them in dust. Though severe sandstorms are rare in the Park, they can be highly dangerous to flora and fauna by violently sandblasting them, and even burying some of them under suffocating piles of sand.

PLANT ADAPTATIONS TO DESERT EXISTENCE

Desert-dwelling plants have developed a variety of mechanisms for living in their harsh environment. These plants can be classified according to their adaptive mechanisms as either *drought-escapers*— those that **avoid** the limited moisture supply—or *drought-resisters*—those that can **withstand** prolonged hot and dry periods. Several examples of these mechanisms are discussed below.

Drought-escaping Plants

Certain plants evade the desert's shortage of water either by living in perennially

Colorado chipmunks (*Eutamias quadrivittatus*), like the one depicted here in a Utah juniper, are found almost everywhere in the Park. This colorful animal is often seen scampering over rocks or foraging for food scraps at picnic sites and in the Devil's Garden Campground. Its head and body are shaded in brownish-orange and pale gray, and distinctively striped with dark brown and white. The rodent is one of the larger chipmunk species, with an overall length of about nine inches. Its native foods include grasses, herbs, and piñon pine nuts. The chipmunk's main enemies are coyotes, gray foxes, and hawks.

Tamarisk (*Tamarix pentandra*). Prior to 1925 there is no record of tamarisk growing along the Colorado River in Utah. Since then, however, this small, bushy tree has become common along the river and its tributaries in the state. Tamarisk is native to the Eastern Hemisphere from western Europe to the Himalayas, and was introduced into the United States from the Mediterranean region in the early 1800s. The tree's name is indicative of its origin, being derived from the Hebrew word *tamarik*, meaning cleanliness, apparently because its branches were used for brooms. Originally grown in the United States as an ornamental, the tree has become naturalized and has spread widely, and is now regarded as a nuisance in the arid and semiarid areas of the Southwest. Its characteristically dense, jungle-like thickets form virtually impenetrable barriers at certain places along many watercourses. And these invasive plants displace native vegetation, in some areas often taking over completely. Tamarisks are water-loving and have long, fibrous roots penetrating to great depths in search of moisture; they consume enormous quantities of ground water. The tree reaches a height of twenty feet or more and is deciduous, with yellow-green, scalelike leaves on delicate, arching branches. Clusters of tiny, pinkish flowers bloom from spring through summer. Because of their tolerance of salt, tamarisks also are sometimes called saltcedars.

wet locations or by timing their life cycles to periods when moisture and temperature conditions are favorable for their growth. In a sense, these drought-escaping plants do not directly meet the desert's challenge to develop mechanisms that will allow them to survive and thrive in a water-poor environment.

A few permanently moist areas exist in the desert which provide a fairly abundant water supply for plants that require constantly damp soil. The major water-rich areas of Arches are along the Colorado River, Salt Wash, Courthouse Wash, and at Freshwater Spring. Prominent among the water-loving plants—or *hydrophytes* —living in the Park are cottonwoods and tamarisks. They are also examples of *phreatophytes*, plants that have long, fibrous roots extending to permanent water. Tamarisk, also called saltcedar, represent still another type of plant: those that are *halophytic*, or salt tolerant, and are able to live in saline soils. Among other species of salt-tolerant plants at Arches are saltbush, greasewood, shadscale, sagebrush, and pickleweed.

Many plants avoid the desert's drought by completing their life cycles only when moisture is sufficiently available and the temperature is propitious. These plants are called *ephemerals*, and include many diverse species. Most ephemerals are small, and usually they are very short-lived. Their seeds may wait several years to germinate, until favorable moisture and temperature conditions combine, generally in the spring. The plants then quickly grow, flower, and produce seed—often in only a few weeks. When ephemerals bloom, they may create showy displays of colorful wildflowers that are tourist attractions in many desert areas.

Drought-resisting Plants

Xerophytes, or drought-resisting plants, have developed diverse mechanisms to survive with a limited water supply. Unlike the drought-escaping plants, the xerophytes have met the challenge by developing ways to tolerate drought.

Some xerophytes have modified their leaves to lessen evaporation. For example, some of these plants have small leaves, which reduce the surface area from which life-sustaining water can be lost. Mormon tea, found in many places at the Park, has exceedingly small, scalelike leaves, occurring only at the joints of the plant's young stems. Most species of cacti have completely eliminated water-losing leaves. Certain xerophytic plants have leaf coatings that retard the evaporation of moisture. Blackbrush, an abundant and ubiquitous plant at Arches, has a waxlike coating on its small leaves, and the yucca, another common Park plant, has a similar coating on its narrow, stiff leaves.

Most xerophytic plants have shallow, spreading root systems that are able to absorb quickly any temporary ground moisture, particularly after brief summer rainfall.

Cacti—the hallmark of desert vegetation—are outstanding water savers. They can retain relatively large quantities of water in their fleshy bodies to last them through extended periods of drought. Cacti also have an almost impervious body covering that prevents all but a negligible loss of moisture. Arches is home to six species of cacti.

The adaptation of plant life to survival in the harsh desert environment is vital, since in the desert, as elsewhere, plants provide the food base upon which all animal life is ultimately dependent. Some animals, the *herbivores*, subsist exclusively on plants. *Carnivores* eat the plant consumers, while the *omnivores* are both plant and animal feeders.

ANIMAL ADAPTATIONS TO DESERT LIFE

Animals, unlike plants, can seek more hospitable surroundings when living conditions become too stressful. Nevertheless, to survive in the desert, animal life, like plant life, must adapt to the harsh environment's two principal threats to survival—aridity and heat. The many ways in which animals adapt to desert living are grouped in two categories: *body mechanisms* and *behavioral patterns*. Some animals have adaptations from both categories. Several examples of these adaptations follow.

Body Mechanisms

Although certain desert animals have body mechanisms that allow them to live with excessive dryness and high temperatures, these mechanisms are not unique to desert fauna. Such mechanisms have been refined in desert-dwelling animals through evolution. These mechanisms are either *physiological*—involving the body's vital processes and functions—or *morphological*— affecting the form and structure of the body. Both types of mechanisms may be present in the same animal species.

Animals obtain their water in one or more ways: by drinking, from moisture in

Ord's kangaroo rat (*Dipodomys ordi*). Abundant in Arches, Ord's kangaroo rats inhabit dry, sandy areas where they dig burrows. Well adapted to arid regions, these rodents can survive without drinking water, relying instead on moisture produced by the digestion of seeds they gather and store in their underground dens. Nocturnal, they hop about on their large, strong hind legs, a characteristic that gives them their common name. When chased by predators, kangaroo rats can leap as far as six feet in attempting to escape. Their hair is yellowish-brown on the upper body, and white on the underside. The long, tufted tail, which has a lateral white stripe, may be five to six inches long, or about one-half the animal's overall length.

food, through *metabolic water* produced chemically by the digestion of food, and by direct absorption through the skin.

Certain desert-dwelling animals can live without drinking water, although they may drink water if it is present. These animals can satisfy their needs entirely from moisture in food and by producing metabolic water. For example, the kangaroo rat, a common resident of Arches, rarely drinks water. These small rodents subsist almost completely on dry seeds, relying for moisture on the meager water content of the seeds and on metabolic water. In the animal's body, the oxidation of one gram of starch yields 0.6 gram of water and one gram of fat produces about 1.1 grams of water. Further, the kangeroo rat practices *caprophagy*, that is, the animal eats its own fecal pellets, thus retrieving their scant water content.

Amphibians—frogs, toads, and salamanders—absorb water through their skins. Consequently they must live in moist areas, the existence of which would seem to be incongruous with desert regions. Yet such hospitable environments are found in many desert settings, including Arches, along permanent and intermittent streams and rivers, at springs, and in temporary pools in potholes and ground depressions. Eight species of amphibians live in the Park: three of frogs, four of toads, and one kind of salamander.

Conservancy of water in the bodies of animals is crucial, especially for those living on the desert. However, loss of this indispensable liquid becomes unavoidable through respiration, by evaporation from the body surface, and through elimination of urine and fecal matter.

To minimize water loss, desert animals employ several morphological and physiological mechanisms. Some animals have body coverings that conserve water. Many species of insects have nearly impervious, waxy body surfaces that give considerable protection against moisture loss. Reptiles have tough, dry skins covered with scales. Although the reptile's skin does not prevent water evaporation, it does impede it.

The spadefoot toad commonly congregates in temporary pools that form after spring and summer rainfall. When these pools evaporate, the small amphibian seeks refuge from desiccation either by entering burrows of other animals, or by excavating its own burrow.

The spadefoot has a single, sharp, black horny spur, or "spade," on the inner side of each hind foot. To burrow, the amphibian moves its hind feet in a circular motion—digging with its spades—and pushes the dirt aside as it backs into the ground.

Safely underground, the spadefoot enters into *estivation*, or "summer sleep," a state of dormancy. This torpid physiological condition results in a lowering of the animal's metabolic rate, thus conserving its energy, body weight, and moisture. In addition, the spadefoot's outer skin forms a sheathing that reduces water evaporation.

Water is lost by all land animals through the excretion of urine and feces. However, reptiles and birds have physiological mechanisms that greatly reduce water losses from the voiding of urine. Such water-saving is especially beneficial to desert-dwelling reptiles and birds. Urine is composed of water, nitrogeneous waste called *urea*, and small quantities of other substances that have been removed from the blood by the kidneys. In reptiles and birds, much of the urine's water content is reabsorbed before elimination, leaving *uric acid*, a whitish, semisolid material that is excreted with the dark-colored feces.

Physiological mechanisms to reduce water loss from excretion are also present in the kangaroo rat. Their kidneys produce highly concentrated urine, so that relatively little water is lost by voiding. Water is also saved by reabsorption in the large intestine, resulting in the excretion of very dry feces.

All animals must adjust to changes in the temperature of their environment to survive. On the high desert these fluctuations may be great—from parching heat to enervating cold—and to withstand such extremes an animal must maintain its body temperature within certain limits. Various adaptations have evolved among animals to cope with temperature stresses.

Most animals are *ectothermic*, or "cold blooded," with body temperatures determined by the temperature of their external environment. All the invertebrates (animals without backbones, such as worms, snails, clams, and spiders) and all the lower vertebrates—fishes, amphibians, and reptiles—are ectotherms.

Cold weather lowers their body temperature, decreasing *metabolism*—the complex of physical and chemical processes that substain life. Exposure to excessive cold will kill ectotherms. The spadefoot toad survives freezing temperatures by retreating into underground burrows and crevices that extend below the frost line. There the small creature enters a state of dormancy termed *brumation*, a type of "winter sleep" that lasts until the weather warms.

If ectotherms are subjected directly to high summer heat and do not take evasive action, their body temperatures may exceed tolerance levels, resulting in death. For example, the lethal body temperature of the desert spiny lizard, a reptilian species occurring in the Park, is about 109°F. This reading approximates the maximum air temperature of many summer days at Arches, and is about fifty degrees below typical daytime temperatures registered on sand and bare rock during the summer.

Birds and mammals are *endotherms*, or "warm-blooded" animals, characterized by a nearly constant body temperature, regardless of the temperature of their external surroundings. The body temperature

The **Great Basin spadefoot toad** (*Scaphiopus intermontanus*) is one of the most common amphibian inhabitants of Arches. The adult is small—about two inches long—and pudgy. It has catlike vertical pupils, one of the characteristics that distinguishes it from true toads of the genus *Bufo*. Another differentiating trait is a single spur, or "spade," on the inner side of each hind foot. These spades are used to dig burrows. During dry periods, the toad uses its spades to burrow backward into the ground [as illustrated], there to lie dormant until the return of favorable moist weather.

of endotherms is largely determined by internal production of heat. Such animals can function in both relatively hot and cold weather.

Certain endotherms possess large appendages that radiate body heat. The blacktail jackrabbit—a common inhabitant of the Park—has large, thinly haired ears. When blood vessels in the ears are dilated, body heat is dissipated into the air.

Body coverings provide insulation against temperature stresses. In warm weather, birds press their feathers against their bodies to transmit heat outward; when temperatures are cold they ruffle their feathers, thus retaining bodily heat within the spaces between the feathers.

In hot weather, the hair of mammals acts as a shield against outside heat; in cold weather, their hair retards heat loss from the body.

Many desert animals have pale coloring which reflects light and heat. This aids them in regulating their bodily temperature and in conserving water.

Some animals are equipped to move considerable distances in the desert to seek water and food, or relief from extreme, prolonged summer heat. Birds can fly to water and shade, while larger and medium-sized mammals, such as mountain lions, mule deer, bobcats, gray foxes, and coyotes—all residents of Arches—can walk many miles to water and food, or to more comfortable temperatures.

Behavioral Patterns

Adaptation of behavioral patterns is even more important than physical adaptations to the survival of animal life in the harsh desert environment.

Reptiles—the evocative symbols of desert animal life—regulate their temperature by behavior. Most lizards forage during the day, maintaining their body temperature within optimal range by seeking shade when it rises too high, or by bask-

ing in warming sunlight when their body temperature begins to drop.

Some animals avoid summer daytime temperatures by being *crepuscular*—active during twilight at dawn or dusk—while others are *nocturnal*—active only during darkness. Tourists at Arches sometimes comment that there appear to be very few animals in the Park. This apparent lack of animal life is largely traceable to the crepuscular and nocturnal habits of many desert-dwelling animals. Such animals spend daylight hours in the protective shade of plants or rocky ledges, or in underground burrows.

Daytime surface temperatures of sandy soil and rock in the desert may rise to 150°F or more when the air temperature reaches 100°F or higher. However, the air temperature is lower in the branches of bushes and trees, where reptiles, small mammals, and birds may seek refuge.

During summer days, many desert animals retreat into underground burrows to escape from the fierce blast of heat. Soil insulates burrows, making them relatively cool refuges in the desert. During the hottest part of the summer day, the bottom of a deep burrow may be 100°F cooler than the temperature of the ground surface. At night, if skies are clear so surface radiation is unimpeded, surface temperatures may drop more than 120°F. Yet the air temperature at the bottom of a burrow that extends more than three feet below the ground surface will not register any fluctuation from day to night.

Desert animals that are *diurnal*—active during daylight—such as most species of lizards and birds, escape from heat by periodically resting under or in plants, under rocky ledges, or in burrows. Some of them avoid the scarcity of water by staying near such rare dependable water supplies as springs, streams, and rivers.

Other animals have adjusted, or timed, their life cycles to coincide with favorable moist conditions. Spadefoot toads lie dormant in underground burrows until spring and summer rainfall occurs. Then they emerge and seek pools of rainwater in which to breed. There the males issue a series of loud, rasping mating calls to attract the females. Since the temporary pools may evaporate rapidly, breeding occurs immediately, and development also is rapid: the eggs usually hatch in one to three days, and the larval stage may last only ten to twelve days—the shortest of any of the toads.

With the return of dryness, the spadefoot again goes underground to avoid the desert's extreme drought, and to await the onset of another favorable moist period.

Some temporary pools are inhabited also by a multitude of tiny animals, such as freshwater crustaceans. When the pools begin to evaporate, the crustaceans instinctively produce eggs. These lie dormant in the hardened mud—often for several years—until the pool again fills, when the eggs hatch and the life cycle is repeated.

Certain mammals and birds escape the rigors of winter on the high desert by hibernating. Many of the small mammals, such as mice and squirrels, enter the coma-like "winter sleep." Well known among the hibernating birds are the poor-wills (*Phalaenoptilus nuttallii*), members of the nightjar family, and related to the whippoor-will of the eastern United States. Poor-wills—named for their melancholy call—inhabit Arches, but because of their nocturnal habits are seldom seen during

Black-chinned hummingbird (*Archilochus alexandri*). Black-chinned hummingbirds are fairly common summer residents of the Park. At the end of summer they migrate to the warmer winter climates of Mexico. Males have black throats underlined by a conspicuous purple stripe. Females lack the stripe and have white throats. Both sexes are green on the upper body surface, and white on the underside. The adult is small, generally about three-and-a-half inches long. Their nests, in which two or three white eggs are laid, are usually made in bushes or small trees.

daylight. The Hopi Indians aptly named the poor-will *hölchko*, meaning "the sleeping one." The bird has been observed hibernating in rocky crevices and niches. During its torpid state, the poor-will's body temperature may fall as much as 50°F, from its normal of about 106°F to approximately 55°F.

BIOTIC COMMUNITIES OF ARCHES NATIONAL PARK

To the casual observer, the dry and rocky terrain of Arches may appear nearly lifeless—merely a scattering of scrubby, stunted plants, and an occasional lizard or bird. But this superficial impression is highly deceptive. The Parkland in fact supports a surprisingly rich variety of plants and animals: 357 species of vascular plants, 128 kinds of birds, 38 types of mammals, 20 kinds of reptiles, 14 fish species, and 8 types of amphibians.

Ecologists term an assemblage of plant and animal species that live and interact in a common area a *biotic community*. The character of each community is determined primarily by its dominant plants. Biotic communities are named for their most outstanding characteristics, such as their predominant species of plants, or conspicuous physical features. Many of the plants and animals that denote a particular biotic community also may be found in other communities, but they are most abundant in the community that they characterize.

In Arches National Park there are three major biotic communities: the piñon-juniper woodland, desert scrub, and grassland. Combined, they cover more than 80 per cent of the Parkland. Several minor but distinctive communities also are present, including the sand dune, hanging garden, streamside, and aquatic.

Piñon-Juniper Woodland

Mixed stands of Utah juniper and piñon pine commonly occur on the Park's rocky ridges and slopes, and between fins. These short evergreens form open woodlands, usually with the trees far enough apart that their branches do not touch. Interspersed with the small trees are shrubs and patches of bare ground and rock. The diminutive stature of the junipers and piñons has resulted in the woodland being aptly called the "pygmy forest." Piñon is often spelled "pinyon," the Anglicized equivalent of the Spanish word.

Most of the piñon-juniper woodland at Arches lies above 4,800 feet altitude where prevailing temperatures are cooler and precipitation is greater than at lower elevations. More Parkland is covered by this biotic community than by any other—almost double the combined acreages for all the other communities. Approximately 32,000 acres, or nearly 45 per cent of the Park's area, is piñon-juniper woodland.

Extensive stands of the woodland are found on ridges bordering Salt Valley—along the eastern ridge from north of Eagle Park, south to the Fiery Furnace—and on the western ridge from the Klondike Bluffs area, south to Herdina Park. Other prominent stands occur in the Petrified Sand Dunes area, on the upland between Willow Flats and Courthouse Wash, and along the tops of the massive cliffs bordering the Colorado River.

More species of plants—about ninety—grow in the piñon-juniper woodland than in any of the other Park communities. Of the two dominant species, the Utah juniper (*Juniperus osteosperma*) is more abundant than the piñon pine (*Pinus edulis*), and it grows at many locales in Arches without the pine. Other plants include the wavy leaf oak, single-leaf ash, blackbrush, mountain mahogany, cliffrose, Mormon tea, scorpion weed, catseye, yucca, snakeweed, moss, and lichen.

Among the mammals inhabiting the Park's piñon-juniper woodland are the piñon mouse, Apache pocket mouse, des-

LICHENS: TWO PLANTS IN ONE

Lichens—small, crustlike plants that grow on the ground, on rocks, and on tree bark—occur at scattered localities throughout Arches, and are common in the Park's piñon-juniper woodland.

Lichens are composed of two individual plants—a fungus and an alga—living together in a partnership. They are a classic example of *symbiosis*—the intimate biological association of two different organisms. Lichen symbiosis results in the development of a new plant body, the *thallus*, that has no resemblance to either the alga or fungus, and that acts as a single plant. Botanists classify lichens as *cryptogams*, which are primitive plants that reproduce by spores instead of seeds.

Often drab brown or gray, these slow-growing plants may display bright shades of orange, yellow, and green, adding color to the rocks on which they grow, and often creating strangely beautiful patterns. Dead plants are white or black, and when they eventually fleck off the rock they sometimes leave intriguing designs lightly etched into the surface.

Lichens can withstand extreme drying. They swell when moistened, and the plant's water-holding capability may increase their weight up to 300 per cent.

Lichens play an important ecological role as plant colonizers in rocky areas. They help to disintegrate rock, contributing to the formation of the soil in which other plants will grow.

ert cottontail, gray fox, coyote, bobcat, mountain lion, mule deer, and porcupine.

Porcupines have damaged or killed many of the piñons in the Park. These spiny creatures feed on the pine's sap-rich *cambium* layer found immediately beneath the bark. While gnawing on the cambium they may inflict severe injury, and occasionally they will girdle the trunk, killing the tree. The harmful effects of the porcupine's feeding habits became evident in 1945, when Russell L. Mahan, then custodian of Arches, reported that "porcupines have been very active in both the Devil's

House finch (*Carpodacus mexicanus*). House finches are abundant in the Park, where they are permanent residents. They are small, sparrow-like birds, about five-and-a-half inches long. Males are distinguished by their red heads and breasts, and have brownish wings and tails. Females are smaller, and brownish. House finches are omnivorous, feeding on insects and seeds.

Garden and Windows sections. In the vicinity of the Pine Tree Arch, in the Devil's Garden, all the pinyons have been badly barked and it looks like they will all die. In the Windows section a good portion of the young pinyon growth, one or two foot high, has been stripped." Mahan added menacingly, "I have not caught up with any of the culprits yet but when I do they will be **severely reprimanded.**"

Common birds of the piñon-juniper woodland at Arches include the piñon jay, scrub jay, plain titmouse, gray vireo, hairy woodpecker, black-throated gray warbler, house finch, and ash-throated flycatcher.

Desert Scrub

Next to the piñon-juniper woodland, the desert-scrub biotic community covers the most acreage in Arches. More than a quarter of the Parkland—about 18,500 acres—is in this community, characterized generally by low, widely spaced, woody-stemmed, and small-leaved bushes, or scrub. These plants are drought resistant, and certain of them are salt tolerant. Although their overall appearance is scrubby, drab, and monotonous, they nevertheless are a significant floristic element of the Park.

Blackbrush (*Coleogyne ramosissima*) is the principal desert-scrub plant of the Park, dominating approximately 90 per cent of the scrubland. It grows in shallow soils that are sandy, often somewhat rocky, and low in salinity.

Stands of blackbrush occur at many localities throughout Arches, including The Windows, Courthouse Towers, Willow Flats, along the southeast ridge of Salt Valley, on the east side of Klondike Bluffs, in the Balanced Rock area, at several places along the four-wheel-drive road between Balanced Rock and Klondike Bluffs, and along the paved Park road from south Park Avenue to La Sal Mountains Viewpoint.

Some desert-scrub plants are adapted to grow in saline soils. Among the salt-tolerant, or halophytic, desert-scrub plants in Arches are four-wing saltbush, mat saltbush, Garrett saltbush, Castle Valley clover, pickleweed, black greasewood, spiny shadscale, and big sagebrush.

Mat saltbush (*Atriplex corrugata*) and Castle Valley clover (*Atriplex cuneata*) are prominent on the gray, alkaline Mancos Shale soils in lower Salt Valley and in

Cache Valley. Garrett saltbush (*Atriplex garrettii*) is *endemic* to the Canyon Lands Section of the Colorado Plateau—that is, the plant is found only there. At Arches, it grows on talus slopes along the Colorado, and is common in lower Courthouse Wash.

Stands of black greasewood (*Sarcobatus vermiculatus*) occur in upper Salt Wash and in Courthouse Wash west of the bridge on the Park road.

Near Wolfe Cabin is a small stand of big sagebrush (*Artemisia tridentata*). This gray-green shrub emits a characteristic pungent aroma, especially after rain. It is commonly between two and four feet tall but, as the "big" implies, it can grow to ten feet or more. Sagebrush is widespread in the American West, and is a popular floral symbol of the vast region.

Spiny or round-leaf shadscale (*Atriplex confertifolia*) occurs in Cache Valley. Also called sheep-fat, it is an important forage plant for livestock.

Other plants of the desert-scrub community include prickly pear, devil's claw, winterfat, peppergrass, Russian thistle, wirelettuce, rabbitbrush, snakeweed, hedgehog cactus, sand dropseed, Mormon tea, brickellbush, yucca, horsebrush, Indian ricegrass, and halogeton.

Halogeton (*Halogeton glomeratus*), a noxious annual weed native to Eurasia, was first reported growing in the Intermountain West near Wells, Nevada in 1935. Now infesting several million acres of rangeland, halogeton is a serious problem for cattlemen and sheepherders. The weed's herbage contains oxalic acid, which is poisonous to livestock when eaten in large quantities.

Among the mammals of the desert scrub are the coyote, Ord's kangaroo rat, blacktail jackrabbit, canyon mouse, whitetail antelope squirrel, desert woodrat, and rock squirrel. Representative reptilian species are the collared lizard, sagebrush lizard, northern plateau lizard, short-

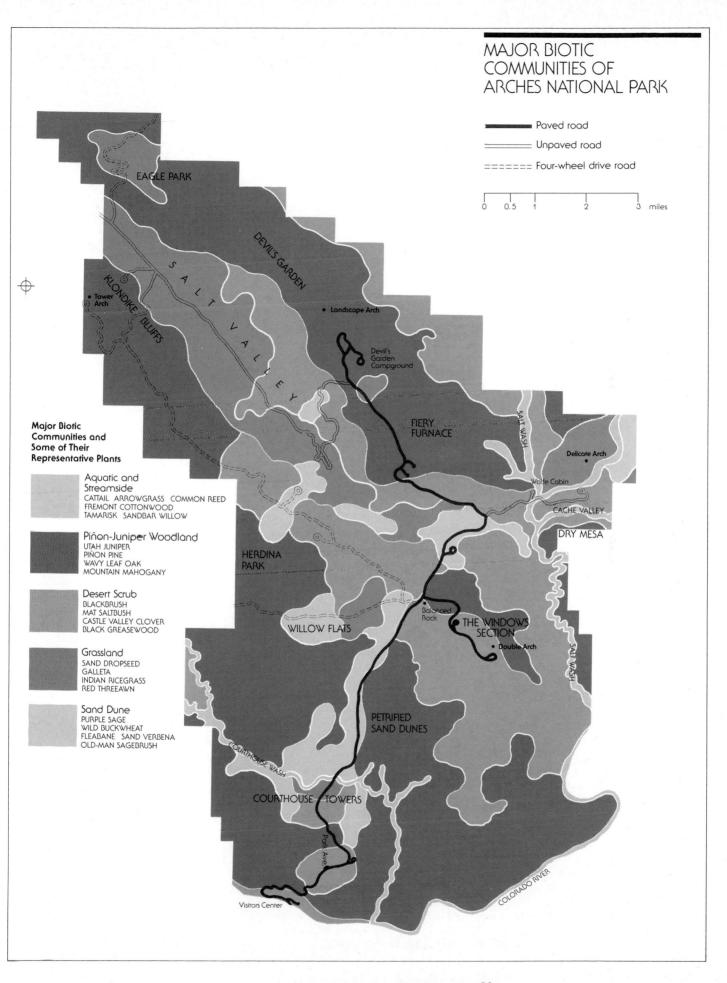

MAJOR BIOTIC COMMUNITIES OF ARCHES NATIONAL PARK

Paved road
Unpaved road
Four-wheel drive road

0   0.5   1   2   3 miles

Major Biotic Communities and Some of Their Representative Plants

Aquatic and Streamside
CATTAIL   ARROWGRASS   COMMON REED
FREMONT COTTONWOOD
TAMARISK   SANDBAR WILLOW

Piñon-Juniper Woodland
UTAH JUNIPER
PIÑON PINE
WAVY LEAF OAK
MOUNTAIN MAHOGANY

Desert Scrub
BLACKBRUSH
MAT SALTBUSH
CASTLE VALLEY CLOVER
BLACK GREASEWOOD

Grassland
SAND DROPSEED
GALLETA
INDIAN RICEGRASS
RED THREEAWN

Sand Dune
PURPLE SAGE
WILD BUCKWHEAT
FLEABANE   SAND VERBENA
OLD-MAN SAGEBRUSH

EAGLE PARK

DEVIL'S GARDEN

SALT VALLEY

KLONDIKE BLUFFS

• Tower Arch

• Landscape Arch

Devil's Garden Campground

FIERY FURNACE

SALT WASH

Delicate Arch •

Wolfe Cabin

CACHE VALLEY

DRY MESA

HERDINA PARK

WILLOW FLATS

Balanced Rock •

THE WINDOWS SECTION

• Double Arch

SALT WASH

PETRIFIED SAND DUNES

COURTHOUSE WASH

COURTHOUSE   TOWERS

Park Ave.

Visitors Center

COLORADO RIVER

Coyote (*Canis latrans*) shown standing behind blackbrush, near Klondike Bluffs. Coyotes are widespread in the western United States, and their characteristic howling and yelping may be heard in the night at Arches. Coyotes are long-legged, and resemble medium-sized, scrawny dogs. An adult weighs from twenty to fifty pounds. Their fur is gray or reddish-brown. The tail is bushy, frequently tipped with black or brown, and carried down when running. Coyotes have a long face and yellowish eyes. Their long ears are pointed and held erect. Although occasionally seen in daylight, coyotes are chiefly nocturnal. They commonly make their dens in rock crevices or in underground burrows. Coyotes are predators and scavengers, and are omnivorous, their diets including such foods as juniper berries, lizards, birds, mice, chipmunks, kangaroo rats, squirrels, rabbits, deer, carrion (dead and decaying flesh), and even rattlesnakes. Coyotes are fast runners, having been clocked at speeds in excess of forty miles per hour over a quarter-mile distance. The name "coyote" is a Spanish-American corruption of the Aztec word *coyotl*.

horned lizard ("horny toad"), desert spiny lizard, gopher snake, and the midget faded rattlesnake. Birds include the black-throated sparrow, sage sparrow, sage thrasher, common raven, and house finch.

Grassland

Approximately 8,500 acres of the Park, or slightly more than 11 per cent of the total area, is grassland. Most of this growth—about 65 per cent—lies in Salt Valley. Smaller tracts are at Eagle Park, Willow Flats, Winter Camp Wash, Courthouse Towers, and the flat between Broken Arch and Sand Dune Arch.

Some thirty-five species of plants grow in this grassland community. Grass species are dominant, with sand dropseed being the most abundant. Other prevalent grasses are galleta, Indian ricegrass, and red threeawn.

The prominence of sand dropseed (*Sporobolus cryptandrus*) is apparently the result of overgrazing by livestock. Cattle and sheep, which once ranged on the present Parkland, prefer the more palatable galleta and Indian ricegrass. As the cover of these two grasses was reduced, the lightly grazed sand dropseed spread and became more plentiful.

Salt Valley was once heavily grazed, and today sand dropseed is common there. Soil erosion also followed overgrazing. In August 1941, Henry Schmidt, then Arches custodian, reported that "overgrazing in the Salt Valley area during the past winter has left the area with little ground cover to prevent a rapid run-off of water, and the heavy rains have washed the road beyond practicable repair."

Among other plants occurring in the grassland are snakeweed, globe mallow, woolly Indianwheat, prickly pear, Mormon tea, stinking milkvetch, winterfat, six-weeks fescue, pale evening-primrose, and two exotic species which are natives of Eurasia: cheatgrass and Russian thistle.

Cheatgrass (*Bromus tectorum*) and Russian thistle (*Salsola kali*) are prominent among the *naturalized* plant species of the Park, that is, those that are nonnative but propagating freely and growing wild.

Cheatgrass is a weedy annual that has spread throughout most of the United States. Also called downy chess and downy brome, cheatgrass derives its common name from its abundance in fields where cereal grains were once raised. After cheatgrass has matured in the spring, it dries to become an extreme fire hazard.

Russian thistle, the famed "tumble-weed" of western song and legend, was introduced into the United States in 1873 or 1874. Seeds from the plant were in a shipment of flaxseed from Russia which was sown near Scotland, South Dakota. From this introduction, the plant has become widespread, infesting many areas of the central and western United States, where it is considered a common weed pest.

This spiny, bushy, round-shaped plant can grow to three feet or more in diameter. An annual, its seeds mature in autumn, with a single plant producing up to 50,000 seeds. After the plant withers, the wind breaks its stem, and then—as its common name implies—the wind tumbles the weed across the ground, scattering its seeds. Piles of tumbleweeds often accumulate in ground depressions or against cliffs, fences, and other barriers.

Mammals of the Park's grassland include the mule deer, coyote, badger, blacktail jackrabbit, Ord's kangaroo rat, valley pocket gopher, deer mouse, and northern grasshopper mouse. Pronghorn, commonly called antelope, and the white-tail prairie dog formerly lived on the grassland but have vanished from Arches.

Among the grassland birds are the horned lark, western meadowlark, mourning dove, loggerhead shrike, common raven, common nighthawk, sparrow hawk, red-tailed hawk, and prairie falcon.

Sand Dune Community

Several hummocky tracts of sand dunes are scattered throughout Arches. Their aggregate expanse covers nearly 4,000 acres, or approximately 5.5 per cent of the total Parkland. Major concentrations of dunes are at Courthouse Towers and Willow Flats, in Salt Valley, east of south Devil's Garden, and along The Great Wall.

Although the dry, sandy slopes of dunes—the epitome of desert landforms—may seem an inhospitable place, certain plants and animals are adapted to living on these wind-rippled mounds.

Geographers classify dunes as either *active* or *fixed*. Active dunes lack vegetative cover, and consequently are readily moved by wind. Fixed dunes are those that are stabilized—anchored—by plant growth, thus prevented from further shifting by wind currents.

About sixty-five species of plants grow on the fixed dunes of the Park. However, the number of species and their composition may vary considerably from one group of dunes to another. Annuals are abundant when moisture and temperature are favorable for their growth, but may be absent when these conditions are not auspicious.

Among plants growing on the dunes are Indian ricegrass, purple sage, wild buck-

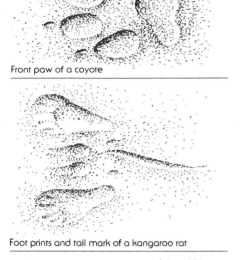

Front paw of a coyote

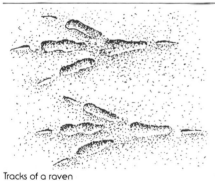

Foot prints and tail mark of a kangaroo rat

Trace of a garter snake

Tracks of a raven

Examples of **animal tracks** commonly found on sand dunes and on other sandy areas of the Park, depicted one-half natural size.

wheat, fleabane, red threeawn, six-weeks fescue, rusty lupine, Mormon tea, dock, little twistflower, spurge, old-man sagebrush, sunflower, Coville bursage, mule's ears, and sand verbena.

Animal life on the dunes is often recorded by tracks left in the soft sand. Telltale tracks of nocturnally active animals usually can be observed after sunrise and until the wind has smoothed the sandy surface. However, tracks made by animals that are active during the daytime may be quickly erased by the wind.

Most desert-dwelling snakes are nocturnal. Characteristically they leave long wiggly lines, the smaller species making narrow and shallow traces while the larger serpents form wider and deeper furrows.

Kangaroo rats are another of the nocturnal animals. As their name implies, they hop about on muscular hind legs. When making short, slow hops, these agile rodents leave tracks of all four feet in a row—the small front feet between the larger hind feet—followed by a slight, linear depression where their long, tufted tail lands. But when the kangaroo rat makes long, fast leaps, only its hind toes touch the sand, simultaneously leaving a series of paired tracks.

Coyotes often prowl about the dunes at night in search of prey. They leave doglike paw prints, and if the sand is firm enough impressions of their claws may show also.

Most lizards are active during the daytime. As they forage, their feet make diminutive prints and their dragging tails leave thin, faint streaks in the loose sand.

Birds usually leave tracks on the dunes in the morning and late afternoon hours, when avian life is most active.

Hanging Gardens

Perched on some of the Park's sandstone cliffs are spring-fed alcoves housing lush vegetation, vividly contrasting with the naked, reddish rock of the precipices. These aerial oases, appropriately called hanging gardens, are the rarest and most distinctive of the Park's biotic communities.

Several of these unique gardens are on the massive cliff behind the Visitors Center. Others are in Freshwater Canyon, and northeast of Wolfe Cabin along the cliff north of the foot trail to Delicate Arch.

Clinging to these cool, moist alcoves are *mesic plants*—those that require a moderately wet habitat—such as maidenhair fern, cave primrose, scarlet monkeyflower, helleborine orchid, columbine, dogbane, bastard toadflax, and poison ivy.

Birds seek the small pools of water that may collect at hanging gardens, and the shelter of their cooling, protective shade. Small mammals frequent those hanging gardens accessible by narrow ledges.

Streamside Community

Dependable and fairly abundant water supplies are obviously rare in desert areas like Arches. But there are limited zones

THE MYSTERIOUS TURTLE OF FRESHWATER CANYON

Several times during the summer of 1964 a turtle was seen at a pool in Freshwater Canyon, a tributary to Salt Wash northwest of Wolfe Cabin. Until these sightings, there had been no record of turtles in Arches. Attempts were made to capture the turtle, but on September 1 of that year, Thomas D. Mulhern, Jr., then the acting naturalist, reported that "so far it has eluded collection." Had the creature been caught, said Mulhern, it would have been "the first turtle to be scientifically recorded" at Arches.

The following year, Dennis L. Carter, who succeeded Mulhern as naturalist, reported that the turtle was sighted on April 14, again in Freshwater Canyon. Since then, no further sightings have been reported, and the fate of the elusive Turtle of Freshwater Canyon is unknown.

Are turtles native to Arches? No. Except for the one seen in Freshwater Canyon, no others have been reported in Arches, nor have they been recorded in the general vicinity of the Park.

How, then, did the mysterious turtle get there? Was it someone's pet that escaped or was freed, or was it put in the canyon pool as a hoax? The answer remains a mystery.

where permanent water is available: along perennial streams and at springs, or along intermittent streams where surface water is present for part of the year or—where there is no surface flow—ground water is readily obtainable at shallow depths year-round. The streamside, or *riparian*, community occurs on constantly moist soil along the margins of perennial and intermittent streams.

The Park's streamside community is concentrated in narrow strips along the right bank of the Colorado River, and lining the borders of Salt Wash and Courthouse Wash. In some places the vegetation is dense, occasionally creating jungle-like thickets. Where these plants are thickly massed, they stand out in striking contrast

Beaver (*Castor canadensis*). These large, semiaquatic rodents were trapped extensively in the early 1800s for their luxuriant fur, and the quest for beaver pelts contributed much to the exploration of the American West. Fur hunters trapped beaver along the Green and Colorado rivers in Utah, and one trapper—Denis Julien—carved his name in 1844 near a natural arch in what is now the Park. Heavy trapping led to the extermination of beaver in many areas, but they have been reintroduced widely in their former range. Beaver are noted for their dam-building ability, but since they cannot dam large rivers such as the Colorado, they instead excavate burrows into the river banks. Entrances to these dens are underwater during spring and early summer, but usually exposed when the water drops in late summer. Beaver have thick, brown fur, and large, chisel-like front teeth. Their hind feet are webbed, and they possess a naked, paddle-like tail that is used as a rudder, and as an aid to fast swimming. Adults are about four feet in length, and weigh up to seventy pounds. They are primarily nocturnal, venturing onto land in darkness in search of food. At Arches, beaver prefer to feed on willow and cottonwood leaves, twigs, and bark, but will also eat tamarisks.

to the generally sparse, low and scrubby plants that are widespread over so much of the Parkland.

Flash floods are a major hazard to plants growing within the confines of desert washes. Muddy, debris-laden torrents periodically rage through these washes after thunderstorms, scouring them of plants and undercutting vegetated banks, causing them to collapse. Few plants survive long in such a precarious habitat.

Common plants of the streamside community at Arches include tamarisk, Fremont cottonwood, sandbar willow, Russian thistle, hackberry, and rubber rabbitbrush. Less abundant are Russian olive and peach-leaf willow. Russian olive, Russian thistle, and tamarisk are naturalized plants. The introduction of tamarisk (*Tamarix*) has caused major and dramatic changes in the character of streamside vegetation in the arid Southwest. This plant has spread widely and become a nuisance by forming dense thickets, displacing native plants, and consuming great quantities of ground water.

The greatest concentrations and variety of animal life in the Park occur within the streamside community. Among the mammals found there are the mule deer, coyote, bobcat, gray fox, porcupine, ringtailed cat, raccoon, striped skunk, spotted skunk, beaver, muskrat, blacktail jackrabbit, desert cottontail, deer mouse, desert woodrat, and canyon bat (western pipistrel).

Many species of birds live along the streamsides, attracted by its readily accessible water, vegetation, and the plentiful supply of insects. Included in the streamside bird population are the great blue heron, snowy egret, mallard, spotted sandpiper, red-shafted flicker, black-billed magpie, house wren, warbling vireo, Bullock's oriole, blue grosbeak, song sparrow, and common raven.

Representatives of all the Park's amphibians also dwell in the streamside community: the leopard frog, bullfrog, canyon treefrog, Great Basin spadefoot toad, Woodhouse's toad, red-spotted toad, Great Plains toad, and tiger salamander.

Reptiles of the community include the western whiptail, leopard lizard, northern plateau lizard, common garter snake, black-necked garter snake, wandering garter snake, racer, Mesa Verde night snake, and midget faded rattlesnake.

Aquatic Community

The presence of an aquatic community in the desert setting of Arches may seem a paradox, yet it exists in the Colorado River, and along the courses of Salt Wash and Courthouse Wash—when these intermittent streams are flowing or have small standing pools—and in temporary pools that form after rainfall in ground depressions and in potholes.

Aquatic plants spend part or all of their life cycles either immersed or submersed in water. Among the aquatic plants at Arches are watercress, sedge, common reed, rush, cattail, and arrowgrass. The leaves of arrowgrass (*Triglochin maritima*) contain hydrocyanic acid, and can cause poisoning when eaten by livestock.

Fifteen species of fish have been recorded from the Colorado River near Arches. Of these, only six are natives: humpback chub, roundtail chub, Colorado squawfish, speckled dace, flannelmouth sucker, and bluehead sucker. The Colorado squawfish and the humpback chub are rare and endangered, while the flannelmouth sucker is abundant. The other three natives are common.

fathead minnow, carp, red shiner, sand shiner, channel catfish, black bullhead, plains killifish, largemouth bass, and green sunfish.

The many small, temporary pools that form in potholes and ground depressions following rainstorms in the spring and summer may teem with tiny lifeforms. Stresses on life are extreme in these shallow, ephemeral pools. The volume, temperature, and chemistry of water in them can change drastically in a very short period of time, and the life cycles of animals living in any of these pools must be completed quickly before the water evaporates.

Among the inhabitants of these temporary pools are toad tadpoles, snails, aquatic insects, and freshwater crustaceans such as copepods, fairy shrimp, tadpole shrimp, clam shrimp, and seed shrimp.

FISH

Fifteen species of fish have been reported in the Colorado River at Arches. Of these, six are native and nine were introduced. One of the native species and one of the exotics are portrayed below.

Colorado squawfish (*Ptychocheilus lucius*)

The Colorado squawfish is native only to the Colorado River system. This fish—the largest minnow in North America and one of the biggest in the world—may attain a length of six feet and weigh up to 100 pounds. The elongated, streamlined body is bright olive-green with a whitish abdomen. Its cone-shaped head has a large, almost horizontal mouth containing raptorial teeth. Long-lived and a carnivorous predator, the squawfish is usually found where the river current is strong and the water is deep and muddy. Spawning occurs from spring into late summer. Construction of dams apparently has been detrimental to the habitat of the Colorado squawfish, and now it is classified as a rare and endangered species and is protected by federal and state laws. Indians and pioneers caught the squawfish for food, and early Moab settlers took the fish from the Colorado in the vicinity of Arches. The Colorado squawfish is also known as the Colorado salmon, whitefish, and Colorado minnow.

Channel catfish (*Ictalurus punctatus*)

Channel catfish were planted in the Colorado River near Arches in 1919, through the efforts of Horace Stone Rutledge, an active sportsman. Rutledge was born in Missouri in 1873, and there during his boyhood enjoyed fishing for channel cats. After settling in Moab—where he became a prominent public official serving in various positions, including three terms as mayor—Rutledge recognized that the Colorado River was suitable for the introduction of channel catfish. In 1919, Rutledge, then Grand County Clerk, applied to the Bureau of Fisheries in Washington, D.C. for a shipment of fingerlings. His application was approved, and several cans of fry were dispatched by train from a government hatchery in Kansas. They arrived at The Denver and Rio Grande Western Railroad depot in Thompson, about forty miles north of Moab, on Sunday, October 12, 1919. There the fingerlings were met by Rutledge and a truck and driver supplied by the Moab Garage, then transported to the Colorado and released just upriver from the highway bridge. Rutledge several years later recalled proudly that the fry were planted "without the loss of a single fish." Three cans of fingerlings were unloaded, from the same train, at Grand Junction, Colorado, and those fry were placed in the river there. Chronicling the planting near Moab, the town's newspaper, *The Times-Independent*, noted prophetically on October 16, 1919, that "within a very few years" the Colorado "should provide good fishing for the sportsmen here." The prophesy was amply fulfilled, and in less than five-and-a-half years, on March 20, 1927, a lengthy article appeared in the sporting section of the Sunday *Salt Lake Tribune* about the channel catfish in the Colorado River near Moab, and stated that the origin of these fish in the river was a mystery. Commenting on the article, the Moab newspaper for March 24, 1927, observed that "the article made interesting reading, but like most fish stories, it was somewhat misleading. As is well known by the people of Moab, channel catfish were planted in the river a number of years ago by H. S. Rutledge." Though now widespread in the western United States, channel catfish are not native to the rivers and lakes of the West. Homewaters for this popular sport and food fish are east of the Rocky Mountains, from southern Canada into northeastern Mexico. But beginning in the late 1800s they were widely introduced into western waters, where they have since flourished and become common permanent denizens. Channel catfish are adapted to living in rapidly flowing rivers, by having enlongated, streamlined bodies and deeply forked tails. However, they commonly dwell also in ponds and lakes. Their scaleless bodies are usually grayish-blue above, fading to white on the underside. Black spots of various sizes and number, according to the individual fish, speckle the sides. At the front of the dorsal fin and each of the pectoral fins is a sharp, stiff spine used in defense against predatory fish. Also, a venom-producing gland is located at the base of each spine. When the channel cat is attacked, these spines are raised and locked into position, giving the fish spike-like, poison-laden weapons. Channel catfish have the potential to grow quite large—specimens weighing more than fifty pounds have been caught. However, average weights are lower, ranging widely from about two pounds for those living in ponds and small streams up to twenty pounds or more in larger lakes and rivers. They are omnivorous, nocturnally feeding on the bottom in shallow water. Their distinctive *barbels*, resembling cat whiskers and giving the fish its common name, are sensitive to touch and taste, and are used in hunting for food. Spawning occurs in the spring, with breeding sites hidden in deeply undercut banks, under rocky ledges, in hollow logs, and other protected places.

Ten species of lizards and ten species of snakes are found in Arches. Turtles and tortoises are not native to the Park. However, in the mid-1960s a single turtle was sighted, but it probably was placed in the area as a hoax. Fossilized bones of Mesozoic Era reptiles have been unearthed at Arches. Three of the Park's more interesting reptiles are depicted here.

Collared lizard (*Crotaphytus collaris*)

This large, colorful lizard lives in rocky, dry areas of the Park. Adults are about a foot long, with the tail usually twice the length of the body and head. Skin color can be light brown, olive, bluish, or greenish. Variegated spots cover the skin, and adult males have a blue-green throat. The collared lizard derives its name from two prominent transverse black bands that ring the neck. These collars break the outline of the reptile, making the head appear detached from the body, while the spots—resembling lichen patterns and simulating rock surfaces—help the lizard blend into its surroundings and escape predators. Collared lizards are pugnacious, swift-footed—often running on their hind legs—and excellent jumpers. They are primarily carnivorous, preying on other lizards, small snakes, spiders, and insects.

Midget faded rattlesnake (*Crotalus viridis concolor*)

A subspecies of the western rattlesnake, the midget faded rattlesnake is the only highly poisonous snake found at Arches. These serpents are small, usually less than twenty-five inches long, and have straw-colored skin with a faint pattern of blotches on the dorsal surface. Like other rattlers, they have bulky bodies, narrow necks, and large flat, triangular heads with keen, catlike eyes. The midget faded rattlesnake is found in a wide variety of habitats. Like most desert-dwelling snakes, it is primarily nocturnal, spending daylight hours in underground burrows or beneath logs and rocks, to escape heat which can raise its body temperature to lethal levels. The snake has been observed climbing into bushes and trees. B. W. Allred of Moab once saw a midget faded rattler stretched along the limb of a tree, about four feet above the ground. All rattlesnakes are classed as pit vipers. They have two heat-sensitive pits, one on each side of the head between the eyes and the nostrils. These special heat receptors are used to locate warm-blooded prey in darkness. The heat-sensing ability of pit vipers is so well developed that they can detect temperature differences of one-fifth of a degree Celsius. The rattler commonly feeds on lizards, birds, and small mammals. Although dangerous, rattlesnakes are preyed upon by some animals. Red-tailed hawks regularly hunt rattlers, and so, to a lesser degree, do eagles. Kingsnakes, racers, and whipsnakes attack and swallow them whole. Bobcats, foxes, and especially coyotes stalk rattlers. Other enemies include deer and pronghorn—which have been seen stomping rattlers to death—and man, who has generally considered them to be evil, slithering creatures manifestly deserving of destruction. However, these reptiles—found only in the New World—are unique, even beautiful, and have been wrongly accused of being vindictive toward man. Though widely despised, they are of economic value to many ranchers and farmers by preying on rodents. Most rattlesnakes try to avoid humans. But if surprised or provoked, they usually—but **not** always—sound their distinctive rattling warning, and may make a swift strike. They have a pair of sharp, hollow fangs hinged at the front of the upper jaw. Ordinarily, the fangs lie against the roof of the mouth, but when the rattler strikes they swing down into a biting position. Most bites suffered by people are on the fingers and hands, with the next largest number of bites inflicted on the ankles. The venomous bite is painful and commonly accompanied by weakness, sweating, faintness, and nausea. A single bite can be fatal. Imprecise statistics exist for the number of people bitten by rattlesnakes annually in the United States. However, it is estimated that 7,500 people are bitten each year, with about 10 of the victims dying.

Mesa Verde night snake (*Hypsiglena torquata loreala*)

In addition to the midget faded rattlesnake, Arches is home for one other species of venomous serpent: the rear-fanged Mesa Verde night snake. This small snake, with its flat and triangular-shaped head, dark patches on the back, and cat-like vertical pupils, somewhat resembles a rattler. Because of these similarities, the night snake is occasionally mistaken for a small rattlesnake by people whose knowledge about reptiles is limited. Unlike the rattler's venom, which is injected by fangs at the front of its upper jaw, the night snake's venom flows down grooves in the rear teeth of its upper jaw, and must be chewed into the victim. Compared with the lightning-quick, needle-like strike of the rattler, the night snake's chewing bite takes a longer time to impart its deadly effect.

Although venomous, the night snake is not considered dangerous to man. The likelihood is virtually nil that this small snake could chew on a person long enough to release a hazardous quantity of poison before being dislodged. Any minor wound the reptile might inflict would probably not be any more harmful than a bee sting. Since the night snake, as its name implies, is nocturnal, it is seldom encountered by people. It frequents rocky and sandy areas, and preys on lizards, salamanders, frogs, and toads. Juvenile specimens also seek insects. These slender, smooth-scaled snakes are usually less than two feet in length. They are gray or beige, with brown or dark-gray blotches on the back. Behind each eye is a prominent black or dark-brown mark.

Teeth of an *Iguanodon*, an Early Cretaceous-age dinosaur, were discovered near Arches in 1968 by Lin Ottinger of Moab. His find was a new species of this dinosaur and it was appropriately named *Iguanodon ottingeri* for its discoverer. The first *Iguanodon* remains—also teeth—were found in England, in 1822. The discovery was made by Mary Ann Mantell, the wife of an English physician, Dr. Gideon Algernon Mantell. They shared a mutual interest in fossil collecting and geology. In spring of 1822, Mrs. Mantell accompanied her husband on a house call near Lewes, in Sussex. While her husband attended his patient, Mrs. Mantell strolled along a road in Tilgate Forest. By the roadside, in a pile of rocks to be used for road repairs, she saw some fossil teeth embedded in one of the stones. She showed the specimens to her husband and, excited about the find, he searched for, and found, more. Later that year, Dr. Mantell published a book about fossils and included a description of the teeth. The name "Iguanodon" was suggested to Dr. Mantell by the Reverend W. D. Conybeare, a pioneer English paleontologist.

PREHISTORIC REPTILES

Fossilized bones of Mesozoic reptiles have been unearthed at several sites in Arches.

Reptiles dominated the world during the Mesozoic Era. Called the "Age of Reptiles," the Mesozoic spanned 167 million years, from 230 to 63 million years ago. Reptiles occupied virtually all of the world's habitats in that ancient era. Some were land dwellers; some were amphibious and others were aquatic and lived in either freshwater or marine environments; still others could fly. Many of them had frightful and bizarre body forms. Dinosaurs, meaning "terrible lizards," were the ruling reptiles of the Mesozoic. They ranged in size from awesome giants—some were more than eighty feet long and weighed in excess of fifty tons, the largest land animals known to have lived—down to chicken-sized creatures. However, there is evidence suggesting that dinosaurs were not "cold-blooded" reptiles as has long been believed, but instead that they were "warm-blooded" creatures, and should belong to a proposed class of vertebrates, Archosauria, that also would include birds and crocodilians (crocodiles, alligators, and gavials). Thus, birds would be considered flying dinosaurs. Birds now have their own class (Aves), and crocodilians are presently an order of the class Reptilia.

At the close of the Mesozoic, all of the dinosaurs and most of the other animals on the land and in the sea became extinct. Why dinosaurs perished is a matter of considerable speculation, with many hypotheses having been offered. Two commonly proposed causes are that the dinosaurs could not adapt to world climatic changes that altered their habitat and food supply, or that they were unable to withstand the development of competition of mammals. Another theory supposes that most of the Mesozoic animals died after the Earth was struck by an asteroid, estimated to have been six miles across. This cataclysmic collision is believed to have created a global dust cloud that obscured sunlight, shrouding the planet in semidarkness for three to five years. Such prolonged gloom would have killed many land plants, and freshwater and marine phytoplankton (microscopic floating plants). This would have disrupted sharply the vital food chain, causing a world-wide famine. According to this fascinating theory, approximately 75 per cent of the animals on the Earth at that time vanished, leaving alive no land animals weighing more than fifty-five pounds.

One of the early dinosaur fossil finds at Arches was made in 1934 by Keith Wright, then seventeen years old, while herding cattle about a half-mile east of Wolfe Cabin. The youth reported his discovery to Frank Beckwith, director of the Arches National Monument Scientific Expedition, who was working nearby. Beckwith excavated the site and removed three sections of vertebrae, including one more than a foot in diameter and about six inches long. Wright was so excited about his find that one night he was overheard talking in his sleep, saying in true cowboy fashion, "Head that dinosaur—he's getting away from me!"

Beckwith also searched Yellow Cat Flat, northeast of Arches, for dinosaur bones and was, he said, "richly rewarded by finding more than a dozen major deposits." On the surface of the Flat, Beckwith discovered about two tons of fossil dinosaur bones.

A bone fragment of an *Iguanodon*, a large, plant-eating dinosaur that lived about 135 million years ago during the Early Cretaceous period of the Mesozoic, was discovered in 1968 a few miles west of the Park, near Dalton Well. Lin Ottinger, of Moab, found part of the dinosaur's posterior right maxilla with two teeth in place. This find resulted in the recognition of a new *Iguanodon* species, appropriately named *Iguanodon ottingeri* in honor of its discoverer.

The *Iguanodon* was the first dinosaur to be adequately described scientifically. It was originally discovered in 1822 near the town of Lewes in Sussex, England. Paleontologists estimate that the *Iguanodon* sometimes reached thirty feet in length, stood up to sixteen feet tall, and weighed between four and five tons. It was bipedal, with powerful legs and three-toed feet. The shorter forelimbs had five fingers including large, bony, spikelike thumbs that may have been used for defense. Apparently the animal's skin was thin and tuberculated. Its tail was flattened, suggesting that this land-dwelling dinosaur may have been able to swim.

Evidence of these monstrous creatures, which are believed to have lived in herds, has been found also in Belgium, France, Spain, Portugal, Tunisia, Australia, the eastern Gobi Desert of Mongolia, and on Spitzbergen.

Today, four reptile orders survive from the Mesozoic: the Chelonia (turtles and tortoises), Squamata (lizards and snakes), Crocodilia (crocodiles, alligators, and gavials), and Rhynchocephalia (now represented by only one species, the tuataras). Of these orders, only one, Squamata, occurs at Arches where it is represented by ten species of lizards and ten species of snakes.

[Opposite] **Tunnel Arch,** partially framed by a piñon pine, pierces a fin of Slick Rock Member of Entrada Sandstone in south Devil's Garden. The arch is east of the main Devil's Garden foot trail, and is easily reached over a short connecting trail. The opening has a span of twenty-seven feet and a height of twenty-two feet. The dominant biotic community in Devil's Garden is the piñon-juniper. This community is the most extensive one in the Park, covering nearly 45 per cent of the area. Junipers are more prevalent than piñons, since they are better able to tolerate warm and dry conditions.

[Below] Three biotic communities occur at **Courthouse Towers:** desert scrub, sand dune, and grassland. Desert scrub and sand dune cover most of the acreage, with grassland restricted to a relatively limited area south of Courthouse Wash, an intermittent stream. The principal monuments of Courthouse Towers are The Three Gossips, Sheep Rock, Tower of Babel, and The Organ. Park Avenue is in the southwest corner of Courthouse Towers. Hole-in-the-Wall, a small arch with a span of twenty-five feet and a height of fourteen feet, is in a fin south of Sheep Rock.

[Right] **Dark Angel,** a spire of Slick Rock Member of Entrada Sandstone, stands prominently on the west side of northern Devil's Garden. Vegetation surrounding the spire consists of a mixture of two biotic communities: desert scrub and piñon-juniper. Due to the open terrain along the western margin of Devil's Garden, as in the Dark Angel area, vegetation there must cope with sunnier and drier conditions than plants within Devil's Garden's broken and shaded interior.

BIRDS

Although 128 species of birds have been recorded in Arches, avian life is somewhat sparse in the high-desert Parkland. The heaviest concentrations are in the streamside community. Illustrations of twelve of the area's common birds follow.

Golden eagle (*Aquila chrysaetos*)

These very large birds of prey are hawk-shaped, but have larger beaks and broader wingspans. An adult may measure more than three feet in length, weigh about fifteen pounds and have a wingspan of nearly eight feet. Neck feathers are golden, and body plumage is a rich, dark brown. Legs are feathered to the talons. Golden eagles prey mostly on rodents and rabbits, but feed also on other small mammals, birds, reptiles, and carrion. These majestic birds are fairly common, permanent residents of Arches, where they usually build their large nests of sticks on ledges on the faces of cliffs.

Common flicker (*Colaptes auratus*)

This jay-sized woodpecker is often called "red-shafted flicker" in the West. The male has a red mustache. Reddish wings and tail linings of the Western flickers are conspicuous in flight. They are year-round residents of Arches, where they are common in woodlands bordering washes and the Colorado River. They nest in natural tree cavities, or chisel holes into trees with their strong, sharp-pointed beaks.

Plain titmouse (*Parus inornatus*) in piñon pine

Undistinguished in appearance except for a small crest of feathers on the head, the plain titmouse has a gray back and light-gray underside. This small, very active bird is a fairly common, permanent dweller of the piñon-juniper woodland at Arches.

Common raven (*Corvus corax*)

Recognized by their glossy, solid-black plumage, and their long, heavy beaks, common ravens look like very large crows. They are fairly common year-round residents of the Park, and are often seen scavenging for food in Devil's Garden Campground and at picnic sites. Ravens have a wedge-shaped tail that shows clearly in their hawklike flight. Very intelligent birds, they are ranked by naturalists on the same intelligence level as dogs. The raven's characteristic call is a hoarse, croaking *kraaak*.

Black-throated sparrow (*Amphispiza bilineata*)

Named for their conspicuous black "bibs," these birds are known also as "desert sparrows" because they adapt well to dry, hot areas. Common summer residents of Arches, these small birds are gray on the upper sides, and white on the undersides.

Mourning dove (*Zenaidura macroura*)

The mourning dove is named for its melancholy cooing, a soft *coo-ah, coo, coo-coo*. These slim, swift-flying birds are abundant at Arches in the summer, often nesting in tamarisk thickets along washes and the Colorado River. Mourning doves have light brownish-gray bodies with darker, pointed wings, and long, tapered tails.

Red-tailed hawk (*Buteo jamaicensis*)

Also known as chicken hawks, these large birds are fairly common, permanent residents of Arches, and often are observed perched on tree-tops, or soaring as they search for prey. They feed on rodents, rabbits, and reptiles—including rattlesnakes—and also are carrion eaters. This hawk is about twenty inches long, with a wingspread of up to four-and-a-half feet. Its call is a loud, screaming *kee-ahrrr*. The red-tailed's nests are made of sticks, usually in tall trees or on cliffs.

Horned lark (*Eremophila alpestris*)

Horned larks gain their name from pointed tufts of black feathers, or "horns," on either side of the head. These sparrow-like birds are permanent residents of the Park, and are commonly seen in Salt Valley. Horned larks are about seven inches long. For nests, they scratch pockets in the soil.

Chukar partridge (*Alectoris graeca*)
near Sheep Rock

Introduced into North America in 1893 from the dry regions of southeast Europe and parts of Asia, this gamebird is named for its call. Chukars are fairly common year-round residents of Arches, where they inhabit open, rocky areas. They roost on the ground, and feed on bulbs, seeds, and insects. Chukars are about a foot long, and have a prominent black band on the face.

Great horned owl (*Bubo virginianus*)

Great horned owls are larger than red-tailed hawks, weigh from three to five pounds, measure about two feet long, and may have wing spreads up to four-and-a-half feet. Their prominent "horns" are tufts of feathers. Silent fliers, these yellow-eyed birds command the night air. They are aggressive and efficient hunters, with strong beaks and powerful talons, and will attack most small animals. Instead of building their own nests, great horned owls appropriate old nests of hawks or other large birds. This owl's low, mournful *hoo, hoo-hoo-hoo, hoo* call is frequently heard at Arches, where they are fairly common, permanent residents. Protected by federal law, this bird is also known as the hoot owl and night owl.

Scrub jay (*Aphelocoma coerulescens*)

Scrub jays are robin-sized birds, and characteristically make short flights ending with sweeping glides. They are crestless, with blue heads, wings, and tails, white throats, and light-gray undersides. These jays are common, year-round residents of the Park.

Canyon wren (*Catherpes mexicanus*)
at Park Avenue

Fairly common at Arches, these small birds usually nest in rocky crevices in canyons. About five inches long, they are brownish with white throats and breasts. Their song is a loud series of descending whistles, slowing at the end: *tee-tee-tee-tee-tee-tee-teer-teer-teer*.

MAMMALS

Thirty-four mammal species inhabit Arches. Among the common mammals are the deer mouse, Apache pocket mouse, Ord's kangaroo rat, desert woodrat, whitetail antelope squirrel, porcupine, gray fox, and mule deer. Four other species are no longer found in the area: the bighorn sheep, pronghorn, gray wolf, and whitetail prairie dog. Black bear on very rare occasions travel through the area. Four of the Park-dwelling mammals are represented here.

Mountain lion (*Felis concolor*) near Tower Arch in Klondike Bluffs

Certainly the most impressive animal of Arches National Park is the mountain lion. Secretive and rarely seen by visitors, this large, powerful cat is primarily nocturnal, and prowls in the remotest areas of the Park. It has a lean, muscular body, with an overall length of six to eight feet including a heavy, round tail up to three feet long. A mature male may weigh in excess of 200 pounds. The adult's color is tawny, with the tail having a dark-brown tip. The cat has yellowish-green eyes, large teeth, and long, sharp, retractile claws. The mountain lion is one of the two large cats native to the Western Hemisphere, the other being the jaguar, which is larger than the mountain lion. Preying mostly on deer, the mountain lion is carnivorous, killing an average of one deer per week either by stalking or by leaping on the victim from overhanging ledges or from tree limbs. It also hunts foxes, porcupines, mice, rats, rabbits, and sometimes livestock. These animals are cannabalistic, and especially will eat their own cubs. Dens are established in rocky caves or crevices, where black-spotted kittens may be born any time

of the year—usually two to four to a litter. Mountain lions are inquisitive, and sometimes will openly follow humans—not stalking, but just out of curiosity. They are, however, fierce and predacious animals, and have been known to attack and kill people. Because of its wide distribution—the most extensive of any New World mammal—this cat has become known by more than forty common names. Probably best known as the mountain lion, it also is called cougar, puma, panther, painter, and catamount. Mountain lions once lived coast-to-coast in the United States, but due to the bounty system and human encroachment have been eliminated over much of their range. They are now concentrated largely in the West. In 1974, a census of these animals estimated their population at 22,000 in the western United States and Canada, about half of them being in the Canadian provinces of British Columbia and Alberta. They are not yet listed as endangered, although their survival in many areas is in serious doubt.

Porcupine (*Erethizon dorsatum*)

Equipped with some 36,000 needle-sharp barbed quills, the awkward and slow-moving porcupine possesses a formidable armor against attackers. These barbed quills are found even on the animal's feet, head, legs, and tail. Contrary to popular myth, the porcupine cannot "shoot" its quills at an enemy. The quills can, nonetheless, damage an attacker seriously, and cannot be dislodged without tearing the victim's flesh. Many predators, including foxes, eagles, and mountain lions, have been found dead after a porcupine's quills have worked their way into the animal's body to pierce a vital organ. Each quill, or spine, is about four inches long. But these yellow-tipped, blackish quills are not always effective in warding off predators. Mountain lions, bobcats, and coyotes will occasionally risk puncture wounds and prey on porcupines by flipping them over to expose the vulnerable, unquilled abdomen. Porcupines are found in both the Old and New World. Although species from the two areas look alike, they are not related. New World porcupines are found from southern South America northward through Central America, Mexico, the United States, Canada, and Alaska. About the size of a small dog, a mature porcupine is stocky, weighing up to thirty pounds. Usually forest dwellers, they are commonly found at Arches in the open pygmy forest of piñon pines and junipers. Their bodies are especially adapted to tree-climbing, and they spend much time in trees, often sleeping aloft on the branches. Primarily nocturnal, they may be active during the day. At Arches, porcupines eat the sappy inner bark of piñon pines, junipers, and cottonwoods. They also feed on twigs, buds, nuts, and berries. Sometimes they will kill trees by girdling them. The word "porcupine" derives from early French and English terms meaning "thorny pig." The animal is, of course, a rodent, not a pig. They sometimes also are called— incorrectly—hedgehogs.

Gray fox (*Urocyon cinereoargenteus*)

Gray foxes are common inhabitants of the Park. Primarily nocturnal and secretive, they frequently establish dens in hollow logs or beneath boulders. About the size of a small dog, an adult gray fox weighs eight to fifteen pounds. Their coat is gray on the back and reddish-brown along the sides. The long, bushy tail has a distinctive black strip on top and is tipped with black. Gray foxes are omnivorous, eating such foods as berries, insects, birds, eggs, and rodents. Enemies include eagles, bobcats, and coyotes. Because they are adept at climbing, gray foxes are also called tree foxes.

Mule deer (*Odocoileus hemionus*) at Balanced Rock

These large deer are common in Arches. Their name derives from the animal's prominent, mulelike ears. An adult may measure four feet high and six feet long, and weigh from 150 to 200 pounds. The mule deer's reddish-brown summer coat changes to blue-gray in winter. The tail, held down when the deer is running, has a conspicuous black tip. Males shed their antlers in mid-winter, regrowing them in the spring. Deer are herbivores, their diet varying with the seasons, and at Arches includes junipers, piñon pine needles, Mormon tea, rabbitbrush, cactus, and wildflowers. Mule deer are fast runners, and have been clocked at speeds up to thirty-five miles an hour. Their distinctive, stiff-legged bounding gait helps them to climb steep slopes rapidly in flight from predators. Mountain lions prey on deer, each lion killing an estimated fifty per year. Young deer are hunted by bobcats, coyotes, and golden eagles. The deer's normal life span is about sixteen years.

PLANTS

The flora of Arches include 357 species of vascular plants of which 322 are native and 35 are exotic. Forty-six species are rare in the Park. Illustrated here are some of the more common plants of Arches.

Mormon tea (*Ephedra viridis*)

This plant's common name comes from the tealike beverage early Mormons brewed from its slender, tannin-rich stems. The sticklike shrub is common in Arches, growing in dry, sandy, and rocky sites. It is low—generally one to three feet tall—and has many greenish, jointed, and furrowed stems with tiny, triangular scalelike leaves at each joint. Yellowish flowers blossom from small cones in spring, with male and female flowers occurring on separate plants. The shrub was used by Southwest Indians and pioneers for several medicinal purposes. Navajos made a cough medicine from its stems, other Indians brewed a drink from it to stop bleeding and as a remedy for intestinal ailments, and both early settlers and Indians used the plant to treat syphilis. Also, Indians roasted the seeds and ate them whole, or ground them and made a bitter bread.

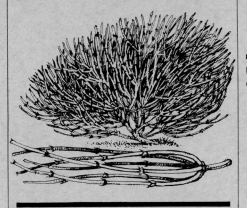

Devil's claw (*Sclerocactus whipplei*)

This barrel-shaped cactus is most commonly found in sandy or gravely soils of the Park's juniper-piñon woodland. It usually has a single stem four to twelve inches tall and between three and five inches in diameter. Also called fishhook cactus, it has central spines up to three inches long and, as the name suggests, hooked at the tip, while the shorter radial spines are straight and needle-like. Showy white, pink, or purple flowers bloom at the plant's apex. The funnel-form blossoms are short, and one to two-and-a-half inches broad.

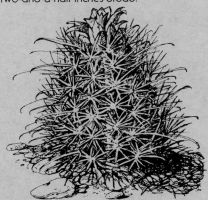

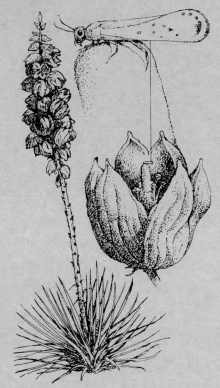

Harriman yucca (*Yucca harrimaniae*)

This low, nearly stemless clumped yucca has long, stiff saber-like leaves, and a tall flower stalk that rises from the plant's center, bearing greenish blossoms. The yucca is a member of the lily family, and the Harriman yucca, the only yucca species found at Arches, is common and widely distributed in the Park. A remarkable biological association exists between the yucca and the small yucca moth (*Pronuba*). Each is entirely dependent upon the other for perpetuation. This symbiosis was discovered by entomologist Charles Valentine Riley in 1872. He observed that the female moth gathers pollen from yucca flowers, forms it into a tiny ball carried under her head, then flies to another yucca blossom, lays her eggs, and leaves pollen which fertilizes the flower. After emerging from their eggs, the moth larvae feed on the plant's seeds, but enough of the seeds remain to mature and to reproduce the plant. Before the pods ripen, the larvae bore their way through the walls, fall to the ground, burrow into it, and remain there until the following spring when the moth emerges to repeat the extraordinary cycle. The yucca was an important plant to the Indians. They ate the buds, blossoms, and flower stalks, and made cord, mats, and sandals from the leaves. Early settlers made soap from yucca roots.

Utah juniper (*Juniperus osteosperma*) at Double Arch

Blackbrush (*Coleogyne ramosissima*)

Blackbrush is the principal plant of the desert-scrub biotic community at Arches. The shrub is the dominant growth on nearly 16,500 acres, about 90 per cent of the scrubland or 22.5 per cent of the total Parkland. The low, woody, drought-resistant plant has rigid branches, often spine-tipped, with small, narrow, dark-green, leathery leaves. Its flowers are small and yellowish.

Utah junipers and piñon pines form the major plant community at Arches. Almost 32,000 acres, nearly half of the Park's acreage, is in this woodland, with the juniper the dominant member. It is a bushy, compact evergreen with thin, fibrous, reddish-gray bark. The tree is usually less than twenty feet tall, with scalelike green leaves, and small berry-like cones. The "berries" are eaten by animals, and have been used by Indians for food and medicine, and as necklace beads. The juniper's soft, lightweight wood is sometimes used for fence posts and fuel.

Piñon pine (*Pinus edulis*) at Skyline Arch

Piñons—also called nut pines—are well-known for their edible seeds, or "nuts." These tasty, hard-shelled seeds are about a half-inch long, mature in the fall, and are rich in protein and in calories. They were eaten by Indians and by early settlers, and the seeds are still gathered, even commercially. The piñon is adapted to life in dry, rocky terrain. At Arches, they usually grow with junipers, and this association—the piñon-juniper woodland—covers approximately 45 per cent of the Parkland.

Mature piñons are short, generally about twenty feet tall, and scraggy. They have reddish-brown bark, and yellow-green leaves ("needles") about an inch-and-a-half long, in clusters of twos. The seed cones are small, approximately two inches long. Porcupines feeding on the inner bark of the piñons injured or killed many of the trees at Arches, particularly in Devil's Garden, in the mid-1940s. The pine's Spanish name, piñon, is frequently spelled "pinyon," the English equivalent.

Fremont cottonwood (*Populus fremontii*)

Tall, spreading cottonwoods are the largest trees in the Park. When mature, they can exceed 100 feet in height, with trunk diameters of about five feet. On older trees, the bark is gray, thick, and deeply furrowed. Cottonwoods need plentiful quantities of water, and have long roots that extend to great depths for permanent water. A single, large tree may consume more than fifty gallons of water per day. Cottonwoods are conspicuous members of the Park's streamside community. Stands of the trees occur near the U.S. Highway 191 bridge over the Colorado River, and along Courthouse Wash. Those growing in washes are subject to flash flooding, with numerous seedlings being destroyed annually. Cottonwoods are rapid-growing trees, and can reestablish themselves after flooding by root-sprouting. This tree's shiny, yellow-green leaves are broad and roughly triangular-shaped, and turn brilliant yellow before dropping in late autumn. Dense clusters of male and female flowers in drooping catkins bloom on separate trees. Only the female trees produce seeds. These tiny seeds are copiously covered with white, cotton-like fibers, which give the tree its common name. The Fremont species was named for John Charles Frémont (1813-1890), a famous soldier and western explorer, and the first Republican candidate for the presidency (1856). Cottonwoods sometimes were used by pioneers in the construction of cabins. Many of the logs in historic Wolfe Cabin are cottonwoods.

The **Gray Wolf** [left] preys on livestock and consequently is considered an economic menace by stockmen. Because of this, these dog-like carnivores have been annihilated over most of their range, including Arches. Although they are not found in the Park, a few of them still live in southeastern Utah.

Whitetail prairie dogs [below] once lived at Arches, especially in Salt Valley. They were exterminated by stockmen, primarily because the rodents competed with range livestock for grass. Whitetail prairie dogs are between twelve and fourteen inches long, and weigh from one-and-a-half to two-and-a-half pounds. Their hair is yellowish-gray, except for the tip of the short tail which is white, giving the species its popular name. Prairie dogs are members of the squirrel family. Their common name comes from the animal's dog-like bark and from their open country habitat. Prairie dogs are gregarious, dwelling in underground burrows clustered in colonies, or "towns." Often the rodents are seen sitting on their haunches by the entrances of their burrows, sunning and watching for predators.

GONE BUT NOT FORGOTTEN

Three familiar mammal species have vanished in historic times from the area of present-day Arches National Park: the pronghorn (antelope), the gray wolf, and the whitetail prairie dog. Fortunately, these animals have not become extinct, and still are found in the vicinity of the Park. With the probable exception of the gray wolf, they may eventually return to Arches—either naturally or with the aid of humans.

Ironically, humans were the cause of their disappearance. Humankind, the universal predator, poses the gravest threat to wildlife. During the settlement of the American West, pioneers were responsible for the deaths of an incredible number of native animals. At least 50 million bison (buffalo) and 100 million pronghorns were destroyed. Some species such as the bison were almost exterminated, and several species have tragically gone over the brink to extinction, among them the Merriam's elk (wapiti) of Arizona and New Mexico which vanished about 1906. Historians have aptly called this bloodstained era "The Great American Slaughter."

Such exterminations may be either *local*—the destruction of an animal species in one or more parts of its range, but with specimens remaining alive elsewhere—or *range-wide*, resulting in extinction of the species. Also, extermination may be *direct*—when man overtly destroys the species, either locally or throughout its range—or *indirect*, when the species dies because man has fatally altered part or all of its habitat, either purposefully or accidentally.

Countless wild animals were killed by early ranchers who believed that certain native animals preyed on livestock. Often their suppositions were wrong, and the decimation of eagles illustrates the fatal consequences of man's ignorance. Eagles feed primarily on small animals and on carrion, but ranchers mistakenly blamed eagles for heavy depredations against livestock. As a result, these majestic birds were shot and poisoned. Today, the golden eagle—a permanent resident of Arches—is listed as a "threatened" species. The bald eagle, the nation's symbol and a winter visitor to the Park, is regarded as "endangered."

Other wild animals unquestionably do prey on livestock. The gray wolf (*Canis lupus*) once was a severe menace to Moab area stockmen. On December 8, 1911, the Moab *Grand Valley Times* reported in a front-page article that wolves "in the past two years . . . have become the stockman's, and especially the cattleman's worst enemy." The account said that wolves were "very numerous and bold" on ranges surrounding Moab, and noted that bounties of $100 were being offered in the area for each wolf killed.

The gray wolf was virtually eliminated over nearly all of its range in the forty-eight adjoining states because it hunted livestock. Today this carnivore is found in

Pronghorns formerly ranged in the area that is now Arches. Driven off by humans and their activities, they may eventually return.

only five small, widely separated areas in the contiguous states: in the Big Bend region of western Texas, a tiny part of southwest New Mexico-southeast Arizona, along the boundary of southwest Colorado-southeast Utah, in extreme northwest Wyoming, and in central Oregon. It also ranges throughout Alaska and Canada, and along coastal Greenland.

Native animals were also directly exterminated by early ranchers if they competed with livestock for range forage. The white-tail prairie dog (*Cynomys gunnisoni*) is one of these animals, and was locally exterminated at Arches. The last recorded observation of this rodent in the area was on June 29, 1966 when one was sighted in Salt Valley, then mostly outside of the boundaries of Arches. They were, however, once numerous. In May 1940, Henry Schmidt, then custodian of Arches, reported that prairie dogs were "very much in evidence in Salt Valley, the Devil's Garden and Delicate Arch sections."

Throughout most of their range they have been either exterminated or their numbers severely reduced. Ranchers have conducted vigorous trapping and poisoning campaigns against these rodents because they compete with livestock for grass. Also, prairie dogs have been killed because livestock sometimes break their legs in tripping over entries to the underground burrows of the rodents, and such accidents are usually fatal for range stock. Furthermore, prairie dogs often are infested with plague-carrying fleas and thus are a potential health hazard.

Today, prairie dogs inhabit several areas close to Arches, and could become reestablished in the Park.

Some wild animals were killed for their furs. Beaver were subjects of direct extermination by fur trappers in many areas of their range. Mountain Men scoured the West in search of beaver, from the 1820s into the 1840s. Some of them, including

Denis Julien, trapped along the Green and Colorado rivers in the Canyon Country of today's Utah. After the decline of the fur trade, sporadic trapping continued in the area. Among the later trappers at the turn of the century were "Nat" Galloway, Charles ("One-eye Smithy") Smith, "Hi" Turner, and one known to history only as "Old Rocky."

Many wild animals have been hunted for meat, others for sport, and some for both. When unmanaged, such hunting can result in the extermination of a species. As an example, excessive hunting of the passenger pigeon for its savory meat, coupled with destruction of the birds' nesting sites due to clearing of American forests, was responsible for extinction of this once abundant game bird.

The pronghorn (*Antilocapra americana*) was hunted to near extinction for sport and meat. Grazing competition from cattle and sheep also has been detrimental to pronghorns. They were once abundant on the grasslands of the West, and formerly ranged at Arches in Salt Valley. However, by the late 1930s they were rare there. Then-custodian Henry Schmidt, with two other Park Service employees, sighted what they believed to be a lone pronghorn in the valley during November 1939. Schmidt reported that stockmen in the area "concur that there are a few of these graceful animals left in this region, and that, under proper protection, they would 'come back.'" The last reported observation of pronghorns in Salt Valley was in September 1941, when four were seen. They still exist in areas near the Park, and may return.

Wild animals have been indirectly exterminated by man's destruction of natural vegetation, drainage of wetlands, damming of rivers, use of herbicides and insecticides, air pollution, the naturalization of exotic flora, and the introduction of domestic animals and their diseases.

ONE THAT ALMOST DISAPPEARED

One of the most spectacular mammals of the American West is the bighorn sheep (*Ovis canadensis*). This regal animal was once nearly extinct, and for many years has been rare in Arches. Bighorn populations declined sharply throughout the West following the introduction of domesticated sheep. Diseases contracted from the domestic variety, principally scabies but also anthrax, decimated the ranks of the bighorn. Further declines resulted as hunters killed them for meat or as trophies, and from the encroachment of human activities on this timid animal's ranges.

In the Park's protective environment, competition from livestock has been eliminated, and hunting is prohibited. Under these propitious conditions, the bighorn may thrive again.

Mark Sakovich

Reported observations of **bighorn sheep** in the Park are rare. But on October 16, 1982, a dramatic observation occurred when visitor Mark Sakovich, of Fort Worth, Texas, photographed a bighorn silhouetted against the sky under an arch in The Windows section. The span, earlier known as Christmas Tree Arch, has been appropriately retitled Bighorn Arch.

PREHISTORIC AND HISTORIC INDIANS

ALTHOUGH THERE ARE no Indians living in Arches National Park today, there is evidence that Indians of several cultures—both prehistoric and historic—once used the present-day Parkland. Apparently, they visited the area on a seasonal or sporadic basis, to quarry chert for making arrow points and other chipped stone implements, and to search for food.

Which of the ancient people were the first to see the natural arches of this region, and what they thought of the arches—if they ascribed any religious or magical powers to them—must, of course, forever be speculation.

PREHISTORIC INDIANS

Man migrated to North America from Asia across the Bering Strait possibly 30,000 or more years ago. These ancient migrants moved across an isthmus or "land bridge" now called Beringia, that then existed be-

tween the two continents. Beringia formed during the Ice Age when so much water was frozen in broad, thick ice sheets that the sea level dropped more than 300 feet, exposing the continental margins. Ancient man spread southward from what is now Alaska, to populate North and South America.

Paleo-Indians

So it was that, about 25,000 years ago, early man reached the present-day American Southwest. These original inhabitants, called Paleo-Indians, were big-game hunters. Their Mongoloid ancestry was evident in their copper-colored skin, wide cheekbones, and straight black hair. Though they were Stone-Age people, they were "modern" in the sense that they had developed a spoken language, and possessed full-sized brains.

The Paleo-Indians entered the Arches region some 11,000 years ago, remaining

[Opposite page] These well-preserved **petroglyphs** were carved by Ute Indians. The panel is located on a low sandstone cliff bordering Salt Wash, east of Wolfe Cabin and north of Delicate Arch trail. Shown in the illustration are bighorn sheep, and Indians mounted on horseback. Not shown, but also on the panel, are two small animals, probably dogs, and two other animal-like figures. The larger figures are six to eight inches high. This panel was carved in historic times after Spaniards introduced horses into the present-day American Southwest.

[Right] **Petroglyph panel** in Arches National Park, near Moab Canyon northwest of Visitors Center. This panel was first reported by George Andersen, of Moab, in 1975. In a crevice alongside the petroglyphs, he found what appears to be a *hammerstone*, a crude pounding device of the kind used widely by prehistoric Indians. Andersen said he discovered the hammerstone "just like someone had put it there and forgot it."

Illustration of **Folsom projectile point** found a few miles west of Arches by Mrs. Dallas Tanner, of Moab, in 1959. This point is about one-and-a-half inches long, and slightly more than one-half inch wide at its base. Folsom points date from between 10,000 and 11,000 years ago. They were made by Paleo-Indians, big-game hunters who were the earliest inhabitants of today's American Southwest. Folsom points were used as spearheads. To throw their spears, Paleo-Indians used a wooden shaft now called *atlatl*. The hunter mounted his spear on the atlatl, and grasped both in his hand. Then—in a motion like pitching a baseball—he threw his arm forward, propelling the spear from the atlatl toward its quarry.

there for nearly twenty centuries, or until about B.C. 7000. Evidence of their presence is based on finds of Folsom projectile points, the spear-tips used by these Indians in hunting. Although no Folsom points have been found within the Parkland, several have been discovered nearby. Their name derives from Folsom, New Mexico, near which the first of these artifacts was found in 1926.

Archaic Indians

Pre-agricultural people now called the Archaic appeared in what is today southeastern Utah at least 8,000 years ago. Their culture lasted in the area for some five millenniums, or until about 3,000 years ago, though temporal ranges varied locally.

These ancient people were hunters and gatherers. Small of stature, the Archaic wandered seasonally to gather seeds, ber-ries, and nuts, and to hunt animals, principally the mule deer. They probably lived together in small, kin-related bands. The Archaic have left unique artifacts of their culture called *split-twig figurines*, fragments of which have been found ten miles southeast of the Park in Moonshine Cave, on the north bank of Mill Creek. These figurines were made from willow twigs that were twisted to resemble animals. Anthropologists suggest that they may have been fetishes, used to invoke magical powers for successful hunts.

Anasazi and Fremont

The Archaic period ended in the Arches region about 3,000 years ago, and it would be nearly twenty centuries before the next known aboriginals inhabited the region. Beginning about A.D. 1000 two groups of prehistoric peoples—the Anasazi and the Fremont—entered the Utah Canyon Country. They were agriculturalists whose origin has not been established, although some anthropologists believe they were descended from the Archaic. The possibility of a third ancient culture called the Barrier Canyon, predating the Fremont, has been suggested by some authorities on Indian antiquity.

Arches lies near the boundary between the territories occupied by the Anasazi and the Fremont. Anasazi territory included the present Parkland, plus the area to the east and south and a narrow strip of land immediately to the west. Areas north and farther west of the Park were in the realm of the Fremont. Pictographs bearing evidence of the conjectural Barrier Canyon culture are all localized in the same general area of Utah, near and in present-day Arches and Canyonlands national parks.

The Anasazi and Fremont cultures in the Arches region were essentially contemporaneous. The earliest Fremont settlements date from A.D. 1000, and their culture lasted some 300 years, ending about A.D. 1300. The Anasazi—famed builders of the magnificent cliff dwellings at Mesa Verde—existed during a parallel period of time. Although they had different languages, the Anasazi and Fremont did engage in trading activities. From studies made of skeletons and mummies at Mesa Verde, some 100 miles southeast of Arches, anthropologists have determined that the average life span for Anasazi females was twenty to twenty-five years, and for the males between thirty-one and thirty-five years. Of stocky build, the adult male averaged 5 feet, 4 inches in height, and the adult female 5 feet, 1 inch. Their skin was light to dark brown, and they had straight brown or black hair. Eye color also was brown or black.

Why the Anasazi and Fremont cultures disappeared is not yet completely understood. Among the reasons advanced to

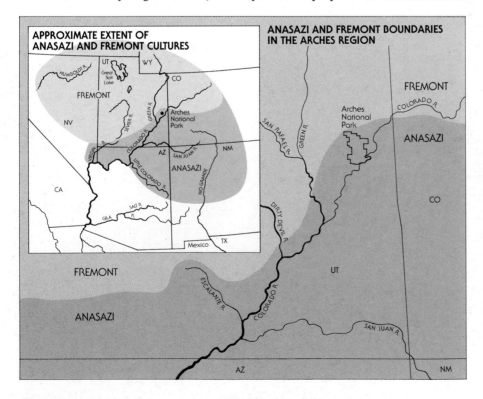

APPROXIMATE EXTENT OF ANASAZI AND FREMONT CULTURES

ANASAZI AND FREMONT BOUNDARIES IN THE ARCHES REGION

One complete **split-twig figurine** and fragments of others have been recovered near Arches National Park. Other examples of these, found elsewhere in the American Southwest, have been radiocarbon-dated, and proved to be between 3,000 and 4,000 years old. Split-twig figurines were crafted by Archaic Indians from single green willow twigs, which they partially split, then twisted into animal shapes. Some of the figurines are pierced by small twigs, probably representing spears, suggesting that they may have been fetishes used in hunting ceremonies. In 1960, fragmentary figurines [top] were found in Moonshine Cave on the north side of Mill Creek, about ten miles southeast of Arches.

Kevin Anderson, of Moab, in 1973 discovered a complete figurine [bottom] on the floor of a *rock shelter* (a shallow, natural cavity on the fake of a cliff) in Seven Mile Canyon, some three miles west of Arches.

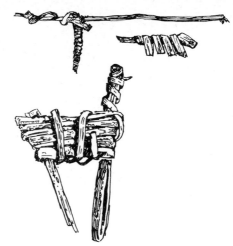

PETROGLYPHS VERSUS PICTOGRAPHS

The names given to rock carvings—*petroglyphs*—and rock paintings—*pictographs*—are often confused, and with reason. They look and sound somewhat alike, and both are tongue twisters. To further complicate the terminology, groups of petroglyphs and pictographs sometimes are called *petrographs* or *pictoglyphs*.

A simple device for remembering the difference is to note that petroglyphs are "pecked" into the rock, while pictographs are painted.

Petroglyphs are also called "Indian writings" and "hieroglyphics." Indian artists usually made them by pecking large rocks or cliff faces with hammerstones or choppers. Desert-varnished rock surfaces were favored for petroglyphs, where the Indians could cut through the darker varnish to expose the underlying lighter colored rock, thus creating intaglios.

Pictographs are made by painting the rock with mineral paints. Red and pink were derived from iron oxides, blues from azurite, green from malachite, and white from gypsum.

Artist's conception of a prehistoric Indian carving **petroglyphs** of deer with a hammerstone. The figures depicted form part of an actual panel at a site in Devil's Garden.

explain their demise are (1) a warming and drying trend of the climate which resulted in lower precipitation and consequently less flora and fauna to support the Indian populations, (2) an influx of hostile Indians, and (3) exhaustion of natural resources. The Anasazi probably are the ancestors of the Hopi Indians, the pueblo dwellers of Arizona.

Although characteristics of the Barrier Canyon rock-art style suggest an affiliation with the Fremont culture, there is no firm evidence yet to link the Barrier Canyon artists with any culture. Some anthropologists believe Barrier Canyon artists preceded the Fremont by more than 5,000 years, dating from at least 4500 B.C. The recurrent form in their pictographs is a long tapering humanoid figure, often lacking appendages. These mummy-like figures may be larger than life-size, and may be headless. When heads are present, they often have ghostly eyes, and sometimes antenna-like projections or crowns. Barrier Canyon pictographs are part of the superb Moab Panel which is just inside the Park's boundary east of Courthouse Wash, on the massive sandstone cliff north of U.S. Highway 191. Tragically, in mid-April 1980 this beautiful panel which had survived for at least 1,500 years was nearly obliterated by vandals.

HISTORIC INDIANS

When the first white explorers reached what is today southeastern Utah in the mid-1700s, they encountered Ute Indians living in the vicinity of Arches. Farther to the south they found Navajos.

Utes

The Utes, whose origin has been traced to what is today Southern California, may have driven out the Anasazi. The date of the Utes' arrival in the Arches area has not been established, but it is known that their ancestors began to disperse from their

Navajos are relatively recent Indian migrants to what is now the American Southwest, probably having arrived in the area during the mid-fourteenth century. By at least the early 1600s, they had extended their range to include the present-day Arches region. In 1916, W. M. Wolsey discovered a probable Navajo burial site in a cave high on the east wall of Courthouse Wash, a few hundred yards north of today's U.S. Highway 191, in what is now the Park. Wolsey's interesting find was reported in *The Grand Valley Times* of Moab on February 25 of that year.

Southern California homeland about A.D. 1000. Utes speak the Numic branch of the Uto-Aztecan language, a large and important language family in Western America and Mexico.

Graphic evidence of the Utes' presence in Arches may be seen today on a low sandstone cliff to the east of Wolfe Cabin, across Salt Wash and north of Delicate Arch Trail. There they carved into the rock a group of petroglyphs depicting bighorn sheep and men mounted on horses. Though these carvings have not been dated definitely, they obviously postdate the introduction of horses into the present-day Southwest by the Spaniards. By 1700, the Utes had become horsemen.

The Ute band that occupied the Arches region—one of seven principal Ute bands—was the Parianuc. In 1855, Indians of this band attacked a colonizing party, the Elk Mountain Mission, sent by the Mormon Church to the site of present-day Moab where they built a rock fort and log corral. Three of the missionaries were killed. The fort was quickly abandoned, giving the Utes a victory. After this blood-letting, some two decades passed before the Mormons made another effort to settle the area—this time successfully, but only after several serious confrontations with the Indians, some episodes resulting in deaths.

Navajos

It is not known when the first Navajos entered what is now the American Southwest. Their origins have been traced to Athabascan ancestors in western Canada. However, it is definitely established that Navajos occupied a site in present-day New Mexico by 1541. Antonio de Espejo, a Spanish explorer, recorded in his journal for 1582 and 1583 a meeting with

---

ORIGIN OF THE COLORADO RIVER AND ITS CANYONS—A UTE MYTH
Recorded by Major John Wesley Powell

"**M**any years ago when wise and good men lived on the earth, the great Chief of all the Utes lost his beloved wife.

Day and night he grieved, and all his people were sad. Then Ta-vwoats appeared to the Chief, and tried to comfort him, but his sorrow could not be allayed. So at last Ta-vwoats promised to take him to a country away to the southwest where he said his dead wife had gone and let him see how happy she was if he would agree to grieve no more on his return. So he promised. Then Ta-vwoats took his magic ball and rolled it before him, and as it rolled it rent the earth and mountains, and crushed the rocks and made a way for them to that beautiful land—a trail through the mountains which intervened between that home of the dead and the hunting grounds of the living. And following the ball, which was a rolling globe of fire, they came at last to the Spirit Land. Then the great Chief

saw his wife and the blessed abode of the Spirits where all was plenty and all was joy, and he was glad.

Now when they had returned Ta-vwoats enjoined upon the Chief that he should never travel this trail during life, and that all his people should be warned not to walk therein. Yet still he feared that they would attempt it so he rolled a river into trail—a mad raging river into the gorge made by the globe of fire, which should overwhelm any who might seek to enter there."

UTĚ, YOO-TAH, UTAH

Utah owes its name to the Ute Indians. *Utah* is actually a phonetic spelling of *Utě*, the singular form for the name of this Indian tribe. It has appeared in various forms— *Yoo-tah, Uta, Eutaw,* and *Utah* among them—but all are synonyms for *Ute.*

An early written reference to the Utes is found in the journal Fray Silvestre Vélez de Escalante kept of his epic exploration of Utah, Arizona, and New Mexico in 1776–77. He wrote of them as the *Yutas.*

OLD NAVAJO BURIAL GROUND DISCOVERED

Bodies of Three Indians Found in Almost Inaccessible Cave Near Moab.

An Indian burial ground, accessible only by scaling a cliff with the aid of ropes, was found the last of the week a short distance north of the Court House bridge, three miles from Moab. W. M. Wolsey, engineer in charge of the repair work on the bridge, discovered the burial ground, which is located in a cave high up in the bluffs on the east side of Court House wash. Mr. Wolsey decided to investigate the cave and with the aid of some rope and a small boy he scaled the wall of the canyon and reached the place. In the cave he found the bodies of three Indians. It was at first thought that the bodies were those of cliff dwellers, but they were later declared to be Navajo Indians. It is thought that the bodies have been in the cave for at least thirty or forty years.

One of the bodies is that of a Navajo baby, presumably about two years old when it died. This body is remarkably well preserved.

One reason for thinking the bodies are Navajos is the fact that their hair is tied with string in the manner all Navajos use.

On Sunday about 100 people made a trip to the cave, and many of them climbed the rope "hand over hand" and viewed the remains of the "good Indians." The burial ground will hereafter be a curiosity for local people, as well as tourists.

A state law makes it a misdemeanor to disturb Indian mummies or relics, and people are warned of the consequences of tampering with the bodies in any way.

The **Moab Panel** is located on the massive cliff forming the east wall of Moab Canyon, just south of Courthouse Wash. This outstanding panel, visible from U.S. Highway 191, is regarded by anthropologists as significant rock art because of the rich diversity of prehistoric and historic Indian art styles represented there. The panel includes pictographs and petroglyphs left by three prehistoric cultures — Barrier Canyon, Fremont, and Anasazi — as well as art created by historic Utes. Because of its archeological significance, the site was listed in 1975 on the National Register of Historic Places. On April 16, 1980, Arches Superintendent Peter Parry and Ranger Thomas Wylie were escorting two federal officials on a tour of the Park: Gus Speth, chairman of the President's Council on Environmental Quality, and Benjamin Zerbey, Utah assistant to the regional director, National Park Service. Ranger Wylie vividly recalls his reaction as the group stopped to view the panel. He remembers "getting out of the car and looking up there, and having a sinking feeling." The once-magnificent work of art had been nearly wiped off the cliff face. In a wanton, mindless act of violence, vandals had almost destroyed the pictographs, probably using stiff brushes to scour them with a chemical solvent. They had also damaged some of the petroglyphs by chipping them, and had pecked obscene graffiti alongside the defaced artwork. This national treasure had survived the ravages of Nature for many centuries, only to be desecrated in a matter of minutes by a senseless act of Man. Restoration work was done on the panel by Connie Silver in August and September 1980. Silver, an expert on restoring damaged artworks, earlier worked for the International Center for Conservation in Rome. She cleaned the panel, removing the scouring agent used by the vandals, but did no repainting. The project, which cost approximately $8,500, greatly improved the images. Photographs below show the panel as it appeared before [top] and after [bottom] the vandalism.

"Querechos" near Mount Taylor in New Mexico, and these Indians may have been Navajos. But Spanish records do not mention Navajos by name until Fray Zárata Salmerón, in 1626, referred to the "Apache del Nabaxu." The Navajos, it appears, were latecomers to the Southwest.

Archeological evidence and oral histories gathered from descendants of the early Navajos indicate that members of that tribe had wandered through what is now southeastern Utah since at least the early 1600s.

Arches was on the Navajo frontier. Possible evidence of their use of the area came to light in February 1916 with discovery of an Indian burial site at Courthouse Wash. W. M. Wolsey, a road engineer, noticed a cave in the cliff on the east side of the wash. He climbed to it and found three bodies. They were presumed to be Navajos because of their hair style.

Harold Leich, who stopped at Moab to reprovision in 1933 on his unsuccessful attempt to run the length of the Colorado River alone, camped briefly at the Peterson ranch north of Moab. Two of Peterson's boys, LeGrand and Weston, took Leich to see the "Mummy Caves."

"I made it after some panting, and hauled the boys up with my rope," Leich later recalled. "In one cave we found a few fragments of bone, apparently human, strewn on a sandy floor among shreds of cedar bark in which the bodies may have been buried. It looked as if curiosity seekers had beaten trained archeologists to the site."

What happened to the remains is not definitely known. In 1934, Frank Beckwith, director of the Arches National Monument Scientific Expedition, reported that "several years ago, a mummy and two skeletons were dug out by amateurs .... From best information we are led to believe that the mummy was taken to Salt Lake City."

HISTORICAL BACKGROUND

THE IDENTITY of the first white man to see the strange landforms in what today is Arches National Park, and the date when he saw them, are unknown. Unfortunately, the story of the earliest penetrations of the region by whites is veiled by the mists of time, and shrouded in missing and incomplete historical records.

JUAN MARÍA ANTONIO RIVERA

Possibly the first white entry into the Arches country — at least the earliest recorded penetration — occurred in 1765. During the summer of that year, Juan María Antonio Rivera, searching for silver, led an expedition from Abiquiu, in New Mexico, northward into Colorado to the Dolores River. Unsuccessful in his search for silver, he turned back at the Dolores to Abiquiu.

Later that year, Rivera organized a sec-

ond expedition. This time, in addition to searching for silver, Rivera was charged by the governor of New Mexico to explore the little-known region and to obtain information about its Indians. Rivera retraced his summer route to the Dolores, then continued into eastern Utah, and reached the southern bank of the Colorado River — across from Arches. However, the party did not ford the river to the Arches side. On their homeward journey — still without having found silver — Rivera's expedition followed the Colorado upstream for an unknown distance before returning to New Mexico by a still unknown route.

During the next sixty-five years, and perhaps earlier, Spanish trappers and traders entered Utah. However, very little is known about their itineraries and activities. Among these elusive *entradas* is one made in 1813. In that year, Mauricio Arze and Lagos García led seven men to trade

Landscape Arch, in Devil's Garden, is the longest natural rock span in the world. According to geographer Dale J. Stevens, the arch's light opening is 306 feet wide—6 feet longer than a football field. The gigantic span is 434 feet long, and the maximum opening height beneath the span is 92 feet above the ground—about the height of a nine-story building. At the span's narrowest vertical point, it is only 16 feet thick, and at its narrowest horizontal width it is 15.5 feet, giving the arch a fragile look. Just when the enormous arch was first seen by white men is not known. This photograph, taken in 1896, is the earliest recorded sighting. Standing in the foreground is a sheepman named Spalding. What the circumstances were of his visit to the arch, and who took this historic photo, are unknown. The first published report of the big arch appeared in 1898 when a short account by Arthur Winslow was printed in the April 22 issue of the journal *Science*. Winslow, who had not seen the arch, had obtained a copy of a photograph of the landform during a visit to Moab. That photo, printed with his article, was the first of the arch ever published. Not until 1934 was the long span given its name. Then Frank Beckwith, leader of the Arches National Monument Scientific Expedition, visited the arch and noted that the scenery seen through its opening was nicely framed, so he named it Landscape Arch.

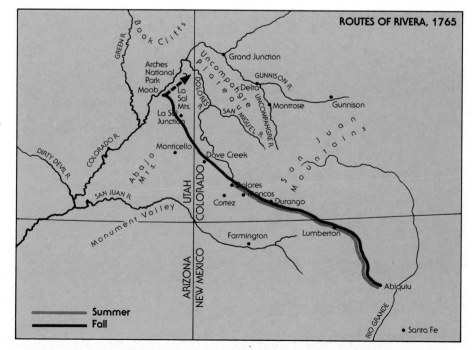

[Right] **The Three Penguins** huddle stiffly together, above the Park's entrance road, on Headquarters Hill. The "penguins" are formed in the Slick Rock Member of the Entrada Sandstone, and they stand upon the Entrada's Dewey Bridge Member. Once this landform was called Trinity Rock.

[Opposite page] **Twin Arch**, in the southern Fiery Furnace, has also aptly — and eerily — been called Skull Arch. The larger opening of this double arch has a span of thirty-three feet and a height of thirty-four feet. Its smaller aperture spans twenty-eight feet and is twenty-one feet high. Cut into the Slick Rock Member of the Entrada Sandstone, this feature is a pothole-type arch.

with Ute Indians on the Sevier River. The party's route is not known. Did they follow Rivera's trail to the Colorado, cross to the Arches side, then skirt by the western edge of today's Parkland on their way north?

The story of one early entry into the Arches country, a tale that was long accepted as fact is now known to be fiction.

THE FABLED "LOST TRAPPERS"
In 1847, David H. Coyner wrote the saga of a fur-trapping party that lost seventeen of its twenty men to Indians and hardships while hunting beaver in the Rocky Mountains. Much of his book concerns the adventures of the three survivors.

Coyner's tale — which he claimed was true — begins in St. Louis in the spring of 1807, when the twenty men headed northwest under the leadership of Ezekiel Williams. With them went Big White, a Mandan Indian chief, whom the party had agreed to escort to his homeland. Leaving Big White at his village, Williams's party entered the Rocky Mountains trapping southward. In time, skirmishes with Indians and other perils reduced their number to three: Williams, James Workman, and Samuel Spencer.

The survivors, unable to agree on a return route to St. Louis, split up: Williams canoed down the Arkansas River, while Workman and Spencer struck out overland for Santa Fe, New Mexico. Heading west, Workman and Spencer crossed the Rockies, then followed the course of the Colorado River. These "lost trappers" — according to Coyner — eventually intercepted a well-used trail where it forded the river. They took the trail southeast, then met and joined a Spanish caravan bound for California — so Coyner claimed.

Many readers of *The Lost Trappers* — including some historians — have accepted the tale as fact. True, some of its events and people were real. Williams, for example — or "Old Zeke" as he came to be

known — was a real Mountain Man, or western fur trapper. But "Workman" and "Spencer" are almost certainly fabricated names — nowhere in the annals of the Mountain Men do these names appear.

Several historians, believing Coyner's fantasy, have identified the trail struck by Workman and Spencer as the Old Spanish Trail, and the ford they saw as the one near present-day Arches National Park in the vicinity of the Moab bridge. But the Old Spanish Trail — which did indeed cross at that site — did not become an established route until the winter of 1830-31, or about

twenty-one years after the "lost trappers" allegedly intersected it!

The Lost Trappers is the story of bold adventure in the western wilderness. But this rousing tale is largely fiction — a fantastic, concocted saga as strange and colorful as the red-rock Arches country in which some of the drama is played in Coyner's book.

OLD SPANISH TRAIL
In the winter of 1830-31, William Wolfskill and George C. Yount led the first party to open a through trail between Santa Fe, New Mexico and Los Angeles, California. This trail became an important overland route for commerce between the two Mexican frontier areas. Commonly called the Old Spanish Trail, the name is a misnomer since the route was opened under Mexican, not Spanish sovereignty, and the first travelers over it were led by two Americans.

The trail forded the Colorado at Arches, yet there is no record of any of the people trekking along the Old Spanish Trail venturing into present-day Arches. The trail's use declined in the late 1840s and by the middle 1850s it was essentially unused.

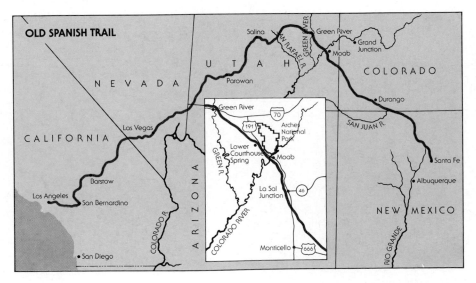

OLD SPANISH TRAIL

HUNTINGTON EXPEDITION

During the fall of 1854, the Mormon Church sent an exploration party under William Huntington into southeastern Utah. The expedition, which consisted of twelve white men, one Indian, and five wagons, followed the Old Spanish Trail southeastward from Manti, Utah.

As the explorers went down Moab Canyon — on the western border of today's Arches National Park — they came to a *jump*, or vertical drop in the canyon's floor. Here the wagons were let down by ropes. The site, named "The Jumping-Off Place," was about a quarter-mile southwest of the Park's Visitors Center. Unfortunately, this historic jump was eliminated by grading for what is now U.S. Highway 191.

From The Jumping-Off Place, Huntington's party continued down Moab Canyon to the Colorado River, crossed to the south bank, and passed through what is now Moab Valley and the future site of Moab. In the upper end of Spanish Valley — the southern continuation of Moab Valley — about fifteen miles from the Colorado, three wagons were cached.

The explorers then continued south, crossed the San Juan River and visited with Navajo Indians before turning north on their homeward journey.

ELK MOUNTAIN MISSION

The following year, 1855, the Mormons sent the Elk Mountain Mission to establish a settlement at what is now Moab. This colonization effort took its name from the mountain range, now called La Sal, that rises southeast of Moab.

Forty men under Alfred N. Billings departed Manti on May 21 with fifteen wagons. When the missionaries reached The Jumping-Off Place, a rough road was constructed around the obstacle. The Colorado was crossed, and the three wagons left by Huntington the previous year were located in upper Spanish Valley.

A site for a fort was selected in lower Moab Valley in a grove of cottonwood trees, on the northwestern outskirts of the present town. The fort had tapering rock walls and was sixty-four feet square.

At first the local Ute Indians were not overtly hostile to the missionaries, and engaged in trading with them. Some Indians were even baptized, but relations began to deteriorate and ultimately led to lethal consequences.

On Sunday, September 23, 1855, at about a half-hour past noon, James W. Hunt went to retrieve his horse, which was grazing about a mile from the fort. A Ute named Charles followed Hunt and shot him in the back. Billings and several other Mormons rushed to Hunt and, while carrying the wounded man to the fort, were charged by Indians. Billings was shot in his right hand, but reached the fort's safety with the other missionaries. While the siege continued, several Utes with Charles at their head left for the La Sal Mountains where they killed two Mormons — Edward Edwards and William Behunin — who had gone there the day before from the fort to hunt.

About 3 A.M. Monday, Hunt died from his wound. Billings concluded the missionaries must withdraw from their fort. So, about 11 A.M. they abandoned the fort and headed for Manti. The mission was never restored.

EARLY RIVER NAVIGATION

At first it may seem incongruous for rocky, high-desert Arches National Park to have a

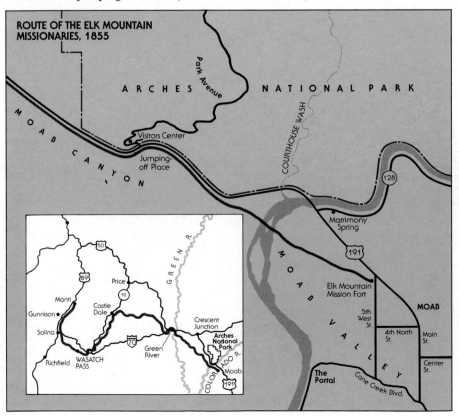

ROUTE OF THE ELK MOUNTAIN MISSIONARIES, 1855

"THE MYSTERIOUS D. JULIEN" — FIRST WHITE VISITOR TO ARCHES?

Strange as it may seem, the first white man believed to have penetrated deeply into the rugged, arid terrain of present-day Arches National Park was a beaver trapper — a hunter of amphibious mammals! Denis Julien left graphic evidence of his presence in the area: he carved his name and the date — June 9, 1844 — on a towering sandstone fin in northern Devil's Garden. Nearby the inscription is an arch, now named for the trapper, that is appropriately eye-shaped — an inanimate witness to Julien's scratching of his historic graffiti.

Who was this beaver trapper, and what was he doing in Devil's Garden?

Denis Julien is certainly one of the more intriguing characters of the Park's history. However, he is a relatively obscure figure in the annals of western fur trappers and traders. Among the several hundred hardy Mountain Men who roamed the wilderness west of the continental divide in the 1820s and 1830s, Julien was a minor figure who would have been little remembered except for one thing: a penchant for carving his name or initials on rocks. This Kilroy-like habit assured Julien a rock-solid

Julien Arch

place in the history of Utah's Canyon Country. In addition to his Arches inscription, Julien left several carvings along the Green River — at least five of them. Two more, and possibly three, were left beside the Colorado River. One of these is still visible. A second — and the questionable third — lie beneath the surface of Lake Powell.

Little is known about Julien's life. Historian Charles Kelly referred fittingly to the elusive fur trapper as "the mysterious D. Julien." While the lack of information about the man is frustrating for historians, it is understandable, for Julien was a relatively unimportant man in his time and lived, for the most part, the isolated life of a frontiersman. Otis R. "Dock" Marston, an historian of the Colorado River, commented pertinently about Julien when he said: "Obscurely he lived and obscurely died."

It is known that the ancestral homeland of Julien's family is France. From there members of the family fled to Ireland and to Canada during the religious wars between the French Calvinists, known as the Huguenots, and the Catholics. The Julien

Mountain Man **Denis Julien** carved his name and the date — June 9, 1844 — over two petroglyphs of bighorns on a fin in northern Devil's Garden, near an arch that is now named for him. This graffiti is the earliest evidence of a white man in what is now Arches National Park. The significance of Julien's inscription was not recognized until July 1977 when Jim Stiles, a seasonal park ranger, saw the carving. Julien's handiwork had been seen before — several others left names and dates carved alongside his inscription. But it was not until Stiles chanced upon and reported the graffiti that its historical importance was realized.

family in the United States was established by immigrants from both Ireland and Canada.

Records at the cathedral in St. Louis, Missouri shed some light on Denis Julien's personal life. Those documents show that he was married to an Indian named Catherine, and that the couple had three children baptized in the cathedral: a daughter, Marie Josephine, born May 5, 1793, and baptized on April 15, 1798; and two sons: Pierre Paschal, baptized on October 25, 1801; and Etienne, baptized on October 21, 1804. Pierre died when he was nine years old, and was buried on February 3, 1809.

Based on these data, an estimate may be hazarded as to when Denis Julien was born. Assuming that he was in his late teens or early twenties (between age eighteen and twenty-two) when his daughter Marie was born in 1793, Julien would have been born between 1771 and 1775. This would have made him about seventy years old when he carved his name at Arches!

Other records show that Julien was listed as an American citizen in 1805 when he was granted a license to trade along the Des Moines River. Julien and his brother Etienne volunteered in 1809 to serve against Indians on the northern frontier of the Louisiana Territory. Julien held licenses to trade on the Missouri in 1816 and 1817. In 1825, at Fort Atkinson on the west bank of the Missouri River in Nebraska, Julien shot a man in the face. Apparently the injury was minor, and there is no record of Julien being tried or punished.

In 1827, Manuel Martínez reported to Governor Antonio Narbona of New Mexico, then a province of Mexico, that a "Dionicio Julián" had been in a party of

trappers from Taos that went to retrieve buried furs "in the direction of the land of the Utes." Just when Julien switched his activities to the Southwest is unknown. He may have gone to New Mexico after hearing about the area from his brother, who had been a guide for Major Stephen H. Long's scientific expedition which entered the northeastern corner of New Mexico in 1820.

About 1828, the Reed Trading Post was established by William "Toopeechee" Reed, near the junction of the Whiterocks River and the Uintah River, about 115 miles north of Arches. Associated with Reed were his nephew James Reed, Denis Julien, and Augustus Archambeau. Ute Indians at the trading post were reported to have called Julien "Julie," and Archambeau "Sambo.' Near the post on what is now called Inscription Rock, Julien carved his name and the date 1831. This is his earliest known inscription.

About 1838, the post was sold to Antoine Robidoux, and thereafter called interchangeably Fort Robidoux and Fort Uintah. Antoine Robidoux was a prominent fur trader who had another post, Fort Uncompahgre, near present Delta, Colorado, about seventy-five airline miles east of Arches. Both posts were abandoned in 1844 after Fort Uncompahgre was attacked by Ute Indians.

That was the same year Julien made the inscription at Arches. What was he doing there? He may have been on a trapping expedition, either going to or coming from the Green River. Some thirty miles northeast of today's Arches was a trail that ran between Fort Uncompahgre and Fort Uintah. A direct route for Julien between the trail and the Green would have been through the present-day Parkland.

What happened to Julien? Once it was believed that he died by drowning in the rapids of the Colorado River's Cataract Canyon. However, there is one conflicting — but tantalizing — report that such was not his fate, and that Julien may have spent his last days in California.

In many respects, the first white man known to have visited Arches remains an enigma.

Is the **Colorado River** Julien's tomb?

history of river navigation. But the turbid Colorado River flows dramatically along the Park's boundary for eleven twisting miles. So, though the river and its navigation are marginal to the Parkland, they form, nevertheless, an integral — and colorful — chapter in the story of Arches.

Ferryboats
Precisely when the first craft plied the river at Arches is unknown. Travelers on the Old Spanish Trail are known to have used rafts to cross the river at that point.

Reportedly, a small ferry was operated in 1880 by Henry Penney at the approximate location of today's Moab bridge, the crossing for U.S. Highway 191.

In 1881 or 1882, Norman Taylor installed another ferryboat which he operated for several years. Later, Grand County took over the service, placing a new, larger ferry on the river in 1897, and running this vessel until 1912, when the first bridge to span the river at Moab was completed.

Historic Raft and Rowboat Trips
In the summer of 1888, three men — Elmer Kane, Frank W. Emerson, and Charles Duke — rafted from Grand Junction, Colorado to Moab, a distance of ninety-six miles. The purpose of their trip was to sightsee and to prospect, and their original intent was to transit the Grand Canyon. It is uncertain how the rafters negotiated the heavy rapids of Westwater Canyon, from sixty to fifty miles above the present Moab bridge. Did they run them, line them, or portage around the canyon? When the trio reached the Moab ferry, they camped on the river's north shore — the Arches side. There they were warned about the dangerous rapids in Cataract Canyon, which begin sixty-nine miles downstream. When they failed in attempts to replace their raft with a more suitable

WHO WERE THEY?

Carved on Park sandstone are nineteenth-century inscriptions that document entries by early frontiersmen into the area. Usually, these old—sometimes faint—inscriptions consist merely of a name or initials, and a date. Certain of the early inscribers are known to history, among them Denis Julien, a mountain man, who—in 1844—carved the earliest inscription by a white man known to exist in the Park. By contrast, the life stories of other early-day inscription cutters are completely unknown. Their enigmatic carvings are intriguing, since they bear witness to penetrations into Arches by white men at a time when the region around the future Park was unsettled, or just beginning to be settled, and long before Arches became a park.

Questions about these early inscribers naturally arise. Who were they? Why were they there? Were others with them? Where did they come from? What happened to them?

Certainly the most perplexing of the mystery inscriptions are those near Freshwater Spring, about a half-mile northwest of Wolfe Cabin. Their wording is identical: the initials, "J. E. D.," and the date, "1860." Significantly, these findings are, after Julien's 1844 carving, the earliest known non-Indian inscriptions in Arches.

Who the initials J .E. D. stand for is unknown, as is the reason this inscriber visited Freshwater Spring in 1860. Most probably, J. E. D. was a man. Was he alone? A prospector? A cowboy? A sheepherder? Regrettably, absolutely nothing is known about him. What was he doing there so early? Moab and Thompson, the nearest towns, were not founded until years later, and there is no record of prospecting or ranching activity in the vicinity in 1860, when the inscriptions were cut. Michael S. Berry, an archaeologist with the Antiquities Section of Utah's Division of State History, offered what he thought was a probable though nonspecific identification. In 1974, Berry and David B. Madsen supervised a field crew on an archaeological survey of northeastern Arches. Berry's report, published in 1975, listed one of the J. E. D. inscriptions, classifying it as a historic petroglyph. Berry concluded that J. E. D. was "probably associated with the initial Mormon settlement of the Elk Mountain Mission in Moab . . . which began in 1854." Unfortunately, Berry's assumption is wrong. The mission, established in 1855—not 1854—was abandoned after only three months following an Indian attack, and five years before the date on the J. E. D. inscriptions. With the exception of the

three who were killed by the Indians, all of the missionaries fled to other Mormon settlements. Further—and conclusive—proof that J. E. D. was not part of the mission is the simple fact that none of the forty-one missionaries had those initials. The intriguing mystery of J. E. D. remains unsolved.

However, there may be the beginning of an answer to the J. E. D. enigma. In 1860, a contingent of soldiers stationed at Camp Floyd, an army post located in northern Utah, near Fairfield, about forty miles southwest of Salt Lake City, was ordered to Santa Fe, New Mexico. Daniel W. Jones, a Mormon, was employed as a civilian guide.

According to Jones, after the troops forded the Green River, at the present town of the same name, the soldiers "suffered considerable" as they toiled east through the arid country. They passed a few miles north of today's Arches National Park, en route to the Colorado River, which was then called Grand River.

Jones later reported that the troops were short of water, and that some of the men who went in search of the vital fluid "got lost. . . ." As they were never found, Jones concluded that "they either perished or fell into the hands of some hostile Indians."

Could it be that J. E. D. was one of the soldiers who went in search of water, and who may have reached what is now called Freshwater Spring, there carving his initials and the year? If so, did this J. E. D. return safely to the troops? Or vanish?

In Devil's Garden is another puzzling inscription. It was first reported by Henry G. Schmidt, custodian (manager) of Arches, in May 1941. Schmidt, on patrol in northern Devil's Garden, found the initials "C R" (without periods), and the date "1878" carved in an arch. Curiously, in his official Park Service report, Schmidt reversed the initials, recording them as "R. C.," and he listed the date as "1876,"—two years earlier than the date inscribed on the arch. Also, Schmidt did not see, or at least did not mention in his report, a second set of initials with the same date left by the mysterious inscriber.

Appropriately, the opening has been named Inscription Arch. But nothing is known about the identity of C. R. or what he (or she) was doing in what is now the Parkland.

Will the mystery surrounding these long-ago "Kilroy was here" carvers ever be solved?

[Right] **Butch Cassidy**, a notorious western frontier outlaw, brushed the history of Arches in 1889. In that year, while fleeing from his first major crime — the June 24 robbery of the San Miguel Valley Bank in Telluride, Colorado — Cassidy (whose real name was Robert LeRoy Parker) and his accomplices Matt Warner and Tom McCarty commandeered the Moab Ferry and crossed the Colorado Then they rode their horses up Moab Canyon along the western edge of the area that is now the Park, thus — in a minor way — riding into the annals of Arches.

Utah State Historical Society

[Below, lower] The **Undine**, an early Canyon Country steamboat that sank in Big Bend Rapid—on the Arches stretch of the Colorado River—is shown tied up near Moab on the south bank of the river, in either late 1901 or early 1902. Across the Colorado, in the background, is present-day Arches National Park.

[Below, upper] For some thirty years, the **Moab Ferry** operated on the Colorado River, crossing just upstream from the present highway bridge. The ferry ran on a cable stretched across the river from its south landing on the Moab shore to its north landing on the Arches side. Ferry service began around 1880 and ended in 1912, when the first bridge opened for use.

Utah State Historical Society

Utah State Historical Society

craft, the trio abandoned their voyage.

In November 1888, Francis M. Shafer and his brother Will assembled a log raft at Cisco, about forty-five miles above today's Moab bridge. The brothers planned to float downstream to Castle Valley, some fifteen miles above the present bridge, and there to prospect for gold. However, the small rapid at Castle Creek prevented them from landing. They finally made shore at Nigger Bill Canyon, across the river from Arches and about eleven miles below their intended destination. From Nigger Bill Canyon the brothers hiked to Moab.

The next year, 1889, Frank C. Kendrick led a survey party downriver from Grand Junction to The Confluence, the point where the Green River joins the Colorado. Kendrick was charged with the responsibility of surveying the river canyon for a water-level railway — the proposed Denver, Colorado Cañon and Pacific Railroad. Plans called for this line to run from Grand Junction down the Colorado to Yuma, Arizona, then west overland to the coast at San Diego.

The survey party, numbering five men including Kendrick, traveled in a single wooden boat. On March 29 they started downstream, and on April 13 portaged around the rapids of Westwater Canyon. Eleven days later, April 24, they stopped at the Moab ferry, and on May 4 reached The Confluence. The men then rowed and pulled their boat up the Green to what was then called Blake, the present town of Green River, Utah.

Two Glenwood Springs, Colorado dentists, Drs. Babcock and Miller, in August 1897 rowed past Arches in a wooden boat seventeen feet long equipped with two water-tight compartments. These adventurous dentists were the first recorded boaters to run the rapids of Westwater Canyon. From Moab, the pair continued downstream to the head of Cataract Canyon, then rowed back to Moab, arriving in mid-September. There, they left the river and returned to Glenwood Springs.

In 1898, Henry Grimm went upstream in a rowboat from Moab about twenty-two miles to near the upriver end of Professor Valley. He returned to Moab, hauling a raft of 6,000 feet of lumber.

Ellsworth Kolb — a famous early river runner — and John Shields, in 1916, embarked in a canoe from Delta, Colorado, on the Gunnison River, and paddled downstream to its union with the Colorado at Grand Junction. Then the canoeists went down the combined flow of the rivers to Moab. However, they portaged around Westwater Canyon.

In September of the same year, with Bert Loper, Kolb departed from Grand Junction in a cedar canoe, ran Westwater Canyon — the second known transit of its rapids — and reached Moab. There they ended the trip.

In 1933, Harold H. Leich planned a solo run of the Colorado from Grand Lake, near the river's headwaters in the Rocky Mountains, to the Gulf of California. For the stretch to Grand Junction, Leich used a folding rubber kayak, but there he constructed a punt which he named the *Dirty Devil*. Leich ran Westwater Canyon, passed by Arches, made a stopover at Moab, then abruptly ended his river adventure in Cataract Canyon when the *Dirty Devil* sank in a rapid. He hiked and swam downstream some thirty miles to Hite — which he found deserted — and from there made the long trek afoot across the arid terrain to Hanksville, Utah — a distance of about fifty miles.

In May 1948, Preston Walker and Otis "Dock" Marston, with their wives, Becky Walker and Margaret Marston, embarked on the Dolores River, at Dolores, Colorado, and made the first recorded run of the river to its junction with the Colorado, about thirty-two miles above the Moab bridge. The Walker-Marston party continued their trip down the Colorado, ending it at the bridge.

Steamer *Undine*
In the late 1890s and early 1900s several commercial powerboat schemes were proposed for Canyonlands stretches of the Colorado and the Green. In 1901, Frank H. Sommeril of Denver had the steamboat *Undine* built in Rock Island, Illinois, and brought by train to Green River, Utah. There the vessel was launched.

The *Undine* was fifty-six feet long, had an eight-foot beam, and drew between twelve and fourteen inches. The vessel was powered by a twenty-two-horsepower,

JOHN WESLEY WOLFE AND WOLFE RANCH

John Wesley Wolfe and his son, Fred, had a small ranch in what is now Arches National Park. They ran Wolfe Ranch from 1898 to 1910.

The senior Wolfe was born in Tennessee on February 17, 1829. Little is known about his early life. Family legend has it that he was a relative of famous frontiersman Kit Carson, and once joined Carson on a hunting trip. Wolfe saw service in the Civil War; he joined the Union Army on July 17, 1862. Army records describe Wolfe as just over six feet in height, of light complexion, with blue eyes and light hair. At the Siege of Vicksburg in 1863, his left leg was injured, crippling him for life. Wolfe received a medical discharge from the army, and returned to his home in Ohio.

Wolfe was twice married. He divorced his first wife, and on February 11, 1869 married Lydia Ault. They made their home in Etna, Ohio, and to their union four children were born: Thomas Fred (on November 16, 1870), William E., Flora May, and Katie Bell.

Wolfe operated a butcher shop in Etna. Then, probably in the early 1880s, he went—alone—to Colorado, where he lived for several years.

Returning to Etna, he picked up his son Fred, and the pair traveled to Utah, where they established their small ranch in 1898. Wolfe Cabin, the ranch's homesite, stands on the west bank of Salt Wash, at today's Delicate Arch trail head. The rustic, one-room structure was built in 1906. Fremont cottonwoods (*Populus fremontii*) were used to construct the walls of the seventeen-foot by fifteen-foot cabin. An earlier cabin was destroyed by a flash flood. In addition to the cabin, they built a corral, a dam for irrigation water, and a root cellar—a rectangular pit roofed over and covered with dirt, and used for the storage of root crops and other vegetables.

In 1910, the Wolfes moved back to

John Wesley Wolfe

Ohio. There at Etna on October 22, 1913, Wolfe died at age eighty-four.

Fred eventually went to Montana, where he had a ranch about sixty miles south of Malta, in what is now the Charles M. Russell National Wildlife Refuge. He died on March 27, 1940, at age sixty-nine, and is buried at Malta.

After the Wolfe family departed Arches in 1910, several other ranchers used the cabin and surrounding area until it was acquired by the National Park Service in 1948. Wolfe Cabin has also been called Turnbow Cabin, after J. Marvin Turnbow, a later owner and the first custodian (manager) of Arches. Because it is a significant cultural feature, Wolfe Ranch has been listed since 1975 on the National Register of Historic Places.

Wolfe Cabin

two-cylinder coal-burning steam engine that drove a stern paddle wheel.

Sommeril had several planned uses for the *Undine*. He wanted to transport freight between Cisco, a station on The Denver and Rio Grande Western Railroad, and Moab, and to carry tourists from Cisco and Green River (also a station on the railroad) to the head of Cataract Canyon. Sommeril also hoped to establish a sanatorium four miles below the start of Cataract Canyon at Cataract (or, Spanish) Bottom.

The *Undine* made two trips to Moab from Green River. On the second, the steamer started from Moab on May 8, 1902 for its initial run to Cisco. But the vessel was able to travel only about six miles up-river, and so returned to Moab. On Wednesday, May 21, another attempt was made to run the steamer upstream. At Big Bend Rapid, about seven-and-one-half miles above the present Moab bridge, the *Undine* capsized. Fortunately, the crew escaped without fatalities. Moab's newspaper, the *Grand Valley Times*, reported the sinking on the front page of its May 23 issue under the bold headline, "A Narrow Escape."

WOLFE RANCH

The first whites known to have settled in what is now Arches National Park were John Wesley Wolfe and his son Fred. In 1898, they established a small, rustic ranch near the junction of Salt Wash and Winter Camp Wash, about one-and-a-quarter miles west of Delicate Arch.

The senior Wolfe was a Civil War veteran, having served in the Union Army. At the Siege of Vicksburg in 1863, he injured his left leg. This injury was to be a continuing health problem for him, requiring the use of a crutch for the remainder of his life. Wolfe was granted a disability discharge, and returned to his home in Ohio.

Why John Wesley Wolfe and his son came to a remote canyon in the red-rock

country of Arches is unknown. Was it for the high-desert's drier climate in which the senior Wolfe's painful leg might improve? An even more intriguing question — also one for which no answer has yet been discovered — is: How did they learn of the out-of-the-way locale?

Fred's sister Flora, her husband Ed

Stanley, and their two children, Esther and Ferol, came from Columbus, Ohio in 1906 to live at the isolated ranch. In 1908, the Stanleys moved into Moab, where on May 23, 1910 their third child, Volna, was born.

In June of the same year, the senior Wolfe, his son Fred, and the Standleys moved back to Ohio.

WHO WAS THE REAL "FATHER OF ARCHES"?

Occasionally a man is honored for his role in originating, founding, or establishing something—a movement, discipline, device, process, or even a nation—by being designated its "father." One familiar example is, of course, George Washington, long honored as the "Father of His Country." Two prominent citizens of early Moab have been called the "Father of Arches": Dr. J. W. Williams, and L. L. Taylor. But the title has most often been applied to Dr. Williams.

Both of these men were well-known throughout southeastern Utah; each holds a special place in its history; each was active in promoting scenic attractions of the area; and each supported the development of Arches.

But does the title "Father of Arches" truly apply to either of these distinguished men?

"Doc" Williams

John W. "Doc" Williams was the area's first permanent physician, establishing his practice at Moab in 1897. Born in 1853 in Pike County, Missouri—in the proverbial log cabin with a dirt floor—Williams crossed the plains to Colorado in 1875 as a cowboy, helping to herd 500 head of cattle. Williams rode the Colorado ranges as a cowhand for the next six years. He then entered the drugstore business at Hugo, Colorado, but twelve years later he quit and moved to Denver to study medicine at Gross Medical College. Following graduation in 1895, Williams first practiced at Ordway, Colorado.

In 1896, Justus N. Corbin, editor of Moab's first newspaper, *The Grand Valley Times*, launched a campaign to attract a physician to the town. Dr. Williams agreed to come to Moab, and opened his office there in 1897. He practiced in and around Moab for twenty-three years until his re-

National Park Service

Alexander Ringhoffer

tirement in 1919. Williams died in Moab in 1956, at the venerable age of 103.

Several honors have been paid to the memory of Dr. Williams for his efforts in promoting conservation of the natural wonders in southeastern Utah, and especially for his interest in Arches. A promontory west of the upper Fiery Furnace, overlooking Salt Valley, was named Doc Williams Point; a bust of Williams sculpted by F. M. Pimpell, of Moab, and cast in bronze in 1958, was placed in the Visitors Center at Arches; and the likeness of Williams's bearded and mustached face is reproduced on one side of a bronze medallion commemorating Arches. The medal was one in a series on national parks sculpted by Frank Hagel and produced under the auspices of the National Park Service and the National Park Foundation Centennial Commission.

"Bish" Taylor

Loren L. "Bish" Taylor was the long-time editor and publisher of Moab's newspaper. His family was among the town's first settlers, and when Taylor was born there in 1892 Moab was still in many respects a frontier outpost.

Taylor became editor of *The Grand Valley Times* (today called *The Times-Independent*) in 1911 and continued in the position for forty-two years. Active in community affairs, he held various posts including town clerk, and was a member of the county commission. Taylor died in Moab in 1972.

Although both Taylor and Williams have been called the "Father of Arches," obviously only one man can be accorded the honor. But does either of these men merit the title? Or does the designation rightfully belong to someone else?

The simple fact is that neither Williams nor Taylor participated in events which led to inclusion of Arches in the national park system, an event which finally occurred in 1929 when President Herbert C. Hoover proclaimed Arches a national monument. Proof that neither of these men was involved in the process is readily available and clearly evident in Park Service Records. Nonetheless, the myth that Williams and Taylor were involved in the establishment of Arches has been related in newspaper and magazine articles through the years, including one by Natt N. Dodge in the April 1947 issue of the widely read *Arizona Highways*.

However, both Williams and Taylor were deeply involved with activities that resulted in enlargement of the monument's area from about seven to nearly fifty-three square miles. This expansion was proclaimed by President Franklin D. Roosevelt on November 25, 1938. Roosevelt thanked Dr. Williams for his efforts on behalf of Arches in a letter dated December 15, 1938, writing to Williams in

DEVIL'S GARDEN: THE CASE OF THE PERAMBULATING PLACE-NAME OR, HOW ARCHES BECAME PART OF THE NATIONAL PARK SYSTEM

Occasionally a name given first to one area will eventually end up designating an entirely different locale. Devil's Garden is an example of such a place-name mix-up. Originally this name was applied to the area now known as Klondike Bluffs, a ruggedly scenic maze of reddish sandstone on the western ridge of Salt Valley. Significantly, it was this locale under its original name — Klondike Bluffs as "Devil's Garden" — that generated the National Park Service's interest in the Arches area, leading to its eventual inclusion in the park system.

Klondike Bluffs was first named "Devil's Garden" by Alexander Ringhoffer. On December 24, 1922, with two of his sons and a son-in-law, Ringhoffer made his first visit to the spectacular area. He was greatly impressed by its many strange and wonderful landforms. In July 1923, Ringhoffer, a Hungarian-born prospector and miner, wrote to officials of The Denver and Rio Grande Western Railroad urging them to send representatives to view the area's erosional features.

Frank A. Wadleigh, the railroad's passenger traffic manager, and George L. Beam, also of the passenger department, met Ringhoffer in September at the railroad station in Thompson, about forty miles north of Moab. Ringhoffer escorted them to the place he called "Devil's Garden," approximately thirteen miles south of Thompson. Beam photographed what is now designated Tower Arch, the principal attraction of the area, thus establishing indisputably the location of Ringhoffer's "Devil's Garden."

After his trip, Wadleigh — obviously awed by what he had seen — wrote to Stephen T. Mather, then director of the National Park Service, suggesting that the area be made a national monument. Interested, Mather requested William Spry, Commissioner of the General Land Office, to have a survey made of the area. The field work was conducted by T. W. McKinley, from July 12 to 14, 1924. However, he could not find anyone at Thompson or Moab who had heard of "Devil's Garden." McKinley then went to Salt Valley but was unable to locate an area fitting Wadleigh's description of "Devil's Garden." So he returned to Moab, where he met Heber Christensen and described to him the place he was looking for. Christensen guided McKinley to a somewhat similar locale, The Windows, a section of today's Park approximately ten air miles from Ringhoffer's "Devil's Garden." McKinley mistakenly concluded that The Windows and "Devil's Garden" were the same.

Moab's newspaper carried a story and photographs about McKinley's examination of The Windows. The July 17 article was seen by Wadleigh, who noted that the location given for The Windows did not coincide with the location of the area he had visited. On August 21 Wadleigh wrote to Mather, calling the

apparent discrepancy to his attention. Arthur E. Demaray, administrative assistant to Mather, replied on August 26, saying that McKinley's report had not yet been received by the Park Service, and promising to write again once the report had been delivered and reviewed.

Demaray sent McKinley's report to Wadleigh on November 10, 1924. After studying the report, Wadleigh was doubtful that the "Devil's Garden" he had been shown by Ringhoffer was the same area as The Windows that McKinley had been shown by Christensen. Wadleigh wrote to Demaray on November 24, stating his suspicions.

On February 14, 1925, Demaray wrote Wadleigh that a new field survey would be made by the General Land Office. The second examination was conducted by F. J. Safley, between June 11 and 14. Safley resurveyed The Windows section and examined an extensive area of fins and arches on the east ridge of Salt Valley which he thought to be Ringhoffer's "Devil's Garden." It was not, but the area has ever since carried that name.

While Safley was engaged in his field investigation, he met Dr. and Mrs. Frank R. Oastler of New York City, who at the request of Mather had just completed a private examination of the original "Devil's Garden" under the guidance of Ringhoffer. Safley did not realize that the area he thought was "Devil's Garden" was not the same locale visited by the Oastlers. Safley never did survey Ringhoffer's "Devil's Garden."

Wadleigh wrote Mather on January 2, 1926, inquiring about the results of the second survey. Mather, who had decided to seek monument status for Arches, responded on January 8 that Hubert Work, Secretary of the Interior under President Calvin Coolidge, was opposed to the establishment of any more national monuments. In fact, Work advocated returning some monuments to the individual states for state parks.

Park Service officials decided to wait

Stephen Tyng Mather (1867-1930), first director of the National Park Service, strongly sought the addition of Arches to the park system. His persistent efforts toward that goal finally triumphed in 1929.

until a secretary more favorably inclined to their goals, including their plans for Arches, was in office. Mather, however, continued to push for Arches, but now concentrating his promoting outside of the Interior Department. He convinced John H. McNeely to prepare an illustrated feature article, using photographs supplied by Dr. Oastler, for *The New York Times Magazine* of May 9, 1926. Mather was quoted in the article as saying: "The national park system contains many marvelous prodigies, yet none of them exceeds in interest the extraordinary specimens of natural sculpture and architecture found in [Arches]." The article also forecast eventual park-system status for the area.

Pressure generated by this article had its effect in Washington, D. C. Secretary Work relented somewhat, and agreed to recommend temporary withdrawal of not more than eighty acres around each of the arches in The Windows section and in Safley's Devil's Garden. Park Service officials recognized that this plan was impracticable, and did not expedite the project while Work or his successor, Roy O. West, were in office.

The election of Herbert C. Hoover in 1928 heralded brighter prospects for Arches. The month after Hoover's inauguration, his Secretary of the Interior, Ray Lyman Wilbur, recommended to the president that he sign an executive order to create Arches National Monument. President Hoover affixed his signature to the order on April 12, 1929. The new monument consisted of 4,520 acres in two detached sections: The Windows, containing 1,920 acres, and Devil's Garden, with 2,600 acres. The monument's name was suggested by Frank Pinkley, superintendent of the Southwestern National Monuments, in a letter to Mather on July 24, 1925. Administration of Arches was placed under Pinkley as its first superintendent.

Ironically, when Arches was proclaimed a monument, it did not include Ringhoffer's "Devil's Garden," the very area that had been the impetus for establishing the monument. Not until President Franklin D. Roosevelt greatly enlarged the monument's area to 33,680 acres on November 25, 1938, did the original "Devil's Garden" — by then called Klondike Bluffs — finally become a part of Arches National Monument.

The next change in the monument's area occurred on July 22, 1960, when President Dwight D. Eisenhower signed a proclamation which added 480 acres but also deleted 720 acres. Just before leaving office, President Lyndon B. Johnson on January 20, 1969, more than doubled the monument's size from slightly more than 52 square miles to about 130 square miles. Finally, Arches became a national park on November 16, 1971 when President Richard M. Nixon signed Public Law 92-155. The same act also reduced the area to approximately 114 square miles, or 73,233.88 acres.

[Opposite page] **Pine Tree Arch** takes its title from piñon pines in the immediate area. Originally, however, it was called Cedar Tree Arch after a Utah juniper that grew at the arch. Junipers are commonly, but incorrectly, referred to locally as "cedars." The arch has a span of forty-six feet and a height of forty-eight feet. It is situated in south Devil's Garden, approximately 1,000 feet north of Tunnel Arch, and is reached by a short path from the main trail in Devil's Garden. From Pine Tree Arch, Crystal Arch can be glimpsed to the northeast.

part: ". . . I have heard of the cooperation you have given the National Park Service of the Department of the Interior in bringing to a successful consummation the project to enlarge the boundaries of the Arches National Monument. On behalf of the people of the United States, I thank you for your assistance in this instance. . . ."

Jesse L. Nusbaum, superintendent of Mesa Verde National Park, on September 12, 1938 called attention to Taylor's role in the enlargement of Arches in a memorandum to the director of the National Park Service, noting that Taylor had "splendidly advanced" the Park Service's plans.

If neither Taylor nor Williams is the "Father of Arches," then who is? To be the "father" one logically must have initiated the long, involved, and at times tedious process that ultimately led to Arches becoming a part of the national park system. Several men played important roles in the drama: Frank A. Wadleigh, passenger traffic manager of The Denver and Rio Grande Western Railroad, who brought the unique area to the attention of the National Park Service in a letter to the director dated November 2, 1923 by urging that the scenic locale be made a national monument; Stephen T. Mather, director of the National Park Service, who agreed with Wadleigh and sought, nurtured, and guided the addition of Arches to the national park system; Ray Lyman Wilbur, secretary of the interior, who recommended to the president that national monument status be given to Arches; and President Hoover, who signed the order establishing the monument in 1929.

There was still another request to the National Park Service to make Arches a national monument. And some people have credited this one as the real impetus which gave Arches its monument status. However, this request cannot be so credited, as it came fifteen months after Wadleigh wrote Mather. Laurence M. Gould,

"UNCLES OF ARCHES"

Arches was a relatively unknown unit of the national park system for the first nine years after it was established in 1929. Even in neighboring Moab, Arches was not fully appreciated by most townspeople in the beginning years. Exceptions, however, were two prominent citizens of the town: Loren L. "Bish" Taylor, long-time editor and publisher of *The Times-Independent*, and Dr. J. W. Williams, Moab's first permanent physician. Both were early and ardent supporters of Arches, and both figured prominently in the campaign to increase its acreage. This effort bore fruit in 1938, when Arches was enlarged by presidential proclamation.

The active and prominent roles played by Taylor and Williams in promoting Arches have brought each of them recognition and praise. President Franklin D. Roosevelt saluted Williams for his efforts to enlarge Arches. Taylor was cited as a "guardian" of Arches, and Bates Wilson, while superintendent of Arches, hailed Taylor as "a real amigo of the National Park Service, especially Arches. . . ."

Loren L. "Bish" Taylor

Both Williams and Taylor have—on various occasions—been called "Father of Arches." But the title is inaccurate. While both men rightly deserve generous applause for their diligent efforts on behalf of the area, neither man was involved in the creation of Arches. The "father" distinction belongs, more appropriately, to Alexander Ringhoffer. For it was Ringhoffer who launched the long, complex chain of events that led ultimately, in 1929, to national-park status for Arches.

While neither Williams nor Taylor may be regarded as the "Father of Arches," both certainly deserve to be remembered as members of the family. Each may be honored as an "uncle" of Arches National Park.

"Doc" Williams at the Garden of Eden.

Mrs. Frank Shields

THE MAN WHO NAMED ARCHES

Arches owes its name to Frank Pinkley. Today, the title seems obvious for the Park. However, people commonly confuse natural arches and bridges. Double Arch, for example, was once labeled Twinbow Bridge. While there are a few bridges in the Park, nearly all of the area's natural rock openings are correctly defined as "arches."

In 1925, Pinkley, who was then superintendent of the Southwestern National Monuments, visited the area now named Arches. At the time, the scenic locale was being considered for inclusion in the national park system. Following his visit, Pinkley wrote on July 24 to Stephen T. Mather, the first director of the National Park Service: ". . . I stopped over a day at Moab and looked into the possibilities of making a national monument out of some formations which lie seven miles north of there."

Impressed by what he had seen, Pinkley described several of the arches in The Windows section. "You will note," he wrote, "that I do not speak of these as 'natural bridges.' They are not formed by the same forces [as bridges] . . . bridges are across canyons and were formed by running water. There is no drainage under these arches . . ."

Pinkley noted: "The local name for them is 'The Castle Windows.'" But, he said, "I do not like this name; it is not descriptive."

Then he wrote: "Should a monument be made, I would suggest calling it 'The Arches National Monument.'" Thus was born a place-name. Pinkley concluded his historic letter by saying: "I would suggest that these arches be made a national monument."

Appropriately, Frank Pinkley was appointed first superintendent of Arches when it was created in 1929.

Pinkley was born on a farm near Chillicothe, Missouri in May, 1881. Later, his family moved into the town, where Frank graduated from high school in 1898, then went to work in a store. In 1900, he fell ill. A physician told the nineteen-year-old youth that he might have tuberculosis, and urged him to seek recuperation in the desert climate of Arizona for about six months.

The young Missourian arrived at Phoenix in September, and set up a camp northeast of the city. After several months, with his health improved, he leased a small ranch for a short time. Then in 1901, he found a job, at $75.00 a month, working for the General Land Office as caretaker of the prehistoric Indian ruins known today as Casa Grande National Monument.

He pitched his tent on the desert near the ruins, but soon found the midsummer heat in his tent unbearable. So, with his own hands and money from his own pocket, Pinkley built a one-room cabin. In his monthly report to Washington, D.C., the industrious employee mentioned his new house. In reply, Pinkley was

complimented for his enterprise, but also was notified that $5.00 a month would be deducted from his paycheck for rent! Each time Pinkley added a room, the government hiked his rent $5.00, until he was paying $20.00 a month for a house he had built and paid for. Fortunately, Pinkley had a sense of humor which helped him to survive both the heat and the bureaucracy.

After the National Park Service was established in 1916, Pinkley rose steadily to become superintendent of the Southwestern National Monuments. Known affectionately as "The Boss," Pinkley in time became a Park Service legend. By 1940, he was administering, from his headquarters near Coolidge, Arizona, twenty-seven national monuments — including Arches — in a domain embracing more than a thousand square miles in four states: Arizona, New Mexico, Colorado, and Utah. He personally described the sights in this realm to nearly a million visitors, and never tired of answering visitors' questions. But now and then a question would stump him. One lady, after viewing some prehistoric Indian dwellings, asked: "Why on earth do you suppose they made their homes out here so far away from the railroad?" That one left Pinkley speechless.

On the afternoon of February 14, 1940 — Valentine's Day — Pinkley delivered an address to the first conference of custodians, or managers, of the monuments under his administration. Proudly, he commented: "This is one of the red-letter days of my life!" Just minutes after he concluded his speech, Frank Pinkley fell dead, victim of a heart attack at age fifty-eight.

Learning of Pinkley's death, L. L. Taylor and Dr. J. W. Williams of Moab, both active boosters of Arches, wrote to Hugh M. Miller of the Southwestern National Monuments on February 14, saying: "Looking back at what he has done for our section, we find it impossible to express our keen personal loss."

Moab's newspaper, *The Times-Independent*, on February 15 carried a front-page announcement of Pinkley's death, and noted: "For the past two decades he was one of the moving forces in the development of the national monuments of the southwest."

Nearly 500 of Pinkley's friends and associates attended his funeral rites, held within half a mile of the Casa Grande ruins where — four decades earlier — his career had begun.

"About the only thing I ever did that was really smart," said Pinkley in 1939, "was to go out in the desert and pick a darned good ruin, and sit down by it for thirty-odd years."

then of the Department of Geology at the University of Michigan, visited The Windows section in August 1924. That summer Gould had been conducting field research on the geology of the La Sal Mountains, southeast of Arches. In Moab he had heard of the unusual landforms at The Windows section, and wanting to see them he engaged J. Marvin Turnbow, later the first custodian of Arches, to guide him. They traveled to the site by horseback. Gould later remarked he was "delighted" by what he had seen.

On February 9, 1925, Gould wrote to Senator Reed Smoot of Utah: "I do not know if any movement has ever been made toward having these interesting natural features made a national monument. It should be done." Smoot sent a copy of Gould's letter to Mather, and in his cover letter, dated February 13, 1925, asked the National Park Service director "to make an examination with a view of recommending, if you think proper, legislation making that part of the State a national monument." Mather replied on February 14 that Wadleigh had previously called his attention to the area, and that although it was still being investigated, the locale had already shown "such unusual scenic quality" that it appeared "worthy of preservation" as a national monument. Obviously, in light of these facts, neither Gould nor Smoot qualifies as the "Father of Arches."

Another persistent myth surrounding the origin of Arches holds that the Lions Club of Moab was instrumental in the establishment of Arches National Monument. This is patently untrue, because the Moab Lions Club was not founded until 1930—a year **after** Arches achieved monument status. However, once the local Lions Club was formed, it was very active in issues affecting Arches. The club was strongly supportive of efforts that resulted in enlargement of the monument in 1938, sought road development to open the area

FRANK BECKWITH — "CHIEF BILLY-GOAT HAIR"

Several of the Park's features, including three of its most prominent landmarks — Delicate Arch, Landscape Arch, and Tower Arch — owe their names to the Arches National Monument Scientific Expedition of 1933-34. The expedition's leader was Frank A. Beckwith, on leave from his duties as editor of a weekly newspaper, the *Millard County Chronicle*, published at Delta, Utah.

Although not formally trained as a scientist, Beckwith nonetheless proved to be a fortunate choice for the position. His close friend, author and historian Charles Kelly, observed that Beckwith "had the mentality of a scientist." He was driven, according to Kelly, by an "almost fanatical desire to pursue any subject to the furthest possible conclusion." Kelly believed that if Beckwith had "followed some scientific profession rather than [journalism], he would have eventually become world famous."

A devout booklover, Beckwith read and reread the classics. When his curiosity was aroused in anything, Beckwith sent "for every book on the subject and began studying them," recalled Kelly.

Beckwith's inquisitive mind was attracted to an astonishing variety of subjects, among them Paiute Indian history and customs, the interpretation of Indian petroglyphs, archeology, trilobites (extinct Paleozoic marine arthropods), the history of Millard County, the geology of the Delta area, astronomy, the Mayan calendar, applied psychology, Hindu philosophy and mythology, and photography.

Though Beckwith never attended college, his scholarly pursuits more than compensated for his lack of formal higher education. Beckwith's interest in trilobites led Kelly to remark that his friend "pursued this study fanatically and in time came to know more about trilobites than the experts." Beckwith accumulated a large collection of trilobite fossils, representing many species. He contributed some 7,000 specimens to the Smithsonian Institution in Washington, D. C.

In 1929, Emory W. John found a fossil west of Delta that resembled a trilobite. He showed the fossil to Beckwith, who — failing to recognize the species — sent the fossil to the Smithsonian. There the specimen was identified as a new species of merostome, a marine arachnoid, along with several tiny brachiopods — also of a new species — that had settled on the merostome and fossilized. The new merostome was named *Obolus johni* and the new brachiopod was designated *Beckwithia typa*, after the two Utah fossil collectors. Later Beckwith said with pride: "I'd rather have that honor than $5,000!"

Beckwith studied the Paiutes living near Delta, and probably "learned more of the lore and mental processes of these Indians than any other white man," according to Kelly. *Indian Joe*, Beckwith's work on the Paiutes was published posthumously in 1975, twenty-four years after his death.

Another of Beckwith's interests, the correlation of the Mayan calendar to known astronomical dates, was pursued "as a mental exercise if for no other reason," Kelly said. Kelly remembered that Beckwith's office "contained bales of sheets covered with calculations which no one in Utah understood but himself." Beckwith wrote several articles for his newspaper on this subject, even though — in Kelly's words — "perhaps not more than half a dozen living men . . . could understand what he was writing about . . ."

Befitting a man of his intellectual interests, Beckwith cultivated a classic professorial feature — a goatee. Because of this distinctive beard, the Paiutes appropriately bestowed on Beckwith the sobriquet Chief Sev-vi-toots, or "Chief Billy-Goat Hair."

Frank Asahel Beckwith was born in the then-Territory of Wyoming at Evanston, near the Utah border, on November 24, 1876. His father, Asahel, was a prominent businessman and rancher. After graduation from high school at age sixteen, Frank worked for several years for his father.

In 1898, Frank married Mary Amelia Simister, of Coalville, Utah. The young couple made their home in Salt Lake City until 1902. Then they moved to Evanston, where Frank worked in his father's bank. In 1907, the couple returned to Salt Lake City. There, over the next several years, Frank was employed in banking, taught at a business college, and worked for *Goodwin's Weekly*. In February 1913, the Beckwiths moved to Delta, a recently established farming community in western Utah. There Frank worked for the Delta State Bank as a cashier. In 1917, the Beckwiths, with their children, went to Oakley, Idaho where Frank was again employed by a bank. They lived in Oakley one year.

Then, Frank—at age forty-two— made a radical decision: to abandon banking, and to pursue a new career in journalism. In February 1919, the Beckwiths returned to Delta where Frank purchased the *Millard County Chronicle* from Charles O. Davis. Beckwith served as the newspaper's editor for thirty-two years, until his death on June 11, 1951, at age seventy-four.

As a non-Mormon in a Mormon community, Beckwith once said he was "tolerated but not loved" by his neighbors. However, he performed many civic duties, including serving as treasurer for the City of Delta from 1937 to 1949. In 1947, he authored a book, *Millard and Nearby*, and gave copies to the Boy Scouts of Delta. The Scouts sold them from house to house to raise funds for their troop.

Beckwith was an even-tempered man. Kelly, who had camped numerous times with Beckwith, recalled: "He never got temperamental, never got angry, and in the toughest situation could always think of a joke."

According to Kelly, Beckwith's greatest disappointment in life was his inability to write successfully about his research. This was due, said Kelly, to Beckwith's "fanatical intensity," which prevented him from realizing that not everyone shared his enthusiasm for his interests. All too often, Beckwith would assume too much knowledge on the part of his readers, thus confusing or alienating them.

During the planning of the Arches National Monument Scientific Expedition in December 1933, the organizers were faced with the problem of finding a suitable leader — one with experience in archeology. The planners, which included then-Superintendent Preston P. Patraw of Zion National Park, and Clifford Presnall, Park Naturalist at Zion, were on the verge of contacting the University of California at Berkeley for a competent archeologist to head the expedition when Beckwith's name was proposed. Patraw described Beckwith as "a man of mature age [who] has indulged in archeology many years and has prepared several publications on the subject."

Presnall later commented on Superintendent Patraw's use of the term "indulged." Calling it an "exquisite" choice, Presnall said: "I know now why all those bone diggers are a little different from common folks, not really foolish, but a little touched; they have been indulging too much in archeology."

While working in the field at Arches, Beckwith contributed several articles on the expedition's activities to Moab's newspaper, *The Times-Independent*. He described the area's features in glowing terms, and documented the naming of Delicate Arch, Landscape Arch, and Tower Arch.

In honor of the expedition's scholarly leader, an impressive sandstone span in the Herdina Park area has been named Beckwith Arch.

Beckwith Arch

Turret Arch, viewed through North Window, has been appropriately called Framed Arch. The prominent "turret" was named Jack's Mummy by Frank Beckwith in 1934. That year in the March 1 issue of the Moab newspaper, *The Times-Independent*, Beckwith reported his scientific expedition had not found at Arches "a real live mummy—one that could talk Indian glibly." But he wrote that Jack YouVon, the expedition's foreman, found "a rock one," which was named for him. Turret Arch is in The Windows section. Its opening has a span of thirty-nine feet and a height of sixty-four feet.

to tourists, and campaigned for national park status for Arches.

Was Wadleigh, then, the true "Father of Arches"? No. The man who **began** the recognition process, the man who introduced Wadleigh to the site—the **real** "father"—was, curiously enough, a Hungarian-born prospector named Alexander Ringhoffer.

In July 1923, Ringhoffer wrote to The Denver and Rio Grande Western Railroad to extol the scenic beauty and strangeness of an area he had recently prospected—today's Klondike Bluffs section of the Park—and to request that someone from the railroad visit the site. The following September, Wadleigh and George L. Beam, another official of the railroad, acted on this request. Guided by Ringhoffer, they visited Klondike Bluffs, then called "Devil's Garden" by Ringhoffer (a place-name which, through later error, was moved east across Salt Valley to designate the area which now bears that name). Wadleigh was greatly impressed with the natural wonders at Klondike Bluffs, saying later that he saw "some stupendous sandstone formations of very remarkable shapes," and calling the site a "beauty spot." Subsequently, Wadleigh contacted Mather, and Mather began the official process which would culminate seven years later—in 1929—in achievement of monument status for Arches and eventually—in 1971—in its designation as a national park.

Arches, then, may have had many "uncles," but naturally it could have had only one real "father": Alexander Ringhoffer. For it was Ringhoffer who provided the seminal impetus, thus initiating the long period of gestation that would one day reach fruition in the birth of Arches.

ARCHES NATIONAL MONUMENT SCIENTIFIC EXPEDITION

In 1933, four years after Arches became part of the national park system, the Park

This photograph, taken by Frank Beckwith in 1934, shows personnel and the pack train of the **Arches National Monument Scientific Expedition** on their way to The Windows section. The hummocky terrain across which they are traveling is part of the Petrified Sand Dunes. The tall, isolated landform in the center is Squaw Pinnacle. On the horizon are the snowcapped La Sal Mountains.

Service organized a scientific reconnaissance of the area. Called the Arches National Monument Scientific Expedition, the party was charged with three primary tasks: (1) to prepare a map, (2) to make a geologic survey, and (3) to conduct an archeological investigation.

Preston P. Patraw, then superintendent of Zion National Park, and Clifford C. Presnall, park naturalist at Zion, were assigned to form the expedition. On December 12, 1933, the pair left Zion for Salt Lake City. The following day they selected Frank A. Beckwith, editor of a weekly newspaper in Delta, Utah, to head the expedition. They also appointed Joseph C. Anderson, of Salt Lake City, as geologist.

Later that day, Presnall went to Price, about 100 miles northwest of Arches, and hired eleven men for the party. On the fifteenth he traveled on to Moab where he employed three more men: Jack YouVon as foreman; J. Marvin Turnbow, who then was Arches custodian, as packer; and Heber Christensen to be the cook. From December 16 to 18, Presnall assembled equipment and established a base camp at Willow Spring. On the nineteenth, he with Beckwith, Turnbow, and Ralph P. Anderson, the transitman, examined the Arches area. They planned the work to be done, and selected camp sites for a mobile surveying party. Presnall then departed for Zion on the twentieth.

The expedition's personnel began their work at Arches. During the field operations, Beckwith contributed several articles to the Moab newspaper, telling about the party's activities, describing the area's scenic attractions, and reporting the discovery of dinosaur bones near Wolfe Cabin. Beckwith named a number of the area's arches and other spectacular landforms, using these titles in his articles.

The expedition's field work was completed by the end of March 1934. Beckwith wrote an official report, and also prepared several articles for publication, including two for *El Palacio*, journal of the Museum of New Mexico. Ralph Anderson drew a detailed map of The Windows section and another map covering the general vicinity of Arches. Joseph Anderson authored a separate report on the results of his geologic survey. Cost of the expedition, including expenses for equipment and labor, was $9,661.60.

The principal legacy of the Arches National Monument Scientific Expedition has come down in the names—some quite colorful—given by Frank Beckwith to many of the area's prominent landforms.

EARLY AUTOMOBILE TRAVEL AND ROAD DEVELOPMENT AT ARCHES

Although Arches became part of the national park system in 1929, it was not until 1958 that the first paved road was opened in the scenic area. However, automobiles had been driven into Arches long before 1958, and even before 1929. Several dirt roads had existed for many years, but they were rough, sandy in places, and in the rainy season were muddy and subject to flooding.

Road conditions at Arches were nearly constant causes of concern to rangers from the earliest days. Harry Reed, custodian of Arches in 1937, reported a decline in visitors that September "due to the poor condition" of the old approach road, which had been damaged by heavy rainfall. The road's sandy stretches also made for "difficult driving," according to Reed. In November 1939, Reed's successor, Henry G. Schmidt, reported in November that he had "spent quite some time filling the ruts, and clearing rocks from the steeper grades" on the old dirt road into The Windows section. The following year, Schmidt described the original route to Devil's Garden as a "desert road . . . not graded, but the tracks are straight and smooth. . . ." However, dirt roads often became corrugated — slowing and bouncing cars, and jarring their passengers — and had to be graded, but only when the soil was moist. Sometimes several weeks would pass during summers before enough rain fell to allow grading.

Flash floods down Courthouse Wash were a major detriment to automobile travel on the old approach road where it crossed the wash. More than once such floods—which occur several times each

[Below] Not all arches in the Park are natural. Shown under construction in 1941 is one of a pair of graceful arches that form the sides of a **Bridge over Moab Canyon Wash** on the Park's entrance road, just east of its intersection with Highway 191. These beautiful arches were built from blocks cut from native sandstone by Civilian Conservation Corps workers. When the entrance road was widened, and extended across the massive cliff seen in the background that forms the east wall of Moab Canyon, one of these stone-and-mortar arches was moved several feet in October 1957 to accommodate the new, broader roadway. This photo was taken by Harry Reed in July 1941.

National Park Service

[Left] Construction of the **entrance road** to Arches began in 1941, but ceased with the entry of the United States into World War II that December. Construction resumed, and the road was completed, in the 1950s. Shown here is a workman using a jackhammer to drill rock on the road's route near the top of Headquarters Hill, the massive eastern wall of Moab Canyon behind the Visitors Center. This photo was taken by Lloyd M. Pierson, then a park ranger, in October 1957.

National Park Service

summer—temporarily stranded motorists. On August 28, 1953, a flood roared down Courthouse Wash, inundating the vehicle crossing. Thirty visitors and eleven cars were stranded on the wash's east side from five in the afternoon until midnight, cut off from access to the main highway. Two gallons of soup were prepared by then-Superintendent Bates Wilson and his wife, and carried across the swollen, muddy stream to the isolated, tired, and hungry visitors. None of the cars were damaged, but one was so firmly mired in the wash that it took two hours of pulling and hauling to free the vehicle. About a month-and-a-half later, on October 12, five cars and their occupants were stranded on the east—or "wrong"—side of Courthouse Wash. Park Service personnel took the passengers to Moab for the night. By the following morning, the water level had fallen enough for the vehicles to cross. Between August 27 and September 27, 1954, heavy cloudbursts occurred on four of the

five weekends, with visitors and their cars halted at the Courthouse Wash crossing of the old approach road. On September 5, fifteen automobiles were stopped on the east side of the wash at 4:00 P.M. by a flash flood. Then-Superintendent Wilson reported: "A Ford sedan was completely submerged in the quicksand twenty feet below the crossing and it was after 10:00 P.M. when all cars were finally pushed and pulled across the wash."

The earliest penetration of present-day Arches National Park by automobile was from the north via Salt Valley, and occurred at least by the early 1920s. The exact date is not known. One early automobile trip—of historic importance—took place in September 1923, when Alexander Ringhoffer, a local prospector, drove Frank A. Wadleigh and George L. Beam, officials of The Denver and Rio Grande Western Railroad, into Salt Valley to the eastern base of Klondike Bluffs. The men hiked to the site—then called "Devil's Garden" by

Ringhoffer—and observed its arches and spires. As a result of this trip, Wadleigh wrote Stephen T. Mather, director of the National Park Service, and suggested the scenic region be added to the park system.

Another historically important early automobile trip into what is now the Park took place in June 1925, when Ringhoffer chauffeured Dr. Frank R. Oastler, a New York City physician, and his wife to Salt Valley. Dr. Oastler was examining the region at the request of Mather, who was then evaluating the area as a possible park site. Ringhoffer stopped his car about half-way down Salt Valley, and led the Oastlers on a climb to Klondike Bluffs. The party returned to the automobile, and continued down Salt Valley to a point where they parked the car and hiked to The Windows, which Ringhoffer called "Window Castles."

The first recorded automobile trip in Arches after the area became part of the national park system occurred when Harry Goulding drove his car to The Windows section on Monday, June 15, 1936. Goulding, a well-known operator of an Indian trading post near the Utah-Arizona boundary, in Monument Valley, was involved in developing tourist attractions in the Canyon County.

Goulding made his historic drive to The Windows seven years after Arches was established in 1929. Since no roads existed to The Windows, Goulding equipped his stock model Ford V-8 touring car with special tires to negotiate deep sand. He began his trip at the main highway leading north from Moab, then designated U.S. Highway 450 but today numbered 191. Accompanying him were his wife "Mike"; Laura Tracy, of Shelburne, Vermont; and two Moab men: Boyd Jorgensen and L. N. Meador. They followed a fair dirt road east from the highway to Willow Spring, a distance of five miles. From Willow Spring on to The Windows, no road then existed

[Below] **Crystal Arch** is located in south Devil's Garden. It can be seen to the northeast from Pine Tree Arch, and is reached from a short side trail off of the Fin Canyon trail section of the Devil's Garden Trail. The arch has a span of thirty feet and a height of twenty-eight feet. Beside it is a much smaller opening (not shown), about six feet by six feet, piercing the Entrada Sandstone fin in which the arch formed.

[Opposite] **Eye-of-the-Whale** is aptly named for its whimsical resemblance to the orb of the mammoth marine animal. Located in the Herdina park section, the arch has a span of thirty-five feet and a height of eleven feet. Eye-of-the-Whale, cut in the Slick Rock Member of the Entrada Sandstone, is one of several Park landforms that derive their titles from fancied likenesses to animals.

[Right] This photograph taken in 1951 dramatically shows the disastrous effects flash floods in **Courthouse Wash** could have at the crossing of the old approach road to Arches. Unfortunately, scenes similar to this one occurred several times, convincingly proving the crucial need for a new entrance road. The present entrance road was dedicated on August 24, 1958.

National Park Service

across the four miles of ruggedly broken and sandy terrain. But the party made the pioneer drive with little difficulty.

The next day, Goulding repeated the drive, taking with him Jorgensen and Meador, plus two other Moab residents: Dr. J. W. Williams and Harry Reed, both enthusiastic supporters of Arches. Reed, a professional photographer, named several features in Arches, and in the late 1930s served as the area's second custodian. Also along on the drive was Harry H. Bergman, a tourist from Aguanga, California.

Goulding made a third trip on June 17, taking with him Meador and Reed; L. L. Taylor, editor and publisher of Moab's newspaper; and Derek Nusbaum, a National Park Service ranger visiting Arches.

In 1958, the present entrance road—the first phase of paved-road development at Arches—was completed. This road runs from U.S. Highway 191 and ascends the towering cliff behind the Visitors Center via a series of switchbacks. Other projects followed, including paved roads to The Windows and to Devil's Garden, and the road at Devil's Garden Campground. When all projects were completed, some twenty-six-and-a-half miles of paved roads had been constructed, providing motorists entry into rugged terrain which previously had been largely inaccessible.

WHAT'S IN A PLACE-NAME?

Name, though it seem but a superficial and outward matter, yet it carrieth much impression and enchantment.

FRANCIS BACON

Buccaneer Rock, Jack's Mummy, The Biscuits, Tower of Babel, Eye-of-the-Whale, Ham Rock, Parade of Elephants, Dark Angel, The Three Penguins—these are but a few of the many colorful place-names in Arches National Park. Once, these and other features of the Parkland had no for-

mal designations. Then man arrived on the scene. Just as a sound exists without a hearer, a place exists whether or not a viewer is there to see it. But a name for it is not intrinsic—a name comes only from man. One authority on place-names, George R. Stewart, put it succinctly: "No names without people!" Names are among the oldest elements of speech. No society has been found that is so primitive it does not use names.*

Descriptive Names Are Common at Arches

Of the Park's thousands of landforms, only fifty-five are officially named on the United States Geological Survey map, *Arches National Park* (1974). Though several place-name categories are represented at Arches, by far the greatest number—forty-eight, or 87 per cent of the landforms named on the map—can be classified as descriptive.

This is scarcely surprising, since most of the area's many peculiar landforms invite comparison with other objects—animate or inanimate. Double Arch, The Great Wall, Khrushchev Rock, Hole-in-the-Wall, Sheep Rock, The Spectacles, and the Petrified Sand Dunes—these and many other descriptive names aptly identify features of the Parkland. Some landforms, like The Phallus, Balanced Rock, and The

---

*Place-names are words or groups of words that designate individual geographical locales or features, and thus distinguish them from others. Place-names are *proper nouns*, that is, they name specific places, and their initial letters are always capitalized.

The study of proper names in all their aspects is termed *onomastics*. It consists of two branches: *anthroponymy*, or the study of personal names, and *toponymy*, the study of place-names. Places are either *natural*, such as an arch, spire, canyon, or river, or *cultural*, such as a building, road, town, or ranch.

Several place-name classification systems have been developed. George R. Stewart devised a comprehensive nomenclature that comprises ten categories: descriptive, associative, incident, possessive, commemorative, commendatory, manufactured, mistake, shift, and folk-etymologies. Some place-names straddle two or more of these categories.

Poodle, are so appropriately named that very little imagination is needed by the viewer to grasp why these features were so titled.

However, the relationship between the actual appearance of some of the Park's landforms and the descriptive names given to them sometimes strains the imagination. Adam and Eve, in the Garden of Eden, is particularly frustrating for most people to envision. Another feature that requires considerable imagination on the part of the viewer is Duck-on-the-Rock, a hoodoo standing southwest of Turret Arch. The weathered top of this rock pillar apparently resembled a duck in the eyes of Harry Reed, the second custodian of Arches, who is believed to have named the landform. However, any likeness to a duck is difficult—even impossible—for most people to see.

Place-Names May Reflect History

Some place-names are inheritances from the past, records of cultural trends and changes. A knowledge of their origins and meanings can enlighten and frequently enliven the study of an area's history.

For many centuries, the future Parkland was known only to Indians. What they called its many fantastic arches and strangely shaped spires is unknown. But certainly the Indians had names for at least some of them.

Much later in time, Spaniards entered the Arches region, followed by the Mexicans, and then the Americans. All bestowed names on selected features of the landscape. The impact of the American presence has been by far the strongest of all these successive cultures, and today only American-given place-names survive at the Parkland.

The Naming Process

Place-naming arises from one basic motive: the desire to identify locales or features and

THE HERDINA OF HERDINA PARK

Jerry Herdina was an avid amateur fossil-hunter. His large collection, today housed in the Field Museum of Natural History in Chicago, consists of 14,191 specimens. It contains several unique species, including two that were named for Herdina during his lifetime: *Herdina mirificus*, a short-winged insect, and *Paleocadums herdinae*, a nautilus-like creature. The collection is well known among American and European paleontologists (scientists that study fossils). Herdina was called the "dean of the Chicago-area fossil collectors" in a 1975 memorial by Eugene S. Richardson, Jr., curator of fossil invertebrates at the Field Museum.

For years, the tall, slim Herdina would periodically visit southern Utah. Besides spending time in the Arches country, he also frequented the areas that are now Canyonlands National Park and Capitol Reef National Park. Richardson said that Herdina "wandered far from the established trails, charting the way to wonders unknown even to the rangers."

A well-educated man, Herdina was a graduate of the University of Illinois at Urbana, and could speak Spanish and Czech. In addition to his intense fascination with fossils, he also was interested in the history of Illinois and Utah.

Following graduation from the university, he was employed by the Ryerson Steel Company in Chicago as an engineer. Many Chicago-area bridges and buildings have steelwork fabricated from Herdina's engineering calculations.

Jerry Herdina was born on January 25, 1905 in the Chicago home of his parents, Joseph and Marie. They had immigrated to the United States from Bohemia (a region in western Czechoslovakia). The family name was originally spelled "Hrdina," but Joseph added the first vowel to Americanize the name.

A few years after Jerry's birth, the Herdinas moved into a large, frame house in the same Chicago neighborhood where he was born. There Jerry resided for some fifty years. A life-long bachelor, he continued to live in the house long after his parents died. In 1969, however, Herdina moved into a yellow-brick house in Berwyn, a near-west suburb of Chicago. He died November 25, 1974, two months short of his seventieth birthday.

Herdina was an active member of the Field Museum. In addition to his outstanding fossil collection, his accumulation of 3,539 color photographic slides and his specialized reference library were donated to the museum.

Russell L. Mahan was the first on-site superintendent of Arches. Previously, the area had been administered by the superintendent of the Southwestern National Monuments, headquartered near Coolidge, Arizona, with a local custodian, or manager, stationed at Arches. Mahan was assigned to Arches in 1944, first as acting custodian and then as custodian. In 1948, he was appointed superintendent of Arches, holding that position until 1949 when he was named simultaneously superintendent of Colorado National Monument and Black Canyon of the Gunnison National Monument.

thus to differentiate them from others. Crucial to the selection of place-names are the reasons for the titles, and their meanings.

Obviously, not all of the features at Arches are named. In areas like the Park, where there is an abundance of unusual landforms, many of these remain untitled simply because they are so common. Usually, designations are given to those features that are in some way distinctive, especially any landform whose physical appearance readily suggests some similarly shaped thing.

Man's impact at Arches before it became part of the national park system was limited because of the area's generally inhospitable environment. Thus, place-names that denote humans or their activities are not common at the Park today. Among such rare designations are: Wolfe Cabin, Julien Arch, Cordova Canyon, Navajo Arch, Doc Williams Point, Beckwith Arch, Herdina Park, Anniversary Arch, and Jack's Mummy.

The reasons why certain natural features are named for people or for human incidents may not be inherently evident in a feature, whereas most titles based on the shape or other characteristics of physical features are usually self-explanatory. The basis for such Park designations as Top-Story Window, Cove of Caves, or Double-O Arch is obvious when those features are seen, but the significance of names like Anniversary Arch, Herdina Park, or Navajo Arch is not apparent.

Anniversary Arch's title dates from September 6, 1962, when Mr. and Mrs. Roby R. Mabery and Mr. and Mrs. Felix Kallis were in the Klondike Bluffs area of Arches. "Slim" Mabery, then a Park ranger, and his wife Juanita were marking their wedding anniversary on that date. Juanita spotted the arch, which has two openings (she did not discover it; the arch certainly had been seen before but was un-

named), and Vione Kallis named it to commemorate the Mabery's wedding anniversary.

Herdina Park is a commemorative name. This scenic area, located northwest of Willow Flats and near the western edge of Arches, honors Jerry Herdina. A steel engineer from Chicago, Herdina was intrigued with the Arches area, visiting it many times before his death in 1974.

In 1952, along with Mr. and Mrs. Harry Sawyer of Helena, Montana, Herdina explored the area that would later be named for him by Bates Wilson, then superintendent of Arches. Herdina and the Sawyers came upon several arches in what is now Herdina Park, including one with a span of forty-seven feet and a height of fifty-four feet. This large opening is now named Beckwith Arch in honor of Frank A. Beckwith, leader of the Arches National Monument Scientific Expedition which conducted surveys and investigations at Arches in 1933-34. Herdina and the Sawyers were certainly not the discoverers of these arches, as cowboys, sheepherders, and prospectors had probably seen them many years earlier. However, Herdina and the Sawyers were the first to bring them to public attention. Moab's newspaper, *The Times-Independent*, on October 15, 1953 in a front-page article reported on the arches, noting as well that Herdina and the Sawyers had found an ancient Indian campsite in the area.

Navajo Arch, in Devil's Garden, was named by Bates Wilson, then superintendent of Arches. One day, Wilson and two Navajo employees were working on the Devil's Garden Trail. During lunchtime, one of the Indians "took a walk," recalled Wilson, and saw the arch. When the Indian returned, he told Wilson about the span, which until then was unknown to the superintendent. Appropriately, he named the feature for the Indian's tribe.

Once a feature is named, there is no

certainty that the appellation will be permanent. Some designations given to features now in the Park have long since been forgotten, and those features are now nameless. Occasionally, names of certain features disappeared from usage for one reason or another, and the features were not retitled. In other cases, names originally assigned to features were replaced—some several times—by new titles. Even widespread publicity does not assure that any given name will become permanent.

Thus, several Park features have had more than one name. For example, the titles given by the Arches National Monument Scientific Expedition in 1934 to four arches in Devil's Garden have since been changed, even though they received publicity at the time they were assigned. Tunnel Arch was first called "Hidden Arch" because, as that name implies, it is partly concealed. Both designations are descriptive, the original characterizing the location and the present name the arch's shape. Pine Tree was originally titled "Cedar Tree Arch." Both titles are examples of associative names, and were derived from flora found at the span. The earlier appellation incorporates a misnomer: locally, "cedar" is often mistakenly used for juniper. Frank Beckwith said that the arch's original name was given because a "fine cedar" grew in it. Today's designation favors the piñon pines present at the site. Partition Arch was named "Pillar Arch" by Beckwith's expedition. Both names embody the same descriptive connotation. Wall Arch was designated "White Cap Arch." Each name is aptly descriptive: this arch is topped by the whitish Moab Member of the Entrada Sandstone, and is cut into a long, narrow, wall-like fin.

Occasionally after a landform is given a fittingly descriptive appellation, the reason for the name ceases to exist, leaving the feature with a title that does not make sense. Owl Rock, also known as Eagle Rock, a tall spire on the west side of the Garden of Eden, was named for a bird-shaped rock that once perched atop the spire. Early in March 1941, this distinctive stone toppled, smashing to bits at the foot of the spire. Today, the spire's name appears illogical to an uninformed Park visitor.

Sometimes a sudden change may radically alter a feature's appearance, and then it may be renamed. Until late in 1940, the opening in Skyline Arch was less than half its present size. Before the arch's dramatic enlargement, it was called "Fallen Rock Arch." Beckwith wrote in his expedition report that this name was given "because a part of the rock mass which fell out still lies in the corner of the arch, partly blocking it." The fall of this block in November 1940 created the greatly expanded opening seen now. Because this large aperture is prominently situated high on the eastern rim of Salt Valley, and can be seen from both sides, it was renamed Skyline Arch.

In the future, more name changes can be expected for features of the Park. Some now unnamed will be given titles, some will have their present names eliminated in favor of new ones, and a few will lose their designations entirely and revert to anonymity.

"The Big Arch": Landscape Arch
Several of the Park's features were named in 1934 by Beckwith as leader of the Arches National Monument Scientific Expedition. In his report on the expedition's work, Beckwith noted that Landscape Arch's name derived from the fact that "through this arch the landscape behind it may be seen. . . ." He offered a more graphic accounting in the March 22, 1934 issue of the Moab newspaper, The Times-Independent: ". . . wind-blown sand rises behind it in a steep slope, covered with cedars [junipers], giving this arch somewhat the appearance of a landscape painted within a frame cut to an arch effect."

The meaning of Landscape's name was again published in the Moab paper a little more than two years later. A photograph of the span by Harry Reed appeared on the front page of the July 9, 1936 issue, and—echoing Beckwith—the caption stated in part: "It was named Landscape from the setting of trees behind it which resembled a painted landscape."

Although Landscape Arch was named in 1934, it had been discovered long before then. The arch—the longest natural span in the world—has been known since at least 1896.

Some people have maintained that originally Landscape Arch was named Delicate, and that the present Delicate Arch was at first called Landscape. Apparently, the basis for this belief is that since Landscape has a slender—delicate—span and since from Delicate Arch there is a sweeping view of the landscape, the names were somehow transposed.

Furthermore, the adjective "delicate" is sometimes used to describe Landscape's span, and this may contribute to the contention that the names for the two arches have been exchanged. Beckwith used the

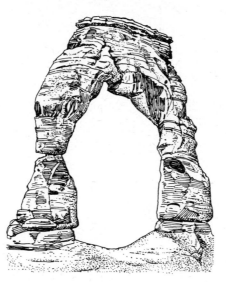

The shape of **Delicate Arch** clearly shows why it also has been called by such colorful names as Chaps, Pant's Crotch, Schoolmarm's Pants, Old Maid's Bloomers, and Mary's Bloomers.

adjective in his report, writing that Landscape "is delicate." Also, he used it in an article for the March 22, 1934 issue of the Moab weekly, characterizing the arch as "very delicate." Another example of the adjective's use in describing Landscape is found in the caption accompanying Reed's photograph of the arch in the July 9, 1936 issue: ". . . from a distance it appears to be so delicate that one marvels that it can stand."

Beckwith located both arches in articles he wrote for *The Times-Independent,* and there are no discrepancies between the locations he cited for Landscape and Delicate in 1934 and their locations today. For example, in Beckwith's January 18, 1934 article, he gave Delicate Arch's position as "about a mile east of Wolf[e] Cabin," which is identical with the location of the arch so named today. And, in the March 22, 1934 issue of *The Times-Independent,* Beckwith located Landscape Arch "in the Devil's Garden area," which is where the striking feature with that name is today.

If the contention were correct that the names for Landscape Arch and Delicate Arch were switched, it would certainly make a good story. Unfortunately, it is not true. Obviously, the names have not been swapped. They are on the same arches now as when they were assigned in 1934.

An interesting sidelight to the naming of Landscape Arch is that Beckwith did not particularly like the name. In an article for the March 22, 1934 issue of the Moab weekly he wrote that the title would suffice for the arch until it is "better named." Beckwith considered calling it "Rainbow Arch," because Landscape "rises like a rainbow." But he concluded that it would be "hardly fitting" to name it "Rainbow Arch" since it would then be confused with Rainbow Bridge—the world's largest natural bridge—which today rises on the east shore of Lake Powell, a few miles north of the Utah-Arizona boundary. In

the same article, Beckwith also referred to Landscape Arch as "Big Arch," but he did not propose this as a name.

"A Beautiful, Delicate Arch"
Delicate Arch—possibly the most famous natural span in the world—has had at least seven other names.

Earliest mention of the span in print is as "Salt Wash Arch"—a name that scarcely does it justice and locates it in the wrong area. This report appeared in the July 1909 issue of *Improvement Era,* a Mormon magazine no longer published. Accompanying the short article is a photograph of the arch. Its location is given incorrectly, but the source of the information, William Howard, admitted he had not been to the arch's site. The following October, the magazine printed another short article about the arch based on information from Flora Stanley, daughter of John Wesley Wolfe, whose ranch was near the arch. Mrs. Stanley correctly reported that the arch is beside what then was called Dry Creek, not Salt Wash. Today, Dry Creek is named Winter Camp Wash.

Other early names were derived from the free-standing arch's distinctive shape. Beckwith wrote in the Moab newspaper for January 18, 1934: "It looks precisely, to borrow the terminology of the cow camps, 'like a bow-legged cowboy's pair of chaps.'" Thus, the arch has been called "Chaps" and "Pant's Crotch"—two rather masculine designations—while on the distaff side it has been known colorfully as "Bloomers Arch," "Schoolmarm's Pants," "Old Maid's Bloomers," and "Mary's Bloomers." Just who Mary was—if in fact

she was a real person—is unknown.

The arch's present name was one of the appellations given to landforms at Arches in 1934 by Beckwith's expedition. He did not use the designation in his January 18 article, although it was hinted at in one of the subheadings, "A Beautiful, Delicate Arch," and when he described the landform as "by far the most delicately chiseled arch in the entire area."

Finally, Beckwith used its present-day title in an article he wrote for the February 1, 1934 issue of *The Times-Independent,* characterizing the arch as "a masterpiece of beauty." He called it Delicate Arch in his official report, noting its "rare beauty" and stating it is "strikingly presented, dominating the field of view."

Tower Arch—or Minaret Bridge?
A curious controversy swirls around the naming of Tower Arch in Klondike Bluffs. This large arch once was called "Minaret Bridge." The debate is not over whether the landform is a bridge or an arch. It is readily classified as an arch, conforming to the classic definition given by Herdman F. Cleland: an arch "does not span an erosion valley" while a natural bridge does. The controversy, instead, revolves around who bestowed the names "Tower" and "Minaret," and when; and why "Minaret" was dropped in favor of "Tower."

Two historic inscriptions appear on the arch. Below the span on its south abutment, carved into the reddish sandstone in large block letters is:

> DISCOV-D.
> BY M. AND
> MRS.
> ALEX RINGHOEFER
> AND SONS
> 1922-3

It is pertinent to note the spelling of the family name in the inscription, since the correct spelling is Ringhoffer.

Tower Arch, in remote Klondike Bluffs, is the "founding" span of the Park. Controversy has surrounded its current name and its original title, Minaret Bridge. Its opening is ninety-two feet wide and forty-three feet high.

The second inscription is under the span, on the sloping base of its north abutment. In small letters is carved "Minaret Bridge." Below those words in faint and even smaller letters and numerals, the name "H. S. Bell" and the date "1927" appear.

Hugh Stevens Bell, then of Willoughby, Ohio, was gathering information and photographs for newspaper articles on scenic areas of the West when he visited the site of what is now Arches National Park, and carved his "Minaret Bridge" inscription.

The present name, Tower Arch, dates from Beckwith's 1934 visit. He wrote in the February 15, 1934 issue of the Moab newspaper that Tower Arch "is so named because immediately behind the sandstone wall [of the arch] rises a tower fully two hundred feet high." He likened this feature to the Tower of London.

From the inscriptions and Beckwith's article it seems clear that Bell gave the arch its first name, Minaret Bridge, in 1927, and that Beckwith originated its present designation, Tower Arch, in 1934.

If the Ringhoffers had a title for the arch, it is not in the "Ringhoefer" inscription. Robert H. Vreeland, author of a booklet about natural rock openings in Arches National Park, claims that the Ringhoffers called the arch "Minaret Natural Bridge" and that this appellation originally formed the first part of the inscription. However, this assertion is not supported by on-site observations made by Beckwith or Bell. When Beckwith visited the arch in February 1934, he transcribed the "Ringhoefer" inscription, and his record does not include the words "Minaret Natural Bridge." Beckwith was infuriated that the arch had been defaced with the inscription, and questioned whether the Ringhoffers were the real discoverers. The arch certainly had been seen by livestockmen and prospectors long before the Ringhoffers encountered it. Curiously, Beckwith did not mention Bell's inscription. Because of that carving's undramatic placement and small size, he may not have seen it.

Bell was questioned in 1985 about the "Ringhoefer" inscription. He declared that the carving did not exist when he visited the arch in 1927. "If I had seen it," Bell commented, "I wouldn't have put anything else down." Because the "Ringhoefer" inscription is conspicuous, it is very unlikely that Bell would have missed it—if the carving had then existed.

The "Ringhoefer" inscription's wording makes it suspect as to when it was cut and who did the carving: Ringhoffer is misspelled, and the date—"1922-3"—is strangely vague for a declaration of discovery. Did a family member misspell his (or her) own name? Or was the inscription carved later by a friend or acquaintance who was unsure of the spelling?

One obvious conclusion is that the inscription was cut **after** Bell visited the arch, to proclaim that the Ringhoffers had been there **before** Bell had left his inscription. And it is in the Bell inscription that the name "Minaret" appears, not in the "Ringhoefer" carving.

If the Ringhoffers had named the arch when they first saw it, or shortly thereafter, and especially if their designation had appeared in the "Ringhoefer" inscription, there is a high probability that the title would have been reported by at least one of two parties Alexander Ringhoffer guided to the span within the next two years. In September 1923 he escorted Frank A. Wadleigh and George L. Beam, both officials of The Denver and Rio Grande Western Railroad, to the arch. Later Wadleigh, passenger traffic manager for the railroad, wrote to Stephen T. Mather, founding director of the National Park Service, urging that the arch and surrounding area be designated a national monument. In this letter and subsequent correspondence, no mention is made of any name for the arch. If the span had then had a title, it would be reasonable to assume that Wadleigh would have cited it.

During the summer of 1925, Ringhoffer took Frank R. Oastler, a New York City physician, to the arch. An article about Oastler's trip appeared in *The New York Times Magazine* on May 9, 1926. Three photographs, including two of what is now called Tower Arch, accompanied the text. Other than the general term "natural arch," no name is given to the span in this article. Since titles are used for several other features (The Spectacles for example, are mentioned), it is logical to assume that if an appellation had then been in use it also would have been cited in the article.

Vreeland, in his booklet, also reports a rumor—incredible as it may sound—that the Park Service did not know the meaning of the word "minaret." Thus, according to this rumor, to avoid the embarrassment of having a term unknown to them in the

ONE STUCK, TWO DIDN'T

Some of the original names given to arches in today's Parkland have survived the years. But other early appellations have disappeared, replaced by titles bestowed by later "name givers."

The story of name-giver Hugh Stevens Bell is a relevant example. During the 1920s, Bell, then a free-lance lecturer and reporter-photographer, made several field trips in the West. He called his excursions the "*Cleveland Plain Dealer* Photographic Expedition" because the Ohio newspaper assisted with financing the trips in return for articles and photographs. In the summer of 1927 Bell, then residing in Willoughby, Ohio, visited Mesa Verde National Park in Colorado. Jesse L. Nusbaum, the park's superintendent, showed Bell a letter he had received from a man in Moab stating that there were many natural arches at a place near Moab called Devil's Garden. The identity of the letter writer is not definitely known. When quizzed for the writer's name fifty-seven years later, Bell thought it probably was Alexander Ringhoffer, the "Father of Arches." Bell's curiosity aroused, he drove to Moab—some 130 miles northwest of Mesa Verde—in his Model-T Ford. Traveling with Bell were two high-school boys from his home town, Robert Lillick and Francis Parks. Both had attended Bell's Presbyterian Sunday School classes in Willoughby.

About twenty miles north of Moab, Bell and his teenage companions stopped at the drill site of an oil exploration company where they met the watchman. He told Bell that there were interesting landforms in the rugged country a few miles east of the drill site. Bell and the two boys camped alongside the watchman's cabin, and for about a week the trio explored what is today Arches National Park, Bell taking photographs and gathering data.

Their hikes over the rough, rocky terrain were made even more arduous by the searing heat of July. They carried, among other items, a twelve-pound tripod, a 5x7-inch camera, and glass photographic plates. On their long, hot hikes "we got awfully thirsty," Bell recalled. "We were stepping on our tongues pretty much!" On one scorching day, short of water, they found a depression that looked as if it might contain water. Digging, they hit damp sand, which they scooped up in their handkerchiefs and sucked in an effort to quench their thirst.

In the course of their reconnaissance, Bell was impressed by three large natural rock openings and named them "Minaret Bridge," "Twinbow Bridge," and "Double-O Arch." As a title, Double-O apparently caught the popular fancy, because it has survived. As for the other two, "Twinbow Bridge" is now called Double Arch, and "Minaret Bridge" has given way to Tower Arch. Although Bell used "bridge" in their names, both landforms are properly classified as arches.

At each of these arches, Bell carved the name he had bestowed upon it. He chose the name "Minaret" because of the minaret-like appearance of a spire which towers immediately north of the arch. He cut the sobriquet "Minaret Bridge," the date "1927," and his name on the arch's northern abutment. This small inscription can still be seen.

At his "Twinbow Bridge," Bell inscribed this name on a loose rock slab measuring about a foot square. Unfortunately, during the intervening years the slab has vanished.

While "Twinbow Bridge" failed to become the landform's official title, the name has appeared occasionally in print. A color photograph of the double spans—labeled "Twinbow Bridge"—was reproduced in the May 1936 issue of *The National Geographic Magazine*. The photograph was taken by Bell on his 1927 trip. "Twinbow" also identified the arch in the October and December 1942 issues of *Natural History* magazine.

Bell carved the title "Double O Arch"— the only one of his three name selections that has stuck—inside the landform's smaller opening, on its north surface. Bell's inscription is still visible.

Bell took what is probably the first photograph of the unique feature. A reproduction of the color photograph was printed in *The National Geographic Magazine* for May 1936.

Hugh S. Bell

Hugh Stevens Bell was born on January 10, 1899 in St. Joseph, Missouri. His father, a physician, had emigrated from Canada. When World War I broke out, Hugh's father went to London where, though a naturalized United States citizen, he joined the Canadian army. After the entry of the United States into the war, he transferred to the American army. When his father left for Europe, Hugh and his mother moved to Willoughby, Ohio, where she had relatives.

Hugh graduated from high school in 1917, entered Allegheny College, dropped out due to illness, joined the navy in 1918, was discharged the following year, and entered Western Reserve University (now Case Western Reserve University), where he graduated in 1922.

After graduation, Bell joined the staff of the Cleveland Museum of Natural History. In the fall of 1922, Hugh married Helen Jessie Rose, whom he had known since high school. They chose October 10 as their wedding day because on that date his parents and maternal grandparents had also been wedded. Hugh and Helen were married for fifty-eight years, and parented four children, all males. Helen died in 1981.

In 1924, Bell left the museum to become a free-lance lecturer and reporter-photographer. It was while he did this work that Bell visited Arches in 1927.

Because his wife's health was adversely affected by Cleveland's smog, Hugh moved his family to Leupp, Arizona in 1930. There, he went to work for the U. S. Indian Service in 1933, as a skilled laborer, first in Leupp, then in Tuba City. Because of the many flowers he planted around government buildings in Tuba City, the Navajos called him *Hosteen Dahatihi*, or "He Who Hovers Over The Flowers."

In 1937, he was hired by the U. S. Department of Agriculture to supervise construction projects for a soil erosion study at Mexican Springs, New Mexico, conducted by the California Institute of Technology.

When the construction was completed, Bell and his family moved to Pasadena, California, where he joined the staff of the California Institute of Technology. In 1948, Bell—a deeply religious man—resigned and moved to Arizona to become a missionary to the Navajos. For about two years, he worked on the Navajo Indian Reservation at Hard Rock. He then established Gospel Broadcasters, in Flagstaff, Arizona, and began manufacturing spring-driven phonographs on which Navajos, living in remote areas without electrical power, could play gospel recordings. Bell produced the records, using Navajo narrators. Later, he moved his operations to Sierra Madre, California, where his work, now called Mission Aides, Inc., is headquartered. His son, Hugh Jr., an ordained Southern Baptist minister, assumed management in 1973. Mission Aides is involved in tape duplication, recording-player equipment, and related technical services for churches and missionary organizations.

The senior Bell, at age eighty-six in 1985, still actively participated in the missionary work he had entered thirty-seven years earlier.

Bell's legacy to Arches is the name Double-O Arch for one of the most spectacular landmarks in Devil's Garden. Eroded into an Entrada Sandstone fin, the upper and larger of the two elliptical openings has a span of seventy-one feet and a height of forty-five feet, while the lower, smaller aperture is twenty-one feet long and nine feet high.

Double-O Arch

Navajo Arch is situated in south Devil's Garden, northwest of Landscape Arch. It has a span of forty-one feet and a height of thirteen feet. The arch was named by Bates E. Wilson, then superindendent of Arches, after he learned of its existence from a Navajo Indian who had seen it while working with Wilson on the Devil's Garden Trail. In the foreground is a Utah juniper, the most prevalent species of tree at the Park.

[Top] **Broken Arch** can be easily seen from the road to Devil's Garden, across Pipeline Flat. The arch's name is a misnomer: it is not broken, although the span appears to be cracked in the middle. Its white cap rock is the Moab Member of the Entrada Sandstone, and the arch's reddish abutments and floor are formed by the Slick Rock Member of the Entrada. The opening has a span of fifty-nine feet and has a height of forty-three feet.

[Bottom] **Partition Arch** is just north and above Landscape Arch. It is really two arches, separated by a narrow partition. The larger opening has a span of twenty-eight feet and a height of twenty-six feet, while the smaller one has a span of only eight-and-a-half feet and a height of eight feet. Partition Arch was originally named Pillar Arch, because of the pillar-like shape of the intervening wall.

"Ringhoefer" inscription, the then-superintendent allegedly ordered an employee to erase the offending words "Minaret Natural Bridge." However, a careful examination of the inscription in 1978 showed no physical evidence that any part of it had ever been altered or removed.

Bates E. Wilson was superintendent in 1967, the approximate year cited for this rumored erasure. Wilson served as superintendent of Arches from 1949 until his retirement in 1972. When he read the allegation that he had ordered an employee to destroy part of the "Ringhoefer" inscription, Wilson set the record straight in a letter to Peter L. Parry, then superintendent of Arches. In this letter dated October 20, 1978, Wilson wrote: "I have no recollection of ever having seen the inscription. Why would I instruct an employee to remove an inscription I didn't know existed? As for our not understanding the meaning of the word 'minaret,' the [National Park Service] supplied every office with a copy of *Webster's Dictionary* . . . and we used it." The former superintendent commented further that Vreeland "does admit that the information in the paragraph is . . . rumor, which might explain the error, but that doesn't excuse poor research." In conclusion, Wilson said he was certain that Superintendent Parry would be willing to lend his copy of *Webster's* to Vreeland "so he can look up the meaning of 'embarrassment'!"

Numbering the Arches

In 1975, David D. May, park ranger and executive secretary of Canyonlands Natural History Association, suggested facetiously that numbers be assigned to all of the arches, thus avoiding controversies over which was named what. However, May readily admitted that under this plan arguments would soon arise as to what number was originally allocated to any

The **Parade of Elephants** — a trio of landforms having a whimsical resemblance to lumbering, ponderous pachyderms — is just south of Double Arch in The Windows section. Two of the "elephants" are on the right and a third is on the left, out of the photograph. The front "elephant" on the right has an unusual double arch: the two openings join inside the elephantine rock mass. The larger opening has a span of twenty-four feet and a height of thirty-six feet, while the smaller one has a span of thirteen feet and a height of forty-one feet. This photo, taken in October 1941, shows Henry G. Schmidt [left center], custodian of Arches from 1939 to 1942, speaking to a group of visitors at the curious march of the stone elephants.

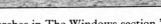

given span: Was Arch 93 really number 93, or was it 107?

While such a system would be neat, logical, and orderly, it would take much of the interest, romance, and richness out of a visit to the Park. What would the area be without arches bearing such colorful names as Elephant, Turret, Flatiron, Gossips, Ribbon, Buttonhook, Diamond, Tapestry, Wineglass, Deception, Crystal, Football, Dutch Oven, Barroom Door, Turban Head, Piano Leg, and Shadow-Box? Who would enjoy calling Eye-of-the-Whale simply "Arch 26"?

Actually, in 1940 a scheme was implemented to number, measure, and mark the area's known arches, although it was not proposed to replace names with numbers. Then-custodian Henry G. Schmidt proposed marking each arch with a surveyor's metal cap, numbering it, and showing the location of each on a map. The acting superintendent of the Southwestern National Monuments, Hugh M. Miller, endorsed the plan, but noted in a memorandum that as new arches were found there could be "no assurance that newly reported discoveries are not duplications of former ones."

So, one hundred caps were ordered and shipped to Schmidt. In June of that year, Schmidt reported receipt of the caps, at the same time observing that their installation "will probably cover quite a period of time." How prophetic!

Sixty days were to pass before the first cap was placed. Schmidt wrote in his report for August: "One bronze marker was placed in The Windows section. More urgent problems demanded my attention this month, making any concentrated effort on this project impossible." In September he reported: "The project to place bronze markers has slowed down to a walk. The necessity of constant road patrol and maintenance made a concentrated effort to continue this job during the month impracticable." But Schmidt was optimistic, commenting that placement of the bronze markers would be continued in October, when "if conditions permit, we hope to complete the marking and locating of all arches in The Windows section."

Success for The Windows was reported in October. "Five man days were spent on the project to place bronze markers at each of the arches," Schmidt wrote. "We have now completed this work in The Windows section . . . 11 markers have been placed and the dimensions of [these] arches determined and registered in a log book. It has given me a good idea of the time required to complete this project and I will consider the work speedily done if all the known 81 arches are marked and measured within one year."

His November report recorded "no work was attempted [during the month] on the project to place bronze markers at the base of each arch." A similar entry appeared in Schmidt's December report, stating that resumption of the project would need to await more favorable weather.

This was his final entry about the markers. In July 1942, Schmidt was transferred to Kings Canyon National Park in California. With his departure, the project ended.

Four students of natural arches, Dale Stevens, Douglas Travers, Reuben Scolnik and Robert Vreeland, have compiled separate listings of the Park's arches and assigned numbers to some of the named and unnamed spans. These numbers, however, were not intended as substitutions for names, but were applied simply for purposes of identification and tallying.

FOOTBALLS AND ARCHES: THE TRAVERS PASSERS

Doug Travers, an electrical engineer from San Antonio, Texas, first visited Arches in 1965. Fascinated by the spans, he began to catalogue and photograph them on subsequent trips. His two older sons, Joe and David, decided to try throwing a football through every arch they visited. Later his two younger sons, Rod and Roy, carried on this tradition. The boys were not always successful in their attempts; the locations of some arches make it very difficult, if not impossible, to throw a football through their openings.

One arch that posed a real problem for the boys was a small, unnamed span in the northern Fiery Furnace area. On their first visit to this arch on July 19, 1975, the boys attempted to hurl a pass, but the football became lodged in the opening. The next day "the football was retrieved," according to the boys' father, "by fishing it through the arch with a pole and line." But the pass was never completed. To mark this incident, the Travers named the landform—appropriately—Football Arch.

TO THE TOP: VICTORY AND TRAGEDY ON LANDSCAPE ARCH

Like Mount Everest, Landscape Arch is the largest of its class. And like the mountain, the arch excites the adventurous climber. Both have been conquered, yet both have been the scenes of tragedy.

Of the attempts to reach the top of Landscape, most have ended in failure. Several of these unsuccessful climbs involved near tragedies, and one is known to have ended in a fatality. Regulations ban climbing on the arch—and other named landforms in the Park—except under special circumstances.

First Recorded Ascent of Landscape Arch

In 1939, members of the Wasatch Mountain Club of Salt Lake City organized a trip to climb Landscape Arch. At the time, there was no record of the arch—the longest natural span in the world—ever having been scaled. Here, then, was a double challenge to these rock climbers: the dangers of the ascent, and the chance to be first on top.

Ten club members left Salt Lake City on Saturday evening September 2 and traveled by car to Moab, where they spread their sleeping bags on the high school's lawn.

After breakfast the next morning, Harry Reed, then custodian of Arches, and Charlie Jones guided the hiking party to Devil's Garden and their objective: Landscape Arch, 106 feet high and 291 feet long.

Philip S. Miner, then a nineteen-year-old student at the University of Utah, and youngest member of the group, investigated many potential routes up the abutments of the arch. Finally he selected a promising approach on the south buttress, and started his ascent. The lean, blond youth reached the span's top in the late

DR. FRED AYRES: THE HIGH-CLIMBING PROFESSOR

Fred Ayres and his sister Irene, on August 19, 1949, made the second recorded ascent and traverse of Landscape Arch. It was his second attempt to scale the arch. The first, in 1947, was unplanned, and abandoned when he concluded that it was too risky for a climber by himself without equipment.

Ayres was a chemistry professor at Reed College in Portland, Oregon. He had extensive climbing experience, having made ascents in the Tetons, Colorado Rockies, Cascades, Sierra Nevada, Canadian Rockies, and the Andes. His record included many first ascents. Mountaineering historian Chris Jones wrote that Ayres had "one of the most impressive mountain records in America, a record largely unknown and wholly unsung." John Oberlin, who had climbed with Ayres, said he was "enterprising and aggressive in the mountains and not easily deterred by technical difficulty, being especially quick on steep rock."

At Arches in 1949, in addition to his ascent of Landscape, Ayres scaled Turret Arch, which he later reported had been climbed several times before. Irene also climbed Turret, and later recalled that she was "more apprehensive on Turret Arch [than Landscape Arch] because an extremely high wind was blowing, and it was rounded and smooth."

However, Fred was unsuccessful on Double Arch, and on North Window and South Window of The Spectacles, though he later stated that he had not explored all of the possible routes. Also, he was unable to find a feasible route to the top of Skyline Arch. He did not attempt Delicate Arch because, he said, "clambering about on this particular one, delicate as it is, would hardly seem appropriate."

In the summer of 1953, with Alex E. Creswell, he returned to Arches when inclement weather forced them to abandon climbing in the Canadian Rockies. Creswell later said that in The Windows section they had "climbed every arch in sight . . . playing in the sunshine." The pair also ascended Elephant Butte by a route that—according to Creswell—"was a beautiful challenge," although they could have reached the summit by a much easier way. Atop the butte, the climbers stood on slender Ribbon Arch but did not cross the fragile span because, as Creswell later said, it would have been "sacrilege if we broke it."

After climbing at Arches, Ayres and Creswell visited the area that is now the northern part of Canyonlands National Park. There, using ropes, they descended to The Confluence of the Green River and Colorado River. From Canyonlands, the pair traveled to present-day northwestern Zion National Park, where they made the first ascent of what is now called Kolob Arch.

With his sister, Ayres made several additional climbing excursions to Arches. In 1955, they scaled Elephant Butte, and by way of it reached the top of both spans

of Double Arch. On another trip, they climbed North Window and South Window. And on their 1951 trip, Fred made a solo ascent of Skyline Arch.

Despite his many climbing accomplishments, Ayres—though athletic—was not a physically imposing man. Of average height and weight, he was modest-mannered and spoke in short, clipped sentences. Creswell, who admitted to idolizing Ayres, noted that he had a "wonderful dry sense of humor."

Ayres had a wide range of interests and a thirst for knowledge which Creswell characterized as a "childlike curiosity." Besides climbing and chemistry, Ayres also delved into archaeology, astronomy, botany, history, photography, and poetry. But climbing was paramount. Creswell said that for Ayres "mountaineering was literally his life."

Fred Donald Ayres was born on Christmas Day, 1906 in Kansas City, Missouri. In 1935, he received a doctorate in physical chemistry from Northwestern University. He joined the faculty of Reed College in 1940, and on sabbatical leave in 1961-62 did research at University College in London. In 1963, he taught at the University of Huamanga in Ayacucho, Peru, on a Fulbright-Hays grant.

Indicative of his interests in mountaineering and science, Dr. Ayres was a member of the Explorers Club, The American Alpine Club, The Arctic Institute of North America, The Alpine Club of Canada, the Mazamas (a Portland, Oregon mountaineering club), and the American Chemical Society.

Ayres was unmarried until late in life. He and his wife, Angela, a native of Peru, had one child, Fred Jr. On July 12, 1970, at the age of sixty-three, Ayres died after a prolonged bout with cancer.

Irene Ayres said that her brother demonstrated "kindness, consideration, and concern for others," and had an "uncanny ability to detect the needs or limitations of those who were with him" on climbs or hikes. "His pack was always as heavy, if not heavier, than anyone's," she also noted proudly.

In a letter to Creswell, Fred Ayres wrote "the time to live is while you are still alive"—a fitting epitaph for an intrepid rock climber.

Very few Park visitors see **Landscape Arch** during or just after a snowstorm. This wintery scene contrasts sharply with the typical hot and dry summer weather experienced by most tourists when they visit the arch in south Devil's Garden. In geological terms, natural arches—like people—pass through three stages: *youth, maturity,* and *old age.* Landscape Arch has reached old age, a stage characterized by such extreme slenderness of the span due to weathering and erosion that collapse may occur at any time.

afternoon of Sunday, September 3, thus becoming the first person known to have climbed the arch. He carried a rope and *pitons,** but he did not need to use either as he worked his way carefully up the steep sandstone abutment.

Following Miner was another climber whose identity is lost, except for a cryptic reference to "Emer" in a front-page article of the October 19 issue of Moab's newspaper, *The Times-Independent.* Was this perhaps a typographical error for Elmer or Emery? When Miner was quizzed more than four decades later for the identity of his climbing companion, he was unable to remember the name.

Once atop the arch, Miner walked across to its north end—the first known traverse of the span, and another record for the teen-ager that day—then crossed again, returning to its south end. Nearly forty-two years later, Miner recalled: "I figured when I got there I just had to cross it." And he did—twice.

The two adventurers were photographed standing on the arch before they *rappelled*† to the ground, ending their historic climb.

According to Reed and Jones, the four ladies in the club's party—identified in the newspaper article vaguely as "Ila, 'Pinky' Lindsay, Ann, and Val"—were the first white women to see Landscape Arch. However, the validity of this conjecture has not yet been established.

Second Ascent and Traverse

The next known attempt to climb Landscape Arch occurred in 1947, when Fred D. Ayres, a noted rock climber, tried the ascent without climbing equipment. Ayres attempted three routes in this effort, but

*A piton is a metal spike with an eye at one end to which a *carabiner*, or metal ring, is clipped and through which a rope can be passed; the piton is driven into a rock crack to provide a climber with security or for direct aid.

†To descend by sliding down a rope.

Bates E. Wilson served as superintendent of Arches for twenty-three years, from 1949 until his retirement in 1972. During that period, Arches changed dramatically: its status was raised from national monument to national park, land area was almost doubled to about 114 square miles, the first paved roads and a new entrance road were constructed, the Visitors Center was built, and yearly visitation rose nearly 1,600 per cent from 13,270 in 1949 to 225,500 in 1972. In addition to his duties at Arches, Wilson was superintendent of Natural Bridges National Monument, and in 1964 was appointed founding superintendent of Canyonlands National Park. He served in all three posts until his retirement. Wilson also was Utah State Coordinator for the National Park Service from 1966 to 1972.

was unsuccessful with each. The most promising route, he concluded, was up a *chimney*, or cleft, in the arch's south abutment. He followed this route some thirty feet, then concluded it was too dangerous for a solo climber without equipment.

Undaunted, Ayres returned to the arch with climbing gear in the summer of 1949. Accompanying him was his sister Irene, also an experienced rock climber.

On Friday, August 19, they started up the chimney route. For approximately the first eighty feet the route was sheer and exposed. To secure themselves, two pitons and two *expansion bolts** were used. At the top of this route, they found a narrow, tunnel-like opening through which they crawled for six feet to a large fissure. They scrambled up the fissure's steep, north side for fifteen feet to the top of the arch.

They then walked across the high, narrow span to its northern end. Fred described the sensation of standing atop the arch as like being "on the wing of a big airplane taking off at a steep angle into the southern sky." Years later, Irene recalled her crossing of the span and remarked—with understatement—that it was "quite narrow and long."

They found no evidence of previous ascents. So, on the summit of the span—a prominent hump near its southern end—the Ayres built a small cairn. Irene later noted that the diminutive rockpile probably did not last through the next winter. Afterwards, they rappelled to the ground.

Tragedy on the Arch

Not quite nine months later, on May 29, 1950, nineteen-year-old Frederick Semisch fell to his death from the north abutment of the arch. Semisch and twenty-five-year-old Gilman Ordway of Darien, Connecticut, were traveling to California, visit-

*An expansion bolt is a piton with a sleeve that increases in diameter when it is driven into a hole drilled into rock.

ing western national parks and monuments on the way. The two young men had met in New York City, where Semisch lived.

They had been in the Arches area for a couple of days before the accident occurred, and had set up a camp beside the Colorado River, near the highway bridge.

On the morning of the accident, Stanley W. Midgley, Jr., a professional photographer and lecturer, then of La Cañada, California, was driving to Devil's Garden in his jeep. He was in the area to shoot scenes for his motion picture, *Jeep Trails Through Utah*. About three miles from the parking lot at Devil's Garden, Midgley found Semisch and Ordway stranded beside the road, their car stuck in the sand. He stopped to help, pulling their vehicle free with his jeep. In retrospect, he said thirty years later: "I should have left them stuck in the sand!"

Midgley went on ahead, planning to photograph Landscape Arch. While he was setting up his camera, the youths arrived. Semisch proposed to Ordway that they try to reach the arch's top, but Ordway was hesitant. Though he finally agreed to start the climb, Ordway soon quit.

Midgley and several tourists (a family) witnessed the tragic drama that followed. Semisch reached the summit of the arch's north abutment, which towers nearly a hundred feet above the top of the span. Standing there he shouted down to Midgley: "You should be up here for a picture!" The youth then called that he was going to climb down to the span. Midgley yelled back, urging him not to attempt the perilous descent.

Midgely then turned away, preparing to photograph the arch, when he heard Semisch scream. He looked to see the teen-ager—still screaming—slipping on the sandstone, then plummeting to the ground. Midgley scrambled to the site, and located the youth's battered body about 400 feet from the abutment's east side, in a

In December 1957, **Cecil M. Ouellette, Jim Eslinger,** and **Mike Borghoff** made the third recorded ascent and traverse of Landscape Arch. Two of the trio are shown crossing the snow-patched span.

National Park Service

narrow chute into which it had rolled. Ordway, north of the arch, had not heard his friend's screams, and was unaware of the accident until he returned about fifteen minutes later and was informed by Midgley of his companion's death.

Meanwhile the other witnesses went to report the tragedy. They found maintenance man Merle E. Winbourn, and told him of Semisch's fall. Winbourn left immediately to notify Superintendent Bates Wilson. Grand County Sheriff J. B. Skewes was called, and he—with Coroner Bert Dalton, Deputy Sheriff George Burck, Winbourn, and Wilson—went to the scene, arriving about 3:30 in the afternoon. Wilson brought a horse to carry out the body. Midgley met the group and guided them to Semisch's corpse.

Their investigation established that the falling youth had struck the abutment and one of the walls of the chute, leaving telltale traces of blood. Semisch's broken body was loaded onto the horse and packed to the parking lot, where it was transferred to Wilson's pickup truck for transport to Moab. From there, the remains were taken to Price, Utah, about 100 miles northwest, where Semisch eventually was buried.

The youth had not obtained permission to climb Landscape Arch. And he attempted the dangerous feat without essential rock-climbing equipment. Wilson noted in his report that the accident "was due to poor judgment and carelessness."

Semisch's death was the first recorded tourist fatality at Arches.

A Near Tragedy

Tragedy nearly struck again at Landscape Arch in August, 1954. An unknown visitor, in an attempt to reach the top of the arch, found himself in a spot where he could climb neither up nor down. He called to another tourist to summon help. His precarious situation was reported to Seasonal Ranger Warren C. Fischer, who

in turn notified headquarters. Superintendent Wilson and Ranger Robert L. Morris left for the arch with—as Wilson later noted in his report—"all the rope we could find." En route they learned that the stranded climber had cut footholds with his hunting knife, and descended safely. Like Semisch, the climber was unequipped and had not obtained permission to climb the arch. Commenting on the potentially fatal incident, Wilson—in an obvious reference to Semisch's death—said that another visitor who "tried this same trick in 1950 was picked up in a blanket."

Another Near Tragedy — Then Victory

The third known ascent of Landscape Arch was made in December, 1957. A trio of experienced rock climbers—Cecil Ouellette, Jim Eslinger, and Mike Borghoff—were granted permission by the Park Service to make the climb.

Standing beneath the arch on the morning of the climb, Ouellette reflected that the span looked like "a strip of sandstone . . . suspended in mid-air . . . remote and far away." Small patches of snow dotted the ground and rocks, a dire portent for Borghoff of the near tragedy to come.

Checking several possible routes to the top of the span, they finally decided to climb its south abutment. The men tied onto a common rope, and with Borghoff in the lead, began their ascent. As they scaled upward, they found a hole that Ayres had drilled for an expansion bolt eight years earlier; the trio were following the same route used by Ayres and his sister.

Reaching the top of the abutment, Ouellete marvelled at the view. He later described what he saw: "Surrounding us was a sculptured country of beautiful natural creations . . . In the distance the massive white towers of the La Sal Mountains glistened in the sunlight. And Landscape Arch shot away from the buttress across a 300-foot expanse of dizzy depth."

Ouellette, in the lead, moved onto the snow-spotted span, and began the crossing—"a traverse across the sky" he would later say. Passage over the narrow, suspended route was hindered by crusted snow. At the half-way point he stopped, sat down, and *belayed* Eslinger to his position. That is, Ouellette used a rope to give Eslinger security; if Eslinger had started to fall, Ouellette would have applied tension to prevent him from falling very far. After Eslinger reached his position, Ouellette moved slowly on to the far side. Once there, he signalled Eslinger and Borghoff to follow him. Borghoff had started across when suddenly his right foot slipped over the arch's edge. He quickly shifted his weight to his left leg, and miraculously held his balance. He had slipped on *verglas*, a thin coating of ice on the rock, hidden beneath the snow. When Borghoff had recovered, Eslinger completed his traverse. Borghoff then followed. At the northern end the trio celebrated and ate a meager lunch, while, as Ouellette later recalled, "the tension of the last few hours drained from our systems." A piton anchor was placed in the rock, and the men rappelled to complete their adventure.

Since the 1957 ascent by Ouellette, Eslinger, and Borghoff, several other individuals have tried to scale Landscape Arch. None are known to have succeeded. Some of these attempts ended when climbers became stranded or hurt and had to be rescued by Park rangers. And none of these attempts were authorized by the Park

It is possible that there were other early daring climbers—perhaps Indians, cowboys, sheepherders, or prospectors—who may have tried to reach the top of Landscape Arch. From inscriptions found on rocks at Arches and elsewhere in the Canyon Country, it is known that some amazing early ascents were made. Whether any of them took place at Landscape—and were successful—is unknown.

PHOTOGRAPHIC ESSAY

[Opposite] **Wall Arch**, located in Devil's Garden, one-fifth of a mile north of Landscape Arch, has a span of sixty-eight feet and is forty-one feet high.

[Right] Spectacular **Fin Canyon**, in Devil's Garden, is a tributary to Salt Wash.

[Left and below] Ancient **Indian petroglyphs** in Devil's Garden.

[Opposite] In seeming defiance of gravity, **Balanced Rock** perches atop its pedestal near the intersection of the main Park road and the road to The Windows. The landform's total height is 128 feet, with the huge balanced rock rising 55 feet above its tapering base.

[Below] Distant view of **Fiery Furnace**.

[Opposite] Detail of **Fiery Furnace** fins. Some
of these fins may tower more than 100 feet
in height.

[Opposite] Astonishing realism of **The Phallus** never fails to attract attention of Park visitors.

[Right] **Park Avenue**, a canyon in the Courthouse Towers section.

[Overleaf] **The Windows** section on a winter's day, Tower Arch on the right, North Window on the left.

[Top] **Double-O Arch** in Devil's Garden. Upper opening has a span of seventy-one feet and a height of forty-five feet. The lower, smaller aperture measures twenty-one feet long and nine feet high.

[Right] Snow blankets **Skyline Arch**.

[Left] Well named, **Hidden Arch**, north of Double-O Arch in Devil's Garden, has a span of thirty-five feet and a height of twenty-five feet.

[Below] **The Spectacles**—North Window (right) and South Window (left)—overlook The Windows section. North Window has a span of 93 feet and a height of 51 feet, while South Window spans 105 feet and rises 66 feet.

[Right] **Turret Arch**, in The Windows section.

[Below] **Eagle Park** (foreground) and the snowcapped La Sal Mountains.

[Opposite] Setting winter sun strikes **Delicate Arch.**

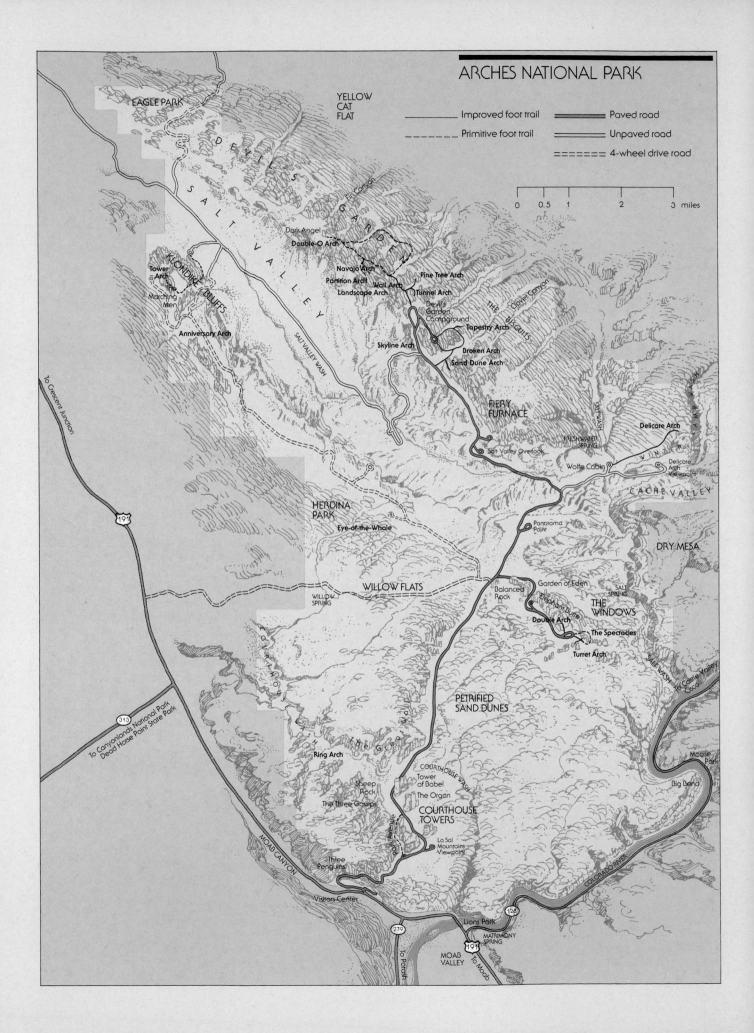

ARCHES NATIONAL PARK

Improved foot trail ———————
Primitive foot trail – – – – –
Paved road ══════
Unpaved road ————
4-wheel drive road ═══════

0   0.5   1   2   3 miles

EAGLE PARK

YELLOW CAT FLAT

DEVIL'S GARDEN

SALT VALLEY

Fin Canyon

Dark Angel
Double-O Arch

Navajo Arch
Partition Arch   Pine Tree Arch
Wall Arch
Landscape Arch   Tunnel Arch

Tower Arch
The Marching Men

KLONDIKE BLUFFS

Anniversary Arch

Devil's Garden Campground

THE BISCUITS

Clover Canyon

Skyline Arch

Tapestry Arch
Broken Arch
Sand Dune Arch

SALT VALLEY WASH

FIERY FURNACE

SALT WASH

WINTER CAMP WASH

Delicate Arch

FRESHWATER SPRING

Salt Valley Overlook

Wolfe Cabin

Delicate Arch Viewpoint

CACHE VALLEY

To Crescent Junction

191

HERDINA PARK

Eye-of-the-Whale

Panorama Point

DRY MESA

WILLOW FLATS

WILLOW SPRING

Balanced Rock

Garden of Eden

SALT SPRING

Elephant Butte

Double Arch

THE WINDOWS

The Spectacles

Turret Arch

COURTHOUSE WASH

313

To Canyonlands National Park
Dead Horse Point State Park

COURTHOUSE WASH

PETRIFIED SAND DUNES

SALT WASH

To Castle Valley
Cisco

Moose Park

Big Bend

THE GREAT WALL

Ring Arch

Sheep Rock

The Three Gossips

Tower of Babel

The Organ

COURTHOUSE TOWERS

Park Avenue

La Sal Mountains Viewpoint

Three Penguins

COLORADO RIVER

MOAB CANYON

Visitors Center

Lions Park

128

279

To Potash

191

MATRIMONY SPRING

MOAB VALLEY

To Moab

ROAD AND TRAIL GUIDE

Arches National Park lies in the colorful Canyon Country of southeastern Utah, immediately north of the Colorado River. About five miles southeast of the Park's entrance, and across the Colorado, is the town of Moab. The high-desert Parkland covers nearly 114 square miles of rough, red-rock terrain. There is so much bare rock in the region that one early cattleman of southeastern Utah, Parley Butts, was reported to once have said: "When God finished makin' the world He had a lot of rocks left over, an' He threw them down here in a pile. . . ." Arches is famed for its many strange and dramatic landforms, and especially for two of its sandstone spans: incomparable Delicate Arch, probably the best known natural arch in the world, and Landscape Arch, the longest natural-stone span on Earth.

ROAD CONNECTIONS
Principal access to the Park is via its only paved entry road, which branches off of U.S. Highway 191, an all-weather, north-south route that skirts the southwestern corner of Arches. This highway intersects with Interstate 70, a major east-west route, twenty-seven miles north of the Park's entry at Crescent Junction, and then continues northward eventually to Montana. South of the Park, U.S. Highway 191 runs to Arizona, where it intersects U.S. Highway 160, an east-west route, and then continues to the south.

MOAB — GATEWAY TO ARCHES
Moab, the seat of Grand County, Utah, has a population of approximately 6,000. The town lies at an elevation of about 4,000 feet between precipitous, red-walled cliffs in Moab Valley. To the southeast rise the La

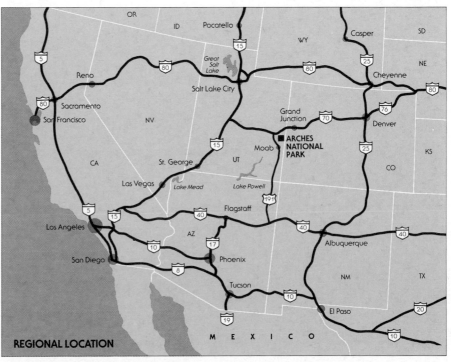

REGIONAL LOCATION

Colorado Historical Society

[Top] **Moab**, looking south on Main Street (also today's U.S. Highway 191) about 1929, the year Arches became part of the national park system.

[Below] **Moab** in about 1938, the year Arches was substantially increased in acreage and its two detached areas were merged. The view is north along Main Street, from Center Street.

Denver Public Library, Western History Department

Sal Mountains, with Mount Peale—the thirteenth highest peak in Utah—towering 12,721 feet above sea level.

Moab is near a strategic point where the canyon-entrenched Colorado River can be easily crossed. The Old Spanish Trail, a major trade route between New Mexico and California from the 1830s to the 1850s, ran through present Moab and forded the river. Then the trail climbed Moab Canyon, along the southwestern boundary of today's Park.

The earliest attempt by whites to settle the area was in 1855, when the Mormon Church sent a party of forty-one men to establish the Elk Mountain Mission, at a site now on the northwestern outskirts of the town. They arrived in June of that year, but in September abandoned their fort when Ute Indians attacked the missionaries, killing three of them.

After the missionaries withdrew, the area was occupied occasionally by trappers and ranchers over the next three decades, but the Indians remained hostile. Not until the late 1870s was permanent settlement achieved, primarily by Mormons.

Moab was named in 1880 by William A. Peirce. He selected the town's title from

the Bible, but Peirce's reason for choosing the designation has been lost to history. Possibly he perceived similarities between the terrain of the Utah locale and that of the Moab cited in the Old Testament. The Biblical Moab lay east of the Dead Sea. Most of that region is an arid, high, rolling plateau with reddish soil. Several deep, precipitous canyons cut the terrain. The Old World Moab has been described as a "cracked and gaping" land.

The settlement grew slowly, its early economy based mainly on agriculture. A frontier town, pioneer Moab had a rough, "Wild West" reputation. In 1891 Frank Sleeper, a silver prospector from Colorado, passed through the isolated town, and in a letter home wrote that Moab was known as "the toughest town in Utah." John M. Cunningham, a prominent cattleman of the region from the late 1880s to the early 1900s, was a partner in a large ranch about twenty-five miles southeast of Moab. But Cunningham and his family lived much of each year in Montrose, Colorado, more than 100 miles away by the shortest route, because (according to a cousin of Cunningham) Moab "was plentifully sprinkled with saloons and grog shops of the lowest

MOAB'S ETYMOLOGY

Moab, the nearest town to Arches National Park, has a curious name. It is an odd-looking and strange-sounding word. Is it an Indian term? Or does it have some other origin? What does Moab mean?

The answer lies in its *etymology*, the branch of linguistics that studies the derivation and historical development of words.

Although Moab may look and sound as if it were of American-Indian origin, it actually derives from the Bible. Moab, mentioned in the Book of Genesis, was the name of a biblical character, and also the place-name of a region east of the Dead Sea. The inhabitants of this ancient land were called Moabites.

Moab's father was Lot, a nephew of Abraham. Lot, his wife, and two daughters lived in Sodom. According to the Bible, when God decided to destroy the wicked cities of Sodom and Gomorrah, Lot and his family were allowed to escape to Zoar, a small city near the southeastern end of the Dead Sea. Before fleeing from Sodom, Lot's wife, reluctant to leave the pleasures of the corrupt city, was warned not to look back. She defied the warning, and was instantly transformed into a pillar of salt.

Lot was afraid to remain in Zoar, so he and his daughters fled into the nearby highland, where they dwelled in a cave.

In the Old Testament account (Genesis 19:30-38), Lot's daughters plied him with wine and then lured him into incestuous relations. Moab was born to the elder daughter, and Ben-ammi to the younger. The descendants of Moab were called Moabites; descendants of Ben-ammi were known as Ammonites.

The etymology of Moab first appeared in The Septuagint, a Greek version of the Old Testament, which dates from the third century B.C. In the English translation of The Septuagint by Charles Thomson, dated 1808, revised by C. A. Muses in 1954, Moab means *"From my father."*

Μωαβ

"Moab" as it appears in Greek in The Septuagint, the earliest version of the Old Testament.

The **Visitors Center** at Arches in 1953 certainly was not inviting to tourists, and illustrated the need for improved, expanded facilities. Robert L. Morris, a park ranger, stands in the doorway. The photograph was taken by Leslie P. Arnberger, Park Service naturalist, on a visit to Arches.

National Park Service

type and the moral standards were below our worst imaginings. . . ."

Another view of early Moab was given by Dr. John W. Williams, the town's first permanent physician. In 1905, "Doc" Williams met Henry L. A. Culmers, a Salt Lake City businessman and publisher. Williams, according to Culmers's diary, said new residents of the town "get Moab fever after the first year. It is so easy to make a bare living and so hard to get rich here. The symptom of Moab fever is chronic laziness."

In 1952 Charlie Steen, a Texas geologist, made his fabulous uranium strike some thirty miles southeast of town. Steen's rich mine—which he called *Mi Vida* (My Life)—attracted hundreds of hopeful prospectors and promoters to Moab, creating a boom-or-bust frenzy reminiscent of the California gold rush a century earlier. Within three years, the population of tiny Moab quadrupled! Facilities in the town were so overtaxed that some residents found it quicker to drive six hours to Salt Lake City than to wait in line to place a long-distance telephone call to that city.

With the fading of the uranium boom, the slack in Moab's economy was taken up by oil and gas exploration, potash mining and milling, continued uranium activity, and tourism generated in part by visitors to nearby Arches National Park.

SERVICES, FACILITIES, AND ACCOMMODATIONS
Arches National Park has only one camping facility—Devil's Garden Campground, located eighteen miles from the Visitors Center. There are no restaurants, lodgings, or automobile service stations in the Park. However, a wide range of such facilities and services is available in nearby Moab, including restaurants, motels, private campgrounds, camping and sporting goods stores, recreational vehicle supplies, guided land and river tours, garages, mar-

kets, clothing stores, and medical and dental care. Moab also has a library, a museum, two city parks, a municipal golf course, and a public swimming pool.

PARK ROADS
Arches is served by sixty miles of roads. Twenty-three miles are paved, twenty-five are graded dirt, and twelve rough miles are suitable only for four-wheel-drive vehicles. The main Park road begins at the Visitors Center and runs northward eighteen miles to Devil's Garden. Along the main road are many scenic turnoffs, and intersections

with several spur roads — some of them dirt — which lead to interesting Park features.

VISITORS CENTER
At the Visitors Center, located at the Park entrance, tourists may obtain information about the area's many scenic attractions, roads, hiking trails, camping facilities, and Park regulations. The Center houses a museum containing geologic and ecologic exhibits, and also the Park's administrative offices. A short, well-marked nature trail begins behind the Center.

HOW MANY ARCHES?

A question commonly asked by Park visitors is: How many arches are there in the Park?

Any inventory of the Park's spans must be based on an agreed-upon definition of "natural arch." While there presently is no widely accepted definition of this term, it is usually applied to natural rock openings with unbroken spans, formed by weathering processes rather than initially by stream erosion, the way *natural bridges* are formed. A major problem encountered in developing a comprehensive definition concerns what difference, if any, there may be between a natural hole through rock and an arch. And, if there is a difference, at what critical size a hole becomes an arch. Thus, depending on what criteria are selected, the number of arches in the Park could vary greatly. Until definitive standards are agreed upon for the term natural arch, the number of these landforms in the Park will remain subject to dispute.

Over the years, as the terrain has been explored and examined, and as further acreage has been added to Arches, more and more natural rock openings have been located and recorded. In May 1938, Harry Reed, then custodian (manager) of Arches, stated that he had "seen" forty-seven spans. Henry G. Schmidt, Reed's successor, in a 1940 report noted that there were eighty-one known natural openings. An article in *The National Geographic Magazine* for August 1947 put the

total at eighty-three, with sixty-four of these in Devil's Garden. *The Salt Lake Tribune* for November 19, 1963, in reporting the discovery and naming of Surprise Arch in the Fiery Furnace, stated that with the finding of this span there were eighty-nine known arches in the area.

In the fall of 1984, Dale J. Stevens, a professor of geography at Brigham Young University, began an intensive study of the Park's arches. His interest in these unusual landforms dated from 1972. Stevens arbitrarily limited his investigations to natural openings measuring at least three feet in one or more dimensions. "There is nothing magical about the three-foot minimum," commented Stevens. "I chose it simply as a convenient cutoff point. Obviously there are many smaller openings that might be considered arches." Each opening studied was photographed, its location mapped, measurements were made of its size, and each was classified into one of ten descriptive categories formulated by Stevens. Also, he assigned names to those openings which did not have titles. By January 1985, Stevens had recorded over 450 such arches in the Park.

Thus, between the observations of Harry Reed in 1938 and the studies of Dale Stevens some forty years later, the number of recorded "arches" in the Park soared nearly tenfold, from 47 to more than 450.

"It seems the supply of new arches is almost inexhaustible," declared Harry Reed in 1938.

The Three Penguins

MOAB FAULT

The Visitors Center sits in Moab Canyon just east of the Moab Fault, a northwest-ward-trending deep fracture dividing the canyon into two mammoth blocks. The fracture developed some 6 million years ago, when what is now the east side of Moab Canyon—the wall behind the Visitors Center—began to be slowly dropped by fault action. The total vertical displacement caused by this faulting is at least half a mile!

As a result of this faulting, individual rock layers, or strata, when traced across the canyon do not correspond between the east and west sides. The fault cut through the strata like a knife through a layer cake, and offset downward the strata on the canyon's east side relative to the west side. Geologists classify this type of fault as a *normal*, or *gravity*, fault. Consequently, the Kayenta Formation which forms the top stratum of the canyon's west wall—the U.S. Highway 191 side—was offset vertically on the canyon's east side so it is now below today's ground level.

HEADQUARTERS HILL

From the Visitors Center, the Park's entrance road climbs in a series of zig-zags up the high eastern wall—Headquarters Hill—of Moab Canyon. About halfway up the road, and above it, tower **The Three Penguins.** The "penguins" are sculpted in the Slick Rock Member of the Entrada Sandstone. An early name for this distinctive feature was Trinity Rock.

Several **hanging gardens**—moist, verdant alcoves—pocket Headquarters Hill. These cliff-face oases shelter the rarest of the Park's biotic communities.

PARK AVENUE

The southern end of Park Avenue is about two miles from the Visitors Center. Park

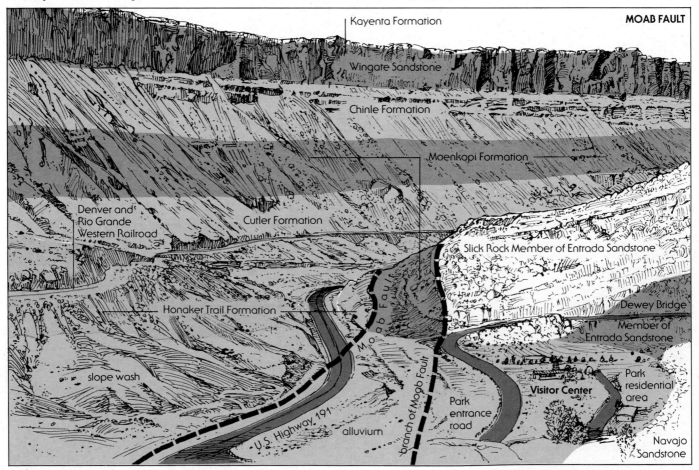

Kayenta Formation   MOAB FAULT

Wingate Sandstone

Chinle Formation

Moenkopi Formation

Denver and Rio Grande Western Railroad

Cutler Formation

Slick Rock Member of Entrada Sandstone

Honaker Trail Formation

Moab Fault

branch of Moab Fault

Dewey Bridge Member of Entrada Sandstone

slope wash

U.S. Highway 191   alluvium

Park entrance road

Visitor Center

Park residential area

Navajo Sandstone

Several **motion pictures** have been filmed at Arches to take advantage of its "Wild West" scenery. In 1960, Warner Brothers Motion Picture Company shot scenes at locales in Arches for one of their productions. This photograph, taken by then Park Ranger Lloyd M. Pierson, shows filming activity at Park Avenue.

National Park Service

Avenue is a narrow canyon with high, sheer walls suggestive of a city street lined by tall buildings.

On its western wall are two prominent balanced rocks: **Queen Nefertiti** and—bearing a more prosaic name—**Sausage Rock,** which has been called also The Popsicle.

Queen Nefertiti is named for the rock's striking resemblance to the famous bust of the fourteenth-century B.C. queen of Egypt, the beautiful wife of King Akhenaton. Queen Nefertiti, higher up on the wall than Sausage Rock, also is called Unjoined Rock because its balanced block is offset on its pedestal. This apparent displacement probably was caused by sandstone blocks falling from the "head" and its "neck." Or, less likely, an ancient earthquake may have shifted the "head" to one side of its "neck." Queen Nefertiti also may be seen from Moab's northern outskirts, along U.S. Highway 191 in the vicinity of Fifth West Street.

Across the canyon from Queen Neferiti,

a large part of the upper wall is said by some people to resemble another monarch, England's **Queen Victoria,** whose long rule lasted from 1837 to 1901. To other observers this rock mass looks more like the elderly woman sitting in profile in Whistler's famous painting of his mother.

The floor—"street"—of Park Avenue along its upper or southern length is formed by the Dewey Bridge Member of the Entrada Sandstone, and along its lower or northern stretch by the Navajo Sandstone. The avenue's walls—"buildings"—are of the Entrada Sandstone, the ledgy and sloping lower part of the softer Dewey Bridge Member, and the sheer upper walls of the harder Slick Rock Member.

COURTHOUSE TOWERS
Northeast of Park Avenue is Courthouse Towers, about four miles from the Visitors Center. Reminiscent of Arizona's famed Monument Valley, Courthouse Towers has a scattering of huge, isolated sandstone monoliths, some of them several hundred

feet tall. Prominent among these landforms are the **Tower of Babel, The Organ,** and **Sheep Rock.**

Between Sheep Rock and the tall fin south of it—and pierced by a small arch called **Hole-in-the-Wall**—there once may have been two large arches in prehistoric times.

Ring Arch, the major opening in the Courthouse Towers section, can be seen to the west from the Park road in the vicinity of the bridge over Courthouse Wash. The arch has a span of sixty-four feet and a height of thirty-nine feet. There is no established trail to it. The span is about a mile and a quarter from the bridge, and a half-mile southwest of the wash. Ring Arch was first reported by Harry Reed in 1940—although it certainly had been seen earlier by cowboys, sheepherders, or prospectors. Reed, an Arches custodian, or manager, in the late 1930s, was then a Moab resident and a professional photographer.

The monoliths of Courthouse Towers were formed as Courthouse Wash and its tributaries cut back into the terrain, leaving huge, isolated rock masses that were weathered and eroded into today's shapes.

THE GREAT WALL
Running north from Courthouse Towers to near Balanced Rock, a distance of some four miles, is a prominent Entrada Sandstone cliff aptly titled The Great Wall.

At several places along the wall are *hoodoos*—weirdly shaped spires and pinnacles created by differential weathering and erosion of strata of varying hardnesses. Three of these hoodoos are striking: The Lovers, The Phallus, and The Poodle. **The Lovers** is less than a mile northeast of Courthouse Wash bridge. **The Phallus** rises—some observers have contended, pornographically—about two miles farther up the road from The Lovers. Another tenth of a mile beyond is **The Poodle.**

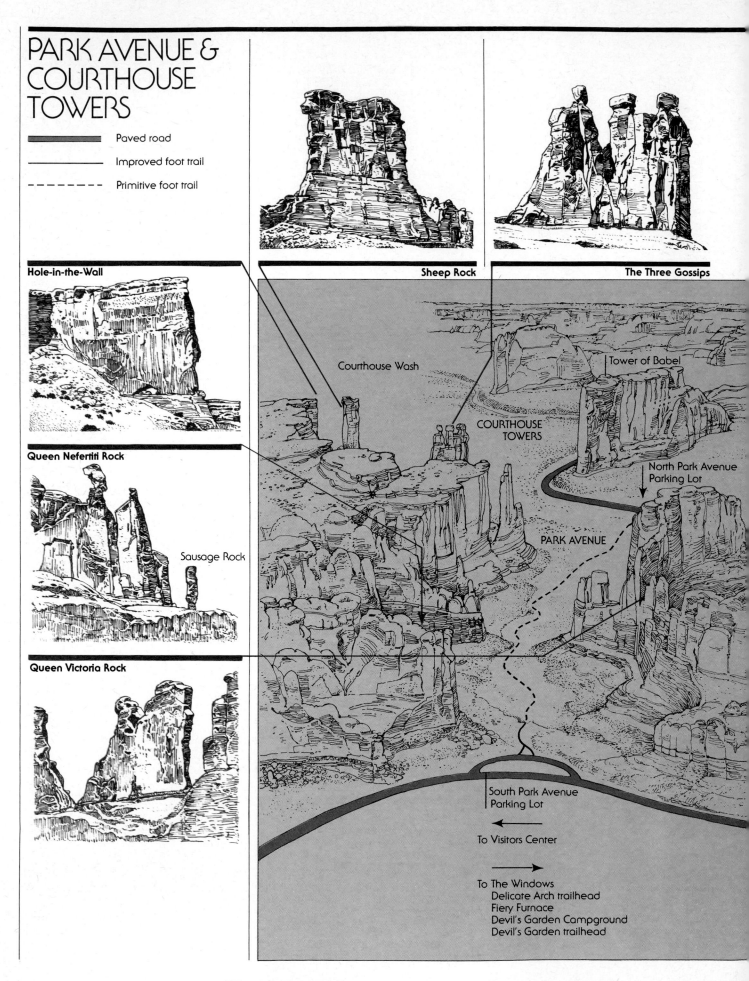

PARK AVENUE & COURTHOUSE TOWERS

Paved road

Improved foot trail

Primitive foot trail

Hole-in-the-Wall

Queen Nefertiti Rock

Queen Victoria Rock

Sheep Rock

The Three Gossips

Courthouse Wash

Tower of Babel

COURTHOUSE TOWERS

North Park Avenue Parking Lot

PARK AVENUE

Sausage Rock

South Park Avenue Parking Lot

To Visitors Center

To The Windows
Delicate Arch trailhead
Fiery Furnace
Devil's Garden Campground
Devil's Garden trailhead

PARK AVENUE TRAIL

The foot trail through Park Avenue is approximately one mile long. It runs from the south parking lot (which lies about two miles from the Visitors Center) to the north parking lot. From the south parking lot, this trail is improved for about 100 yards to an observation point, from which there is a view through Park Avenue to Courthouse Towers. From this viewpoint the trail is unimproved. It takes off from the west side of the point, descends to the canyon's floor, and generally follows the usually dry creekbed to the north parking lot. This lot lies at the base of The Organ, one of the lofty monoliths in Courthouse Towers.

The Lovers

LANDMARKS ALONG THE GREAT WALL

The Great Wall parallels the west side of the main Park road, from Courthouse Towers to a point about one mile southwest of Balanced Rock. This conspicuous escarpment of Entrada Sandstone is approximately three miles long. More than 300 feet tall at its southern end, the cliff decreases in height northward until it merges into the rocky terrain.

On The Great Wall or standing close by its face are many striking erosional features. While several of them have been named, most of these landforms remain untitled.

THE GREAT WALL

— The Organ

Visitors Center

La Sal Mountains Viewpoint

Schmidt Arch

The Phallus

Arch of Motion

The Poodle

The original entrance road to Arches ran passed Willow Spring. A **visitor contact station** was erected there in 1939. Construction on the small, one-room wooden building began on December 15 and was completed five days after. Henry Schmidt, custodian (manager) of Arches, helped a hired carpenter to build the structure. Schmidt took this photograph of the station on February 3, 1940.

National Park Service

Two significant arches are cut into the wall. The larger, **Schmidt Arch**—about a mile and a half from the Courthouse Wash bridge—has an opening twenty feet wide and fifteen feet high. It was named for Henry G. Schmidt, custodian (manager) of Arches from 1939 to 1942. Schmidt made the first report of the arch in 1940.

The other opening, immediately north of The Phallus, is called **Arch of Motion.** Its name is derived from an optical illusion. Difficult to see from the road, the opening's position relative to the observer's line of vision is camouflaged by rock seen through the aperture. But as the observer moves toward the arch, its opening becomes increasingly visible. An appropriate variant name is Hard-To-See-Arch. Its opening has a span of twenty-three feet and is ten feet high.

PETRIFIED SAND DUNES
Lying east of The Great Wall are the Petrified Sand Dunes. The "dunes" are outcroppings of crossbedded Navajo Sandstone, formed originally from the compaction and cementation of ancient sand dunes that accumulated about 200 million years ago.

BALANCED ROCK
Standing near the intersection of the main Park road and The Windows section road is Balanced Rock, about nine miles from the Visitors Center.

Balanced Rock is a classic example of a *hoodoo*, a rock spire composed of horizontal strata of varying hardnesses that weather and erode at different rates, thus often creating strange shapes. The Entrada Sandstone's relatively soft Dewey Bridge Member forms the pedestal, while the Entrada's much harder Slick Rock Member composes the large boulder that gives the prominent landform its descriptive title. The "balanced" block is not resting loose on its pedestal, but is physically attached

to the base. The feature's total height is 128 feet, with the huge boulder atop the pedestal standing 55 feet.

The "balanced" rock weighs an estimated 3,577 tons, or the equivalent of about 1,600 full-sized automobiles.

Lloyd Pierson, a former park ranger, recalled one suggestion that the landmark be redesignated "Undecided Rock." This prompted Pierson to comment: "Some day it will probably make up its mind with a loud and resounding crash."

Balanced Rock also has been called Pinnacle Rock—certainly a much less descriptive and dramatic title.

Bates Wilson, a former superintendent of Arches, remembered a strange—potentially fatal—event that occurred at Balanced Rock. One day he encountered an elderly man at the landform who asked Wilson if the whitish-colored rock on which the "balanced" block rests were concrete. Wilson answered no, but that "didn't satisfy him because he was convinced it was concrete," Wilson said. The then-superintendent left the area, but was called back by tourists who told him a man was stuck on Balanced Rock. Wilson got a rope and rescued the visitor, who—once he was safely down—admitted: "I'm convinced now it's not concrete!"

WILLOW FLATS AND WILLOW SPRING
Lying about two miles west of Balanced Rock is Willow Flats, one of the Park's grasslands. Just over four miles from Balanced Rock, beyond Willow Flats, and approximately a half-mile from the Park's western boundary, is Willow Spring. At this site was the headquarters camp for the 1933-34 Arches National Monument Scientific Expedition. The spring was also used by ranchers to water their livestock. Originally, the entrance road to Arches passed by Willow Spring, where the Park Service maintained a visitor-contact sta-

tion. From Willow Spring, the old route then crossed Willow Flats to Balanced Rock. This entrance road was replaced in 1958, when the present paved route from the Visitors Center was opened.

Willow Flats and Willow Spring are accessible by vehicles over the old entrance route. Now a four-wheel-drive road, it begins at Balanced Rock, from the north side of the main Park road. For about a mile, the dirt road is the same route that runs north to Herdina Park and to Klondike Bluffs, where the road meets an intersection: north to Herdina Park and Klondike Bluffs, or west to Willow Flats and Willow Spring. From this intersection to Willow Flats is approximately a mile, to Willow Spring about three miles, and to the Park's boundary nearly three-and-a-half miles. Beyond the boundary, the rough road runs four miles to U.S. Highway 191, reaching it about eight miles north of the present entrance road to Arches.

HERDINA PARK
Situated in western Arches, Herdina Park can be reached only by vehicles over four-wheel-drive roads. From the main Park road at Balanced Rock, nine miles from the Visitors Center, a dirt road leads west about a mile where it divides. The west branch crosses **Willow Flats** about three miles to **Willow Spring.** The other branch — a four-wheel-drive road — runs north about two miles to Herdina Park.

Herdina Park was named for Jerry Herdina, a noted amateur fossil collector from Chicago. He visited Arches regularly for many years, including the area now named for him.

Two major arches are found in Herdina park: **Eye-of-the-Whale,** with a span of thirty-seven feet and a height of twelve feet; and **Beckwith Arch,** with a span of forty-seven feet and a height of fifty-four feet. It was named for Frank Asahel Beckwith (1876-1951), leader of the 1933-

Pothole Arch

Buccaneer Rock

34 Arches National Monument Scientific Expedition.

THE WINDOWS SECTION

Nine miles from the Visitors Center is the spur road to The Windows section. It begins just north of Balanced Rock. The Windows route is three miles long and is a dead-end road. Among the arches in the section are **Alcove, Arch-in-the-Making, Bighorn, Cove, Double, Elephant, Little Duck Window, North Window** and **South Window** (collectively called **The Spectacles**), **Pothole, Ribbon, Serpentine,** and **Turret.**

Ham Rock and Pothole Arch

The Windows road curves around the north and east sides of a large unnamed butte, with Ham Rock—named for its obvious shape—standing on its summit.

On the north side of the butte, Pothole Arch can be seen from the road. Named for its type by Stanley W. Lohman of the U.S. Geological Survey, this arch has a span of ninety feet and a height of thirty feet.

Garden of Eden

Southeast of the Ham Rock butte, and about one mile from The Windows road intersection with the main Park road, is the Garden of Eden. This area contains a large group of hoodoos, including **Adam and Eve, Devil's Golf Ball,** and **Owl Rock.** The distinctive bird-shaped rock that gave Owl Rock its title fell from its perch in March 1941.

Also in the Garden of Eden is **Serpentine Arch.** Its opening has a span of ten feet and a height of thirteen feet.

Elephant Butte

Beyond the Garden of Eden is Elephant Butte. Its summit elevation is 5,653 feet, the highest point in the Park. On the butte's top, near its northern end, is in-credibly thin **Ribbon Arch.** At its slimmest, the fifty-foot span is a mere eighteen inches wide and one foot thick!

Cove of Caves

On the west side of Elephant Butte—two miles along The Windows road from the main Park road—is the Cove of Caves, a large curved recess in the butte. Several caves—from which the cove gains its title—indent the east wall, and at each end of the cove is a large arch. **Cove Arch,** on the northern end, has a span of forty-nine feet and a height of thirty-four feet. At the cove's southern end is the smaller of the two openings which form **Double Arch.** It has a span of sixty feet and a height of sixty-one feet.

Double Arch

The larger span of Double Arch is 163 feet in length and rises 105 feet above the ground—the second biggest arch in the Park. The smaller opening has a span of 60 feet and a height of 61 feet.

Climbers Fred D. Ayres and Alex E. Creswell, from Oregon, reached the top of the larger span on August 8, 1953. Ayres and his sister Irene climbed both spans of Double Arch on August 27, 1957.

Double Arch has also been called Double Windows, Double-O Arch, The Jug Handles, and Twinbow Bridge.

Buccaneer Rock

Standing south of Double Arch is Buccaneer Rock. Named by Frank Beckwith, this monolith reminded him of "a grizzled Spanish buccaneer, with pirate cap, a la Liberty style. . . ." Such a cap is brimless, fits snugly around the head, and has a soft crown. In 1934, Beckwith's Arches National Monument Scientific Expedition camped near the rock's base.

Archaeological Cave

Cut into the southern side of Elephant Butte, east of Double Arch, is Archaeological Cave. There is evidence that this large, prominent cavity was used by prehistoric Indians. According to a report by Frank A. Beckwith, leader of the Arches National Monument Scientific Expedition, "cedar bark, a few squash seeds, and some bone awls had been taken from it" by Ezekiel "Zeke" Johnson, the first custodian of Natural Bridges National Monument. Beckwith did not note the year Johnson found these items. When the expedition investigated the site in 1934, they found four holes in the cave's floor which had been dug by artifact hunters. Beckwith and his party conducted a "thorough digging" of the cave, but it "yielded no results." Unfortunately, Beckwith concluded, "whatever of value the cave might once have held, nothing remained."

National Park Service

THE WINDOWS SECTION

▬▬▬▬▬	Paved road
═════	Unpaved road
─────	Improved foot trail
‑ ‑ ‑ ‑ ‑	Primitive foot trail

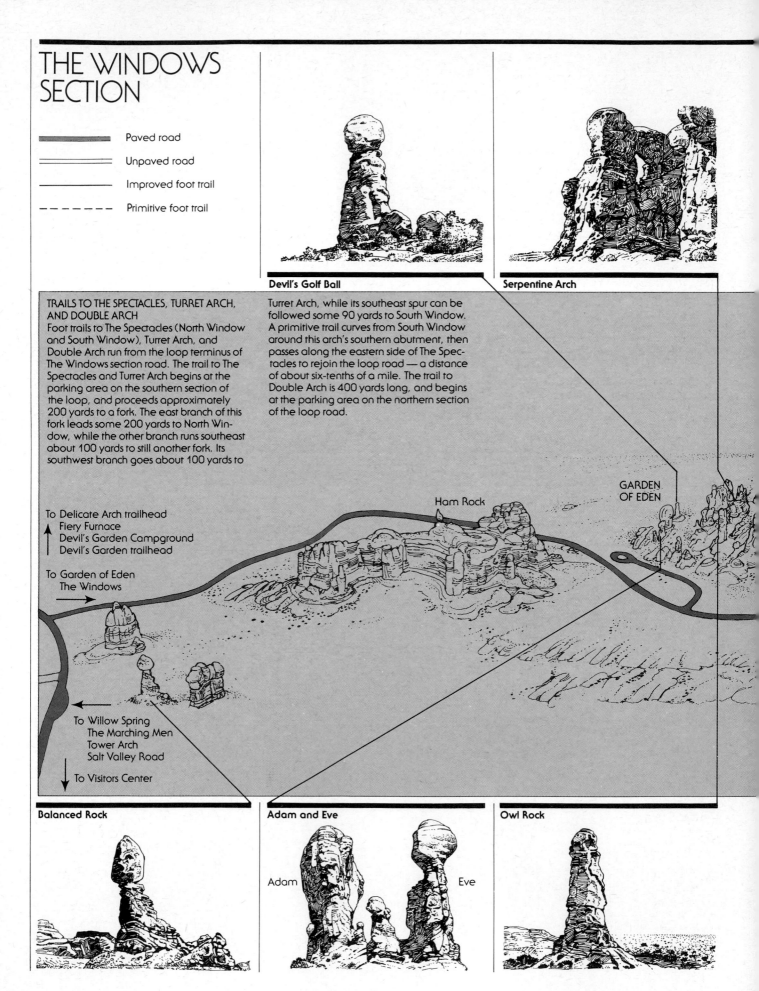

Devil's Golf Ball

Serpentine Arch

TRAILS TO THE SPECTACLES, TURRET ARCH, AND DOUBLE ARCH

Foot trails to The Spectacles (North Window and South Window), Turret Arch, and Double Arch run from the loop terminus of The Windows section road. The trail to The Spectacles and Turret Arch begins at the parking area on the southern section of the loop, and proceeds approximately 200 yards to a fork. The east branch of this fork leads some 200 yards to North Window, while the other branch runs southeast about 100 yards to still another fork. Its southwest branch goes about 100 yards to Turret Arch, while its southeast spur can be followed some 90 yards to South Window. A primitive trail curves from South Window around this arch's southern abutment, then passes along the eastern side of The Spectacles to rejoin the loop road — a distance of about six-tenths of a mile. The trail to Double Arch is 400 yards long, and begins at the parking area on the northern section of the loop road.

To Delicate Arch trailhead
Fiery Furnace
Devil's Garden Campground
Devil's Garden trailhead

To Garden of Eden
The Windows

To Willow Spring
The Marching Men
Tower Arch
Salt Valley Road

To Visitors Center

Ham Rock

GARDEN OF EDEN

Balanced Rock

Adam and Eve

Adam

Eve

Owl Rock

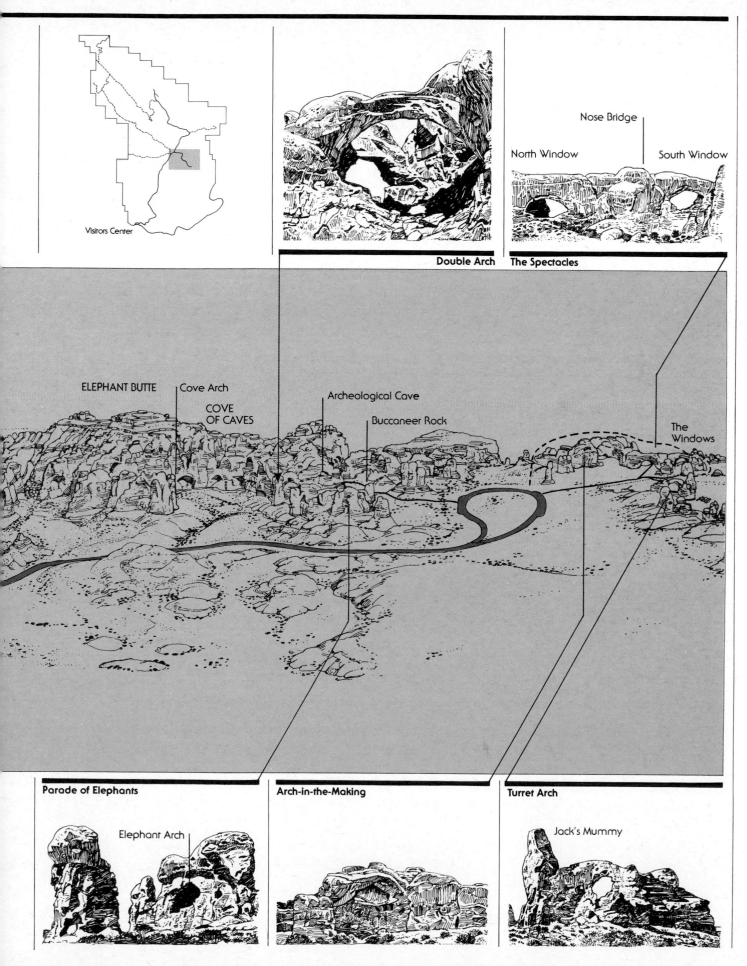

Visitors Center

Nose Bridge

North Window   South Window

Double Arch   **The Spectacles**

ELEPHANT BUTTE   Cove Arch

COVE
OF CAVES

Archeological Cave

Buccaneer Rock

The
Windows

Parade of Elephants   **Arch-in-the-Making**   **Turret Arch**

Elephant Arch

Jack's Mummy

Archaeological Cave · Aunt Emma

Aunt Emma

Just east of Archaeological Cave is a projection of Elephant Butte colorfully called Aunt Emma by that prolific name-giver, Frank Beckwith. He readily admitted: "I am one of those unfortunates endowed with a vivid imagination, and 'see things' with only a hint. . . ." To him, the rock resembled a very proper, aristocratic grande dame "in all her high-brow puritanical smugness . . . slightly disdainful of mere mortality . . . high bulging brow, hair 'tidied' as Boston high-borns are wont to bob it. . . ."

The Spectacles

Formed by **North Window** and **South Window**, The Spectacles stand southeast of Double Arch and east of Turret Arch. The rock mass between North Window and South Window is called **Nose Bridge**, for the analogous part of a pair of glasses. North Window is 93 feet long and 51 feet high; South Window spans 105 feet and rises 66 feet—the third longest arch in the Park.

Although the two "lenses" of The Spectacles are called windows, they are more properly designated arches, and have variant names which incorporate that term: for example, North Window has also been called Massive Arch, and South Window has been titled Oval Arch. The Spectacles have also been called Two Spans Arches.

South Window can be seen also from Wolfe Cabin, from the lower section of Delicate Arch Trail, and from Delicate Arch. North Window can be viewed also from U.S. Highway 191 on the eastern horizon, from many points along the route, beginning near the head of Moab Canyon, north to the Dalton Well area.

Turret Arch

West of The Spectacles is Turret Arch. This distinctive landform has three open-

ings, the principal one with a span of 39 feet and a height of 64 feet. The two smaller openings are, respectively, 12 by 13 feet, and 8 by 4.5 feet.

Turret Arch has been known by seven other names: Double-O Arch, Framed Arch, Jail Entrance, The Jug Handle, Kneeling Camel, Pillar Arch, and Profile Rock.

Among other features observable from the loop road are **Archaeological Cave**, east of Double Arch; **Aunt Emma**, east of Archaeological Cave; **Parade of Elephants**, south of Double Arch; **Elephant Arch** in the Parade of Elephants; **Buccaneer Rock**, east of the Parade of Elephants; **Arch-in-the-Making**, north of North Window; and **Duck-on-the-Rock**, several hundred feet west of Turret Arch.

SALT VALLEY

From the intersection of The Windows road, the main park road descends down the southwest flank of Salt Valley. This large landform has a northwest-southeast trend, and is eighteen miles long and up to two miles wide.

Salt Valley, is a collapsed *salt anticline*. That is, it was an elongated upward-folded structure with a huge salt core. When ground water dissolved the salt under the anticline's crest, the summit collapsed. This caving in produced a type of parallel fracturing termed by geologists *jointing* in sandstone along either side of the anticline—today's Devil's Garden and Fiery Furnace on the northeast, and Klondike Bluffs and Herdina Park on the southwest. Weathering and erosion on the surfaces of some of the joints produced fins in which today's arches and spires eventually develop, and in which others may form in the future.

WOLFE CABIN

About twelve miles from the Visitors Center is a graded dirt spur road to Wolfe

Cabin, the Delicate Arch trailhead, and Delicate Arch Viewpoint. Wolfe Cabin and the trailhead are two miles from the main Park road.

In 1898, John Wesley Wolfe and his son Fred settled along **Salt Wash**, close to its junction with **Winter Camp Wash**. They had come to the isolated locale from Ohio, possibly so the senior Wolfe's left leg, which had been injured in 1863 while he served in the Union Army at the Siege of Vicksburg, might improve in the warm, dry high-desert climate.

The Wolfes ran a small ranching operation, the "Bar DX." Their first cabin was destroyed by a flash flood in 1906. A new cabin, the one standing today, was constructed in the same year. After twelve years, the senior Wolfe sold the ranch in 1910, and with Fred returned to Ohio.

GREEN ROCKS

At several places in the Park—especially in the **Wolfe Cabin area**, along the road to **Delicate Arch Viewpoint**, and in **Salt Valley**—colorful outcrops of blue-green rocks brighten the landscape. One visitor, recounting his 1978 trip to the Park, said he was more impressed by the blue-green rocks than by the arches!

These brilliantly hued rocks are from the Brushy Basin Member of the Morrison Formation. The Brushy Basin Member, which erodes to form slopes, is composed of shale with thin sandstone and conglomerate beds. Dinosaur bones are found in some of the sandstone beds. Petrified wood and chert also occur in the Brushy Basin Member.

Rocks of the Brushy Basin Member usually are drab, but traces of copper have imparted a prominent blue-green tint to them at several locations in the Park. This vivid color has been believed—mistakenly—by some people to be caused by glauconite, a green clay mineral related to mica. Glauconite occurs only in sed-

A BRIDGE, AN ARCH—OR, A DINOSAUR?

Double Arch ranks high among the Park's principal attractions. Easily seen from The Windows section road, the impressive feature's larger opening has a span of 163 feet—the second longest in the Park—and a height of 105 feet—the highest in the Park. The smaller opening's span is 60 feet long with a height of 61 feet.

These dual openings are technically arches. However, they sometimes have been incorrectly called bridges; one early title given to them was "Twinbow Bridge." People commonly confuse natural arches and bridges, and this is understandable since the two landform types are much alike in appearance. Even though they look outwardly similar, arches and bridges have distinctly different origins.

An article discussing the origin of one type of bridge—the kind that forms on meandering streams—was carried in the October 1942 issue of *Natural History* magazine. Entitled, "Rainbows of Rock," the article exemplifies the confusion that surrounds the difference between bridges and arches. The article's author, H. E.

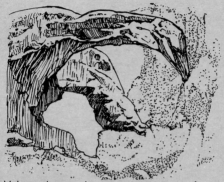

Vokes, who was then associate curator of fossil invertebrates at The American Museum of Natural History, correctly identified the geologic process by which natural bridges are created on meandering streams. He cited examples of bridges, but wrongly included several arches. Of these, four are in the present Park: Double Arch, South Window, Double-O Arch, and Landscape Arch (referred to as "Landscape Arch bridge").

Alexander Seidel, a resident of Plainfield, New Jersey read and reacted to the article. In a letter published in the maga-

zine's December issue, Seidel said that he had noted "with great interest . . . [Vokes's] explanation of how Nature carved . . . natural bridges."

"As I am not a scientist," Seidel stated, "but only a dreamy artist, I have my own ideas about the origin of [Double Arch], depicted on the cover of *Natural History*."

Facetiously, he remarked: "I am convinced that a nice old dinosaur knew already about the slogan 'Keep smiling,' and consequently kept smiling in a most pleasant pose—until he got petrified." Then Seidel commented seriously: "I won't require that you accept my hypothesis [for the origin of Double Arch] . . . . But maybe you can use it as a warning not to seize upon the most obvious explanation when dealing with scientific problems." Printed with Seidel's letter was a drawing he had made showing a dinosaur-like beast forming the two large openings.

Whether Seidel knew that Vokes was wrong to have classified Double Arch as a bridge is not clear, but it is evident that he recognize the danger in basing conclusions on what seems "obvious."

THE LIFE CYCLE OF NATURAL BRIDGES ON MEANDERING STREAMS

Although the Park is known for its many arches, the area also has a few small natural bridges. Often confused with arches, natural bridges are a separate type of landform and begin in a different manner.

Sipapu Bridge in Natural Bridges National Monument, about 120 miles south of Arches, exemplifies the *meander cut-off bridge*, and illustrates how that type of bridge differs from an arch.

The first stage [**left**] in the formative process of this unusual type of landform begins when a winding stream cuts downward and deeply entrenches its curving channel. The stream's ability to erode its banks is greatly increased at outside curves where centrifugal force propels running water against the outer edge of the channel. Where the stream loops to almost double back on itself, with two outside curves separated only by a narrow neck of

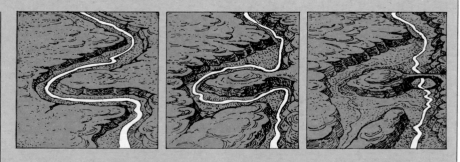

land [**middle**], the hydraulic and abrasive action of the stream may eventually cut a small hole through the neck, forming an incipient natural bridge. The stream, seeking the shortest course, then will flow through this cut-off and enlarge the bridge's opening [**right**]. As the stream continues to cut its bed downward, simultaneously the bridge's opening is further

expanded by the same weathering and erosional processes that create natural arches: the chemical action of air and water, and such physical or mechanical effects as temperature changes, frost wedging, and gravity. These processes, though slow, are unrelenting, and eventually the bridge's span will collapse.

═══════ Unpaved road

────────── Improved foot trail

imentary rocks of marine origin. Since the Brushy Basin Member was laid down in a non-marine environment, on floodplains and in lakes, during the Late Jurassic (about 140 million years ago), the rocks cannot contain glauconite.

DELICATE ARCH VIEWPOINT

From Wolfe Cabin the graded dirt road off of the main Park road continues to Delicate Arch Viewpoint, fording en route Salt Wash and Winter Camp Wash. The lookout is one and a half miles east of Wolfe Cabin, on top of a ridge above **Winter Camp Wash**. At this viewpoint, **Delicate Arch** can be seen to the northeast. This beautiful freestanding arch — the symbolic landform of the Park — has a span of thirty-three feet and a height of forty-five feet. It is formed in the Entrada Sandstone, with the Slick Rock Member composing all of the feature except the top five feet of cap rock, which is of the Moab Member.

In Winter Camp Wash, below the viewpoint, stands a large rock mass—the **Rock Settee**.

FIERY FURNACE

About fifteen miles from the Visitors Center is the Fiery Furnace, a maze of fins, spires, and chutes (narrow passageways). It was named for the warm, reddish glow which the area's Entrada Sandstone often seems to radiate in late afternoon sunlight. Significant natural arches in this confusing

Twisted Doughnut Arch

Ute Indian petroglyphs

Wolfe Cabin

DELICATE ARCH TRAIL

An improved foot trail runs from the parking lot at Wolfe Cabin to Delicate Arch, a distance of one and a half miles. Just past the historic cabin the trail crosses Salt Wash on a swinging suspension bridge 100 feet long. Then the route runs to the base of a cliff, and begins the climb to Delicate Arch. On this cliff, northwest of the trail, are several Ute Indian petroglyphs. Near the top of the trail at Delicate Arch is a small span — Twisted Doughnut Arch — which is fourteen feet long and eleven feet high. Through it can be seen Delicate Arch. Another arch, unnamed, is northwest of the trail and across a canyon, and has a span of seventeen feet and a height of twelve feet.

"ARCHES GOLF CLUB"?

In the fertile imaginations of golfing humorists Tom Hepburn and Selwyn Jacobson, emerald-green fairways wend through the Parkland's red-rock spires to form a whimsical "Arches Golf Club." In their fantasy, a putting green is perched precariously atop the crest of Delicate Arch, and Double Arch forms an obstacle worthy of the driving skill of a Pebble Beach champion. In their spoof, *America's Most Difficult Golf Holes*, the course's fourth green sits on the crown of Delicate Arch. For the intrepid golfer to drive his ball successfully to this lofty green, which is surrounded by sheer drops of fifty feet or more, unfailing accuracy is required.

Not only do Hepburn and Jacobson rank Delicate Arch as one of America's most nightmarish holes, they also class it among Earth's very worst, including it in their comical volume *The World's 72 Toughest Golf Holes*.

Double Arch poses a nerve-racking obstacle to the course's seventeenth hole. Lying on the brink of a high cliff behind the larger span of Double Arch, the green confronts even the boldest golfer with a dilemma: either drive over the span, or under it, to reach the flag. This hole has been aptly titled "Double Trouble."

It is true that sand traps abound in the Parkland, that rocky roughs are commonplace, and that water hazards follow every rainfall. But there is, in real life, no Arches Golf Club. If there truly were, a course at Arches would unquestionably rank among the toughest golfing challenges in the world.

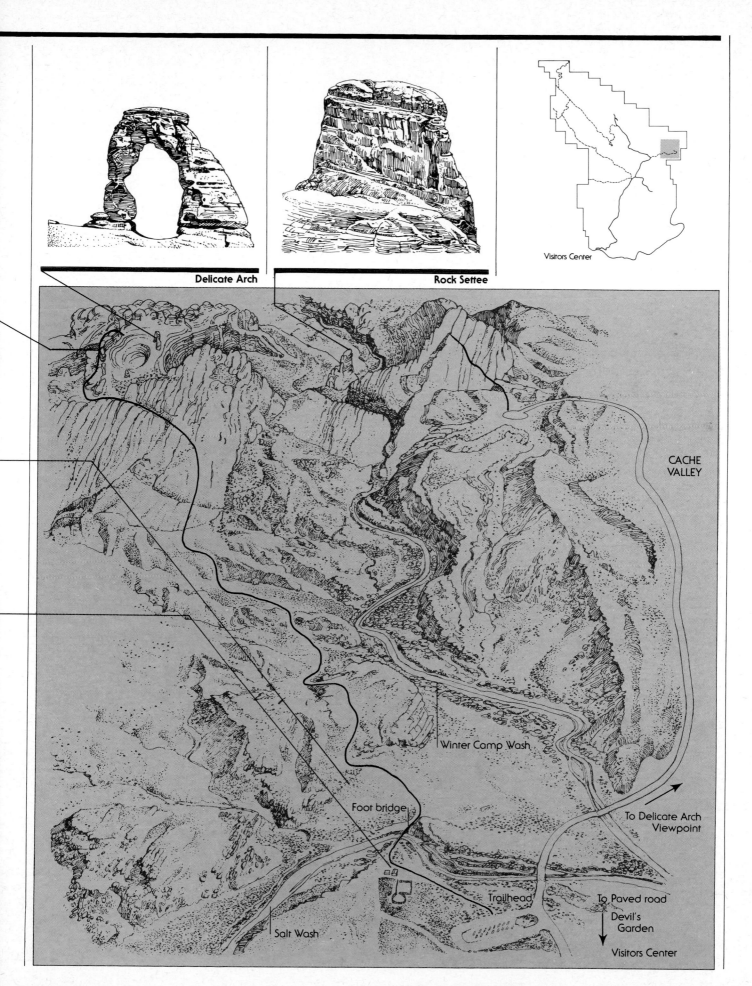

Delicate Arch

Rock Settee

Visitors Center

CACHE VALLEY

Winter Camp Wash

Foot bridge

To Delicate Arch Viewpoint

To Paved road

Devil's Garden

Visitors Center

Trailhead

Salt Wash

jumble of rock are Twin, Surprise, and Cliff.

For good reason, **Twin Arch** is also called Skull Arch because its two openings seem to resemble the eye sockets in some giant skeleton's cranium. The larger "socket" has a span of thirty-three feet and a height of thirty-four feet, while the smaller opening spans twenty-eight feet and is twenty-one feet high.

Surprise Arch was discovered in 1963 by then-superintendent Bates E. Wilson. On Friday, December 13 — certainly not an unlucky day that year for him — Wilson, with Chief Ranger Roby R. "Slim" Mabery and maintenance man Harold J. Shoemaker, was examining the Fiery Furnace for a suitable trial route for visitors. Wilson, who had split away from Mabery and Shoemaker, suddenly — and unexpectedly — came upon the span. "My word," he recalled exclaiming, "look at this arch!" The landform had not been recorded until then, so Wilson dubbed it — fittingly — "Surprise Arch." Its span measures sixty-three feet long and has a height of fifty-five feet.

Cliff Arch, in the eastern Fiery Furnace, is also called Abbey's Arch, after Edward Abbey, a well-known author. Abbey was a seasonal ranger at Arches in the 1950s when he first reported the landform. This arch has a span of twenty-four feet and a height of twelve feet.

Among other arches in the Fiery Furnace are **Bench, Flatiron, Box, Cloister, Dream, Elephant Chin, Fiery Pothole, Football, Hole-in-Fin, Kissing Turtles, Lazy Jughandle, Roadside, Sand Dune, Queue Jughandle, Unseen, Webbing,** and **Wineglass.** There is also a small natural bridge, named **Walk-Thru Bridge.**

PIPELINE FLAT

Lying east of the main Park road, about seventeen miles from the Visitors Center, and two miles south of the road's end at

DELICATE ARCH: TO STABILIZE OR NOT TO STABILIZE?

Delicate Arch, as its name aptly implies, is slender and fragile. This superb natural feature was given its title in 1934 by Frank A. Beckwith, leader of the Arches National Monument Scientific Expedition. Beckwith said that the "delicacy" of the arch's carving, especially of its legs, was the most pronounced among all the natural openings in that region. And he noted that Delicate Arch's east leg "is almost cut in two."

Normal geological processes of weathering and erosion caused this pronounced—but beautiful—narrowing of the arch's east limb, its so-called "weak leg."

In November 1947, then-custodian Russell Mahan, concerned about the stability of the arch, discussed with Carl W. Alleman, Park Service landscape architect, the possibility of reinforcing the landform's east leg. Alleman prepared a report, dated January 22, 1948, in which he noted that "many [visitors] class [Delicate Arch] and its setting as one of the most spectacular erosional exhibits in the national park system." He observed further: ". . . if stabilization [of Delicate Arch] will retard erosion and spare it for an additional generation or two it is a Park Service obligation to give it this protection." Alleman then urged: ". . . if erosion can be checked or retarded without molesting [the arch's] general appearance and setting, prompt steps [should] be taken to carry out these protective measures."

However, no action was taken on Alleman's proposal. Fifteen months before his report, the National Park Service Advisory Board at their October 22, 1946 meeting recommended that no attempt be made to stabilize natural features "solely because of their interest as freaks."

In 1951, Leslie P. Arnberger, Park Service naturalist, visited Arches. In a memorandum dated May 15 to the general superintendent of the Southwestern National Monuments, Arnberger stated that Delicate Arch "certainly would rank among the most impressive erosional features of the entire country," but that it was "inevitably doomed to destruction by natural forces of erosion, unless measures are taken to prevent this." Arnberger said he understood that stabilization of the arch had been "suggested in the past." And while he was "fully aware of the [Park] Service policy of not interfering with the natural processes of nature," Arnberger said he nevertheless felt that "because of the absolutely irreplaceable nature of Delicate Arch . . . an exception could well be made in this case."

M. R. Tillotson, regional director of the National Park Service, wrote to the Park Service director on June 15, 1951, reporting that "the matter of stabilizing Delicate Arch was discussed at our Staff Meeting of May 15, when some of our staff members felt that the proposal is worthy of reconsideration and additional thought before it is

ruled out entirely and finally." Tillotson said he was "of course" aware of the Advisory Board's recommendation against stabilizing natural features, and that he "fully [agreed] with this recommendation." But he noted that some people "feel the policy should not be so rigid as absolutely to preclude any attempts at preserving certain natural features which are so rare, irreplaceable, and uniquely illustrative of natural phenomena as to remove them from the category of being mere freaks." Delicate Arch, wrote Tillotson, was considered by these people as of "much more than freak significance and that it is anything but a commonplace natural feature."

Tillotson also reported that the arch "is in imminent danger of collapse." The east leg, he said, "is being eroded away quite rapidly and unless measures are taken to retard this wear, the arch may fail in the near future."

Tillotson said that stabilization "would doubtless present technical difficulties." He reported that members of his staff had suggested the "best method might be to strengthen the weak portion of the arch and prevent further wear by filling in the badly eroded section with waterproof concrete or cement plaster, to be colored and molded in such a manner as not to detract from the natural appearance and beauty of the arch."

Park Service Director A. E. Demaray replied on July 13, 1951 that there was "no evidence of unnaturally accelerated deterioration of Delicate Arch." Demaray stated he preferred "not to take action with regard to Delicate Arch until further study produces accurate details on its condition." He concluded by saying: "We must give consideration to the possibility that a partial collapse might produce a feature equally unique in character."

John M. Davis, general superintendent of the Southwestern National Monuments, in a memorandum to Tillotson dated August 23, 1951, said: "It is our feeling that the erosion on Delicate Arch may have already reached the critical point when high winds, or any unusual stresses or strains, may bring about the collapse of this feature."

Hugh M. Miller, assistant regional director, visited Arches in the summer of 1952. In a report to Tillotson, Miller announced: "I have decided to join, as a result of this trip, those who believe that stabilization of Delicate Arch is warranted." He favored putting a "simple plaster jacket . . . over the weak point in the arch. . . ."

In a December 22, 1952 memorandum to Tillotson, Davis also urged that Delicate Arch be stabilized, saying: "To allow this unique formation to fall without making some effort to prolong its existence would be to lose forever an integral part of the story justifying the existence of Arches. . . ."

Tillotson, in a February 6, 1953 memorandum to the Park Service director, reported that the engineering division had a plan to stabilize Delicate Arch with a sheath that would "be hardly distinguishable and would not in any manner detract from the natural appearance of the Arch."

David N. Van Pelt, Park Service landscape architect, visited Arches in 1954 to evaluate the stabilization of Delicate Arch. He noted in his March 9 report that "Delicate Arch, in its setting, is unquestionably one of the outstanding scenic and geological features of the National Park System." Van Pelt outlined two options available:

(1) That the arch should not be stabilized. "This view arises," he said, "not out of indifference nor apathy, but from a consideration of the uncertain benefits of stabilization, of the very real possibility that more harm than benefit may be done, and in the knowledge that Delicate Arch is 'in extremis,' its collapse only deferred by the efforts of man."

(2) That the arch should be stabilized. Van Pelt commented that "the contention that nothing should be done is prey to the equally defensible argument that, since the patient is doomed anyway, we are justified in making some attempt to prolong his life."

If the decision were made to stabilize, Van Pelt recommended that the weak leg of the arch should be sprayed with a colorless substance that would penetrate and bind the sandstone grains together to resist erosion, and would allow the rock to expand and contract when freezing and thawing.

An alternative method, Van Pelt noted, was one suggested by J. R. Lassiter, a Park Service engineer. That proposal was to ring the narrow section of the weak leg with a concrete collar, which would be shaped and colored to blend in with the natural sandstone. Van Pelt felt that if

"carefully done, such a solution should satisfy the requirement of 'invisibility'."

Robert L. Morris, acting superintendent of Arches, reported in early 1954 that "plans are underway to treat the badly eroded section of the weak leg of the arch. . . ." On April 23, 1954, the superintendent, Bates E. Wilson, reported tests would be made of materials for their possible use in stabilizing the arch. He applied several liquid preservatives to rock near the arch and found them unsatisfactory, either turning white, scaling off, or both. Years later, Wilson, who was opposed to the project, said: the "best thing I got out of it was an extension ladder I'd been wanting for years."

In the end, no stabilization work was done. But contrary to the dire predictions of Tillotson and Davis, Delicate Arch still stands entire and intact, majestically surveying the Parkland from its precarious perch on the brink of a sheer, towering canyon wall.

The narrow east limb, or "**weak leg**," of Delicate Arch has raised concerns that the magnificent feature—"trademark" of the Park—is on the verge of collapse. Several examinations have been made of the the arch by the Park Service. This photograph was taken in March 1954 during an evaluation conducted by David Van Pelt, landscape architect, Dale King, naturalist, and Bates Wilson, superintendent of Arches. For nearly a decade the Park Service debated whether or not the arch should be stabilized, and finally concluded to allow geologic processes to take their natural course.

Devil's Garden, is Pipeline Flat. It is a *park*, a term that in this usage designates not a cultural unit such as Arches National Park, but a topographical feature, characterized by a level grassland surrounded by rougher, broken terrain.

On the north side of Pipeline Flat is the lower (or southern) end of Devil's Garden; on the flat's south side is the upper (or northern) end of the Fiery Furnace.

Running east and west across Pipeline Flat is a prominent scar—the trace of a buried natural-gas pipeline, which gives the flat its name. This scar also is clearly evident where the pipeline crosses Salt Valley west of the main Park road.

Popularly known as the "Scenic Inch," the Pacific Northwest Pipeline was constructed in 1955-56 by the Pacific Northwest Pipeline Corporation. The twenty-six-inch-diameter main pipeline is 1,487 miles long, with lateral lines totaling more than 800 additional miles. Natural gas is transported via the line from wells in New Mexico, Utah, Colorado, and Wyoming to the Pacific Northwest.

Sand Dune Arch

In the northern end of the Fiery Furnace, near the southern edge of Pipeline Flat, is Sand Dune Arch. This span cannot be seen from the road. Its name comes from the sand dune at the site. The opening is thirty feet long and eight feet high.

Broken Arch

Visible from the road, on the Devil's Garden side of Pipeline Flat, is Broken Arch. The opening was given this name because its span appears to be cracked in the middle, but the title is really a misnomer since the span's rock is not broken. The aperture is fifty-nine feet long and forty-three feet tall. Reddish Slick Rock Member of the Entrada Sandstone forms the feature's abutments and the lower part of the span, and the whitish Moab Mem-

DEVIL'S GARDEN CAMPGROUND & PIPELINE FLAT

The **Pacific Northwest Pipeline,** a natural-gas transmission line running from New Mexico to Washington state, crosses the Parkland's middle in a northeast direction. Constructed in 1955-56, the pipeline's route through Arches is marked by prominent scars on the scenic terrain. This photograph, taken by Harold Ratcliff in November 1955, shows pipe being laid at Arches.

——————— Paved road

——————— Improved foot trail

National Park Service

ber of the Entrada caps the span.

SKYLINE ARCH

Skyline Arch rises alongside the main Park road about one-half mile north of the pull-off for the foot trail to San Dune Arch and Broken Arch. It looms prominently east of the road, nearly seventeen miles from the Visitors Center.

Until late 1940, this landform was called Arch-in-the-Making, because a large sandstone block — then lodged in the present opening — filled more than half of the space. In November of that year, the block fell out, giving the arch its present shape. The span now is sixty-nine feet long and forty-five feet high. The arch's present name is derived from the fact that the span stands high on the skyline, and is visible from many points in the Park. It can be viewed to the southwest from Interstate 70, in the stretch lying between seven and thirteen miles east of Thompson.

DEVIL'S GARDEN

At the end of the main Park road, eighteen miles from the Visitors Center, is Devil's Garden. Many arches are found in this scenic area that stretches for about nine miles along the eastern rim of Salt Valley.

The paramount landform in Devil's Garden is **Landscape Arch.** Measured by geographer Dale J. Stevens in 1984, Landscape is ranked as the world's longest natural span—it stretches an incredible 434 feet! The light opening beneath the span is 306 feet wide, and at its maximum height the span's underside is 92 feet above the ground. At its thinnest vertical point, the span is only 16 feet thick, and at its narrowest horizontal width it measures 15.5 feet.

Landscape Arch rises eight-tenths of a mile from the parking lot at the Devil's Garden trailhead. The huge span can be glimpsed from the loop terminus of the main Park road, in the vicinity of this road's intersection with the campground road.

The arch was named in 1934 by Frank A. Beckwith, leader of the Arches National Monument Scientific Expedition. Beckwith said the landscape seen through the opening to the west was framed by the arch, hence his choice of the title.

On May 29, 1950, the first recorded tourist facility in Arches occurred at Landscape Arch. Nineteen-year-old Frederick Semisch, during an unauthorized attempt to reach the span's top, fell to his death.

Wall Arch, two-tenths of a mile north of Landscape Arch, was the sight of the first serious visitor accident. On September 1, 1948, Oras Krumboltz, a professor at Arizona State College (now University), fell thirty feet from the arch. Krumboltz, who had climbed to the span's top to have his photograph taken by a companion, lost his footing and plummeted to the ground. He suffered a broken pelvis and other internal injuries, plus multiple bruises and abrasions, and a badly sprained left ankle.

Wall Arch has a span of sixty-eight feet and a height of forty-one feet. As is Landscape Arch, it is formed in the Entrada Sandstone. While Landscape is composed entirely of the Entrada's reddish Slick

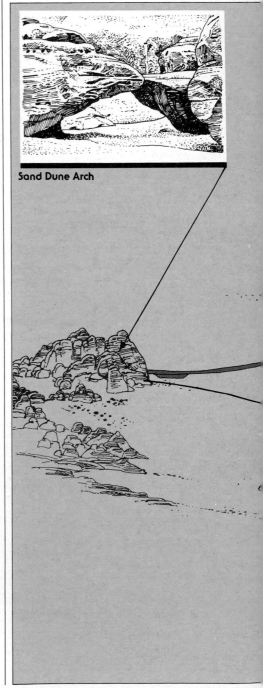

Sand Dune Arch

Visitors Center

TRAILS TO SAND DUNE ARCH, BROKEN ARCH, AND TAPESTRY ARCH

Sand Dune Arch, Broken Arch, and Tapestry Arch can be reached via either of two routes. (1) One trail begins at the main Park road, at the upper end of the Fiery Furnace, about sixteen miles from the Visitors Center. This trail runs 125 yards to a fork. The south branch of the fork leads about 200 yards to Sand Dune Arch in the Fiery Furance. The northeast branch runs about 400 yards across Pipeline Flat, which separates the Fiery Furnace from Devil's Garden, then intersects another trail. (2) The second trail — a loop route — starts at the terminus of the Devil's Garden Campground road. Its eastern branch runs approximately 400 yards to a 300-yard-long spur to Tapestry Arch. From the Tapestry Arch spur the trail leads about a half-mile to and

through Broken Arch, then passes Mammoth Rock, and to the junction with the trail (1) from Sand Dune Arch. The trail then continues northwest about a half-mile to the campground, passing through chutes between towering sandstone fins.

DEVIL'S GARDEN CAMPGROUND

On the east section of the loop road in Devil's Garden, at the end of the main Park road, is the entry to Devil's Garden Campground. This facility provides improved campsites with tables, pulloff spaces for vehicles, cooking grills, and trash cans. Restrooms with running water and flush toilets also are available in this campground. A campfire circle is situated at the base of Skyline Arch, which rises dramatically on the campground's western edge.

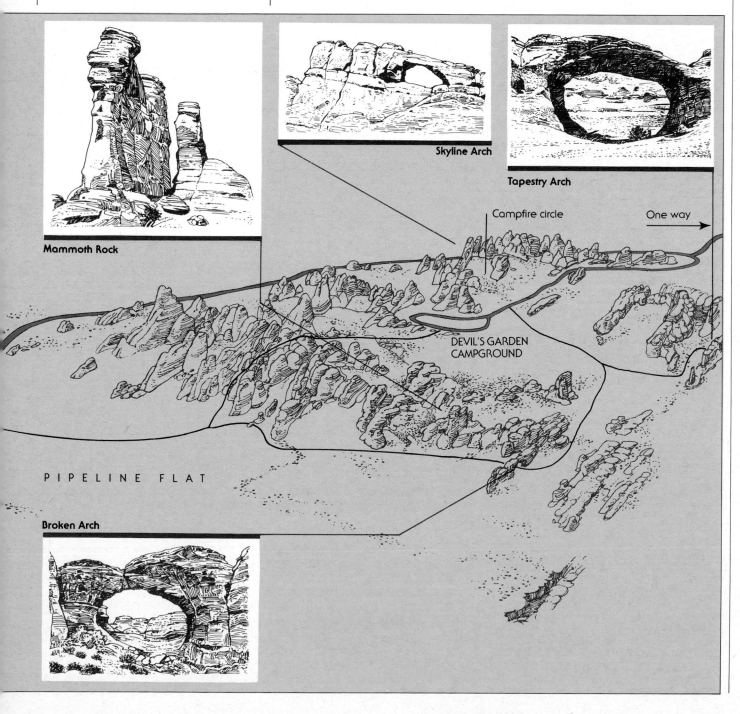

Mammoth Rock

Skyline Arch

Tapestry Arch

Campfire circle

One way

DEVIL'S GARDEN CAMPGROUND

PIPELINE FLAT

Broken Arch

Bighorn sheep are rare, year-round residents of the Park. These majestic mammals inhabit the more rugged and remote sections of the rocky terrain.

Rock Member, Wall's cap rock is the Entrada's white Moab Member while the rest of the arch is of the Slick Rock Member.

Dark Angel, a prominent spire, stands on the western edge of Devil's Garden, overlooking Salt Valley. It formed in the Slick Rock Member, and is the remnant of a high, narrow fin. The isolated shaft is two and a half miles from the Devil's Garden trailhead.

Among the many colorful arch names in Devil's Garden are **Aladdin's Lamp, Arch de Triomphe, Bat Guano, Coke Oven, Gothic, Indian Head, Phantom, Piano Leg, Rubble, Shadow Box, Submarine,** and **Turban Head.** Several small natural bridges also are found in Devil's Garden, including **Oval Canyon Natural Bridge.**

KLONDIKE BLUFFS

According to Samuel J. Taylor, publisher and editor of Moab's newspaper, *The Times-Independent,* the name "Klondike Bluffs" owes its origin to the area's winter weather which some have compared to the bitter and blustery subpolar climate of Canada's Klondike region. Taylor learned of the name's origin from his father, Loren L. "Bish" Taylor, editor of the Moab weekly from 1911 to 1953.

Located in the remote northwestern corner of the Park, rugged Klondike Bluffs is accessible only by dirt roads or foot trails. The only route suitable for standard passenger cars is the Salt Valley road; the others can be traveled solely by four-wheel-drive vehicles. The Salt Valley road branches off to the southwest from the main Park road about seventeen miles from the Visitors Center, near Skyline Arch.

Eight miles from the intersection near Skyline Arch, the Salt Valley road intersects with a four-wheel-drive road to the west. This rough route is three and a half miles long. At its terminus is one of the two trailheads to Tower Arch. En route

from Salt Valley to the trailhead, the road passes **The Marching Men,** an impressive line of towering spires, and intersects with another four-wheel-drive road. This second route runs southeast eight miles, passing **Herdina Park,** to the main Park road, which it meets at Balanced Rock about nine miles from the Visitors Center.

Tower Arch, the major span of Klondike Bluffs, is the "founding" arch of Arches National Park. In 1923, Alexander Ringhoffer, a prospector and miner — and the "Father of Arches" — wrote to The Denver and Rio Grande Western Railroad urging them to send representatives to observe the wonders of the Klondike Bluffs — which Ringhoffer called "Devil's Garden" — and to investigate the possibility of offering scenic tours to the area from the railroad's station at Thompson, Utah, about seventeen miles north.

Frank A. Wadleigh and George L. Beam, representing the railroad, went to view Klondike Bluffs, and were guided by Ringhoffer. Wadleigh, impressed with what he had seen, contacted the National Park Service, and in 1929 Arches was proclaimed a national monument by President Herbert C. Hoover. In 1971, President Richard M. Nixon signed the Congressional bill that established Arches National Park.

Among other natural sandstone openings in the area, in addition to Tower Arch, are **Overlooked, Parallel, Wine Bottle,** and **Anniversary,** a double span, south of the four-wheel-drive road and about a mile from the Tower Arch trailhead. This arch was named to mark the wedding anniversary of Mr. and Mrs.

Roby "Slim" Mabery, who first saw the landform on the date of their anniversary.

Another trail to Tower Arch begins at the end of a one-mile-long spur road off of the Salt Valley road. This spur — passable to standard cars — is only one-tenth of a mile north of the four-wheel-drive road to the other Tower Arch trailhead.

From the mile-long spur road to the Tower Arch trailhead, the Salt Valley road runs about one and a half miles northwest to the four-wheel-drive road north to Eagle Park. Then the Salt Valley road continues northwest, crosses the north boundary of Arches, and eventually — through connections — goes either west to U.S. Highway 191 or northeast to Interstate 70 at Thompson.

EAGLE PARK

In the extreme northern end of Arches lies Eagle Park, a relatively flat area of grassland surrounded by rougher, broken terrain. Principal access is via a foot trail that runs from the Salt Valley road. The trailhead is about one-and-a-half miles north of the short spur road to the Tower Arch trail from Salt Valley. From the trailhead to Eagle Park is approximately two miles over the trail. The first half-mile is across Salt Valley to its east wall, then the foot trail climbs to the ridge, and enters Eagle Park.

Sheep were once grazed in Eagle Park, and at several places are inscriptions that were carved on the rocks by sheepherders. There is also an oil exploration drill site on the eastern edge of the area.

Eagle Park was named in 1968 by Bates Wilson. At that time, the grassland was not part of Arches, but was under consideration for addition. The then-superintendent was locating survey section corners, and noticed two golden eagles soaring overhead. Since the flat was nameless, he decided to call it Eagle Park. Lyndon B. Johnson added the area to Arches by presidential proclamation in 1969.

IS LANDSCAPE THE WORLD'S LONGEST ARCH?

Landscape Arch has been recognized as reigning monarch of the world's rock spans for several decades, and has been listed as the longest natural span on Earth in the *Guinness Book of World Records*. However, since 1952 Landscape Arch's status as the titleholder has been seriously challenged by another great span in southern Utah's red-rock country: Kolob Arch, in Zion National Park.

The earliest published reference to Landscape Arch, in the April 22, 1898 issue of the journal *Science*, claimed an exaggerated length for the span. Arthur Winslow, the article's author, had not personally seen the then-unnamed arch but he had obtained a photograph of it, which was reproduced in the journal. Winslow reported that the photographer had "estimated" the span's length at "about 500 feet"—almost a tenth-of-a-mile long!

After this limited publicity, the great arch returned to near obscurity, where it remained for almost thirty-six years. Not until Frank A. Beckwith, leader of the Arches National Monument Scientific Expedition, visited the striking landform in 1934 was it again publicized. Also—worthy of note—is the fact that he named and measured the huge span. That year, in the March 22 issue of Moab's newspaper, *The Times-Independent*, Beckwith stated he chose the name because the terrain "behind" the arch was framed by its opening, and he reported—in capital letters—that Landscape's span measured "TWO HUNDRED AND NINETY-ONE FEET!"

Beckwith did not claim Landscape was the world's longest arch in his official report, or in articles he wrote for *The Times-Independent*. Who crowned the arch with its regal title is not definitely known, although it may have been Harry Reed, the second custodian (Park Service manager) of Arches. Possibly the earliest published reference to the title appeared in an article on the front page of Moab's weekly for July 9, 1936. The story's headline, "The Longest Natural Bridge In The World," made a common error in calling the arch a bridge. The two landforms are distinct types, with different origins, and the two terms are not synonymous. A photograph of the arch, taken by Reed, accompanied the article.

Curiously, *The Times-Independent* report described Landscape as "294 feet long," or 3 feet longer than Beckwith's measurement. A picture postcard of the arch, produced by Reed, also cited the longer dimension, and credited Landscape with being the world's longest.

In 1941, still another length for Landscape was reported. Henry G. Schmidt, Reed's successor as custodian of Arches, noted in his monthly report, dated March 23, that "a large boulder slipped from the north end of Landscape Arch sometime during the winter months, making the arch approximately 305 feet in length instead of 291 feet."

However, it was Beckwith's figure of 291 feet that became accepted as the span's "official" length for half a century. Then, in 1984, remeasurement of the span produced a new figure. This new calculation appeared, for several months, to have toppled the old monarch from its throne, in favor of Zion's Kolob.

The challenge to Landscape's rank really began thirty-two years earlier. On July 11, 1952, Victor R. Fritz and George H. Riley, both of Philadelphia, Pennsylvania and Wilford B. Morris, of Logan, Utah took the first measurement of Kolob Arch. Fritz reported the length to be 315 feet, and declared that Kolob was therefore "the largest natural span in the world."

The following year, on August 12, Fred D. Ayres and Alex E. Creswell, two seasoned rock climbers from Oregon, made the first known ascent of Kolob. At the request of the Park Service, the climbers returned to the arch two days later and measured its great span. Their rough calculation gave it a length of "about 290-310 feet." Interestingly, though their measurements for Kolob varied from 1 foot shorter to 19 feet longer than the accepted length for Landscape, no effort was made at the time to obtain accurate figures for both spans, and thus to determine definitively which had the greater length, and was therefore the world's longest arch.

It was not until 1983-84 that such comparative measurements were at last made. Victor L. Jackson, chief park naturalist at Zion, had for several years wanted Kolob accurately measured. Finally, in March 1983, Levi A. Crocker, acting superintendent of Zion, wrote Reed Blake at Brigham Young University, and expressed his desire that "a professional survey crew provide a sound, defensible measurement of the arch." Crocker suggested that Blake assemble a voluntary survey party from the university. A team of faculty and students was organized, including Clyde R. Naylor, who then taught surveying at the university. Naylor was also Utah County's surveyor and engineer.

On July 28, 1983 the survey crew measured Kolob. After the field figures were evaluated at the university, Kolob Arch was found to have a span of 310 feet—19 feet longer than the accepted length of Landscape Arch. Significantly, the measurement obtained by the university crew was identical to the maximum approximate length of the span that Ayres and Creswell had calculated thirty years earlier!

About ten months later, Kolob was measured again. A team headed by Dale J. Stevens, professor of geography at Brigham Young University, made the measurement on May 8, 1984. Stevens reported that the span was 431 feet long, and that the "widest light opening" beneath the span measured 292 feet.

Was Kolob really longer than Landscape? Possibly Beckwith's 1934 figure was incorrect, and a new measurement of Landscape would reveal a longer length, and thus the arch would retain its title. So on July 26, 1984 Blake and a team from Brigham Young University measured Landscape. Its span was found to be 287 feet—a loss of 4 feet from the accepted length, and 23 feet shorter than Blake's figure for Kolob's span. Thus, according to Blake's measurements, Kolob was longer than Landscape.

About three-and-a-half months later, on November 8, 1984, Stevens, aided by his father Lawrence, also measured Landscape. Stevens calculated the span to be 434 feet long, exceeding by 3 feet his figure for Kolob. Stevens also established that Landscape's widest light opening was 306 feet, or 14 feet wider than Kolob's. Based on measurements by Stevens of the two arches' spans and widest light openings, Landscape surpasses Kolob in both categories.

By these criteria, Landscape still reigns as the world's longest natural arch.

Three members of the **Arches National Monument Scientific Expedition** sit on their horses below Landscape Arch in 1934. The party, under the leadership of Frank A. Beckwith, made the first measurement of the great arch.

National Park Service

DEVIL'S GARDEN

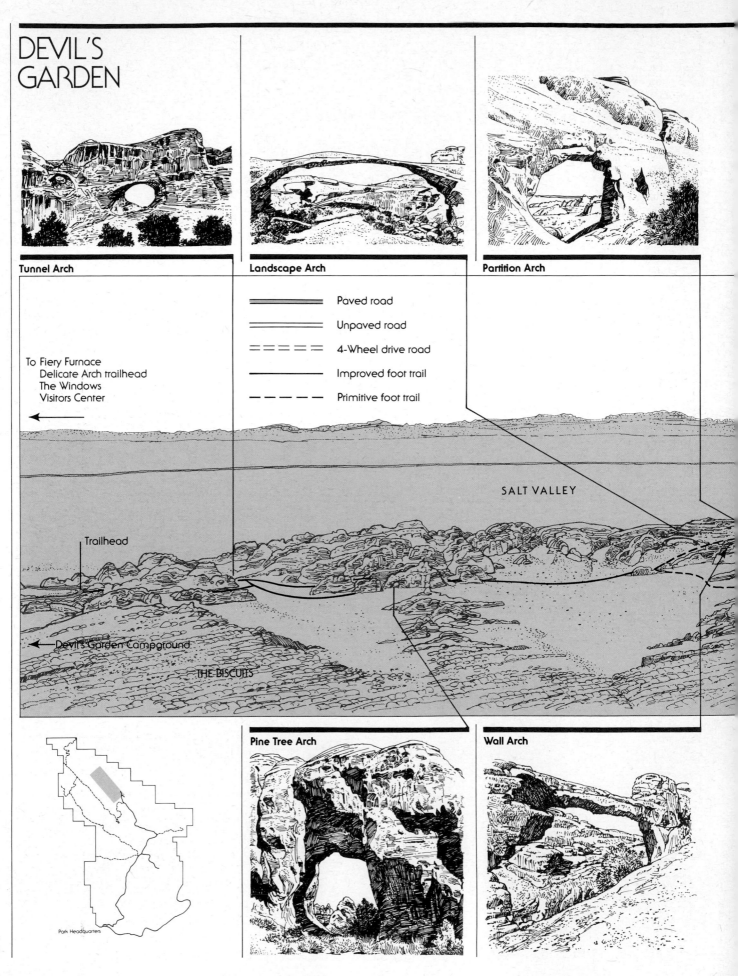

Tunnel Arch

Landscape Arch

Partition Arch

	Paved road
	Unpaved road
=====	4-Wheel drive road
———	Improved foot trail
– – –	Primitive foot trail

To Fiery Furnace
   Delicate Arch trailhead
   The Windows
   Visitors Center

SALT VALLEY

Trailhead

Devil's Garden Campground

THE BISCUITS

Park Headquarters

Pine Tree Arch

Wall Arch

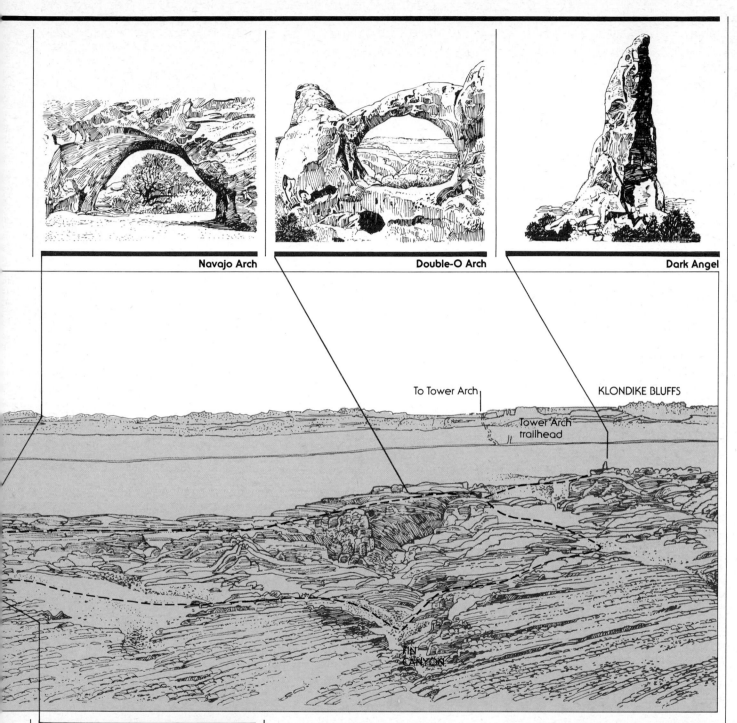

Navajo Arch

Double-O Arch

Dark Angel

To Tower Arch

KLONDIKE BLUFFS

Tower Arch trailhead

FIN CANYON

Crystal Arch

DEVIL'S GARDEN TRAIL

The Devil's Garden trailhead is at the end of the main Park road, eighteen miles from the Visitors Center. This trail includes both improved and primitive stretches, plus several spur trails and a long loop trail. From the trailhead, an improved pathway leads about 400 yards to a junction. A side trail leaves the main trail and goes east 100 yards to a fork, the south branch of which runs approximately 100 yards to Tunnel Arch, while the northeast branch goes 225 yards to Pine Tree Arch. From the Tunnel Arch-Pine Tree Arch junction on the main trail, Landscape Arch is about a half-mile north, or a distance of eight-tenths of a mile from the parking lot. At Landscape Arch the improved pathway ends, and a primitive loop trail begins. On the western branch of this loop is Wall Arch, two-tenths of a

mile north of Landscape Arch. Beyond Wall Arch, about a half-mile, the trail has another junction. A side trail leads about 100 yards to a fork: the south branch runs approximately 285 yards to Partition Arch, while the west branch goes 350 yards to Navajo Arch. From the Partition Arch-Navajo Arch junction on the loop trail beyond Wall Arch, the trail continues north to Double-O Arch — a total distance of two miles from the trailhead at the parking lot. Beginning at Double-O Arch a primitive trail runs northwest about 750 yards to Dark Angel, a prominent spire. Also at Double-O Arch, the loop trail swings back to Landscape Arch, crossing Fin Canyon, and passing by or close to several spans including Shadow Box Arch, Hidden Arch, Top Story Window, Box Arch, Black Arch, Debris Arch, Crystal Arch, and White Fin Arch.

APPENDIX

PARK PLACE-NAMES AND VARIANTS

Feature	Variant Name
Arch of Motion	Hard-to-See Arch
Balanced Rock	Balance Rock
	Pinnacle Rock

Feature	Variant Name
Beckwith Arch	Herdina Arch
	Leaping Arch
Bighorn Arch	Christmas Tree Arch
Black Arch	Fin Canyon Arch
Black Cave Arch	Pizza Pan Arch
Box Arch	belephant Chin
Cliff Arch	Abbey's Arch
Colorado River	Grand River
Cove of Caves	Cove of Six Caves
Dark Angel	Thumb Rock
Delicate Arch	Bloomers Arch
	Chaps
	Mary's Bloomers
	Old Maid's Bloomers
	Pant's Crotch
	Salt Wash Arch
	Schoolmarm's Pants

Feature	Variant Name
Diamond Arch	Campground Arch
Double Arch	Double Arches
	Double Windows
	Double-O Arch
	The Jug Handles
	Twinbow Arch
	Twinbow Bridge
Double-O Arch	Double Arch
	Double Deck Arch
Elephant Butte	The Massif
Football Arch	Teardrop Arch
Garden of Eden	The Fingers
	King Row
	Toadstools
Hole-in-the-Wall	Archette
	Baby Arch
	New Arch
Jack's Mummy	Old-Man-of-the-Mountain
Julien Arch	Big Eye Arch
	The Eye
Klondike Bluffs	Devil's Garden
	Klondike Ridge
	The Palisades
	Red Bluffs
Marching Men, The	Figure Fin
	The Fingers
Moab Canyon	Red Canyon
North Window	Massive Arch
	North Spectacle
	West Spectacle Arch

Feature	Variant Name
Organ, The	The Great Organ
	Red Buttes
Owl Rock	Eagle Rock
Partition Arch	Hole-in-the-Wall
	Pillar Arch
Pine Tree Arch	Cedar Tree Arch
Pipeline Arch	Clover Canyon Bridge
	Magic Mystery Arch
Queen Nefertiti	The Egyptian Face
	Unjoined Rock
Queen Victoria	Whistler's Mother
Red Window	Far Out Arch
Ribbon Arch	Small Bridge
Sausage Rock	The Popsicle
Schmidt Arch	Bean Pot Arch
	Cupola Arch
	Donut Arch
Serpentine Arch	Garden of Eden Arch
Shadow Box Arch	Black Arch
	First Window
Sheep Rock	The Lion
	The Sphinx
Skyline Arch	Arch-in-the-Making
	Fallen Rock Arch
South Window	The Big Window
	Great Oval Arch
	Oval Arch
Three Gossips, The	The Three Graces
Three Penguins, The	Trinity Rock
Spectacles, The	The Domino
	Two Span Arches
Top Story Window	Texas Arch
Tower Arch	Minaret Bridge
Tower of Babel	Cathedral Spire
Tunnel Arch	Hidden Arch
Turret Arch	Double-O Arch
	Framed Arch
	Jail Entrance
	The Jug Handle
	Kneeling Camel
	Pillar Arch
	Profile Rock
Twin Arch	Skull Arch
Twisted Doughnut Arch	Delicate View Arch
	Frame Arch
Walk-Thru Bridge	Fiery Furnace Bridge
	Little Bridge
Wall Arch	White Cap Arch
Windows, The	The Arches
	Window Castles
Winter Camp Wash	Dry Creek
Wolfe Cabin	Turnbow Cabin

NAMING THE COLORADO RIVER

The Colorado River, which borders Arches National Park for eleven miles, was discovered at its mouth on the Gulf of California by a Spaniard—Francisco de Ulloa—in September 1539, almost forty-seven years after Columbus landed in the New World. Ulloa apparently did not name the great river he discovered. But over the next century and a half, at least four titles were given to the watercourse by Spanish explorers. By about 1700 its present name was in use, although the identity of the designator is unestablished.

Colorado is a Spanish adjective meaning reddish. When the river was first called Colorado, its far-upstream geography was largely unknown to the Spaniards—a *Tierra Incógnita*. Later two large rivers were discovered and named: the Green—descriptively titled *Río Verde* by the Spanish because vegetation along its banks contrasts with the otherwise generally barren country through which the river flows in its lower course—and what was initially called the Grand—a tribute to its size. Subsequently, they were found to join and their combined flow to create what was farther downstream known as the Colorado. Thus, the Colorado was originally formed by the union of two other rivers, just as the Ohio is formed by the junction of the Allegheny and Monongahela at Pittsburgh, Pennsylvania.

The junction of the Green and what was first known as the Grand is now called The Confluence. It is in Utah, in the heart of the rugged wilderness of Canyonlands National Park, sixty-four miles downstream from Arches, and about 1,120 miles above the Colorado's mouth in Mexico.

First bridge across the Colorado River at Arches was constructed in 1911-12. An improved span replaced the original in 1955.

At The Confluence, the Green enters from the north, and what was originally the Grand from the northeast. Of the two, the Green, which rises in the Wind River Range of southwestern Wyoming, is longer, and drains a larger basin than the former Grand. But the Green has a somewhat smaller average annual discharge due to relatively lighter precipitation over much of its basin.

The river once called the Grand has its headwaters on the western slope of the Colorado Rocky Mountains. Its length is only about one-half that of the Green, and most of its course was in Colorado state.

Usually, the longest tributary of a river is considered its main stem, and carries the system's principal name. Accordingly, the Green should have been originally called Colorado. In 1921, a bill was introduced in the Utah legislature to change the Green's name to Colorado, but the measure was defeated.

The state of Colorado and its predecessor, the Territory of Colorado, was named for the river. However, when in 1861 the territory was created and named, there was no river with that title in the territory! It was then believed—mistakenly—that the famous Colorado River flowed in the territory. Fifteen years later, in 1876, when Colorado gained statehood there still was no river by that name within its boundaries.

For sixty years the geographical inconsistency existed. Finally, sensitive to this discrepancy, Coloradans campaigned to change the Grand's title to Colorado, thus extending the great river's name upstream into the state. Their efforts were crowned with success in 1921 when the Colorado legislature passed an act that was approved by the governor on March 24, and Congress enacted a bill signed on July 25 by President Warren G. Harding, changing the Grand's designation to Colorado.

Whatever its name, the river always was, and always will be, grand—the grand Colorado!

SUGGESTED READINGS AND MAPS

BOOKS

Geology

Baars, Donald L. *Red Rock Country*. Garden City, New York: Doubleday/Natural History Press, 1972.

Baars, D. L., and Molenaar, C. M. *Geology of Canyonlands and Cataract Canyon*. Durango, Colorado: Four Corners Geological Society, 1971.

Stokes, William Lee. *Scenes of the Plateau Lands and How They Came To Be*. Third edition. Salt Lake City, Utah: William Lee Stokes, 1973.

Plants and Animals

Behle, William H., and Perry, Michael L. *Utah Birds*. Salt Lake City, Utah: Utah Museum of Natural History, University of Utah, 1975.

Dodge, Natt N. *Poisonous Dwellers of the Desert*. Globe, Arizona: Southwest Parks and Monuments Association, 1974.

Earle, W. Hubert. *Cacti of the Southwest*. Phoenix, Arizona: Desert Botanical Garden of Arizona, 1963.

Elmore, Francis H. *Shrubs and Trees of the Southwest Uplands*. Globe, Arizona: Southwest Parks and Monuments Association, 1976.

Heymann, M. M. *Reptiles and Amphibians of the American Southwest*. Scottsdale, Arizona: Doubleshoe Publishers, 1975.

Jaeger, Edmund C. *Desert Wildlife*. Stanford, California: Stanford University Press, 1961.

Johnson, Carl M. *Common Native Trees of Utah*. Logan, Utah: Agricultural Experiment Station, Utah State University, 1970.

Olin, George. *Mammals of the Southwest Mountains and Mesas*. Globe, Arizona: Southwest Parks and Monuments Association, 1971.

Shaw, Charles E., and Campbell, Sheldon. *Snakes of the American West*. New York, New York: Alfred A. Knopf, Inc., 1974.

Sigler, William F. *Fishes of Utah*. Salt Lake City, Utah: Utah State Department of Fish and Game, 1963.

Welsh, Stanley L. *Flowers of the Canyon Country*. Provo, Utah: Brigham Young University Press, 1971.

Welsh, Stanley L., and Moore, Glen. *Utah Plants*. Third edition. Provo, Utah: Brigham Young University Press, 1973.

Indians

Ambler, J. Richard. *The Anasazi*. Flagstaff, Arizona: Museum of Northern Arizona, 1977.

Dutton, Bertha P. *Indians of the American Southwest*. Englewood Cliffs, New Jersey: Prentice-Hall, Inc., 1975.

Jefferson, James; Delaney, Robert W.; and Thompson, Gregory C. *The Southern Utes: A Tribal History*. Second edition. Ignacio, Colorado: Southern Ute Tribe, 1973.

Lyman, June, and Denver, Norma. Edited by Floyd A. O'Neil and John D. Sylvester. *Ute People: An Historical Study*. Salt Lake City, Utah: Uintah School District and the Western History Center, University of Utah, 1969.

Schaafsma, Polly. *The Rock Art of Utah*. Cambridge, Massachusetts: Peabody Museum of Archaeology and Ethnology, Harvard University, 1971.

History

Crampton, C. Gregory. *Standing Up Country: The Canyon Lands of Utah and Arizona*. New York, New York: Alfred A. Knopf and University of Utah Press, in association with the Amon Carter Museum of Western Art, 1964.

Peterson, Charles S. *Look to the Mountains: Southeast Utah and the La Sal National Forest*. Provo, Utah: Brigham Young University Press, 1975.

Miscellaneous

Abbey, Edward. *Desert Solitaire: A Season in the Wilderness*. New York, New York: McGraw-Hill Book Company, 1968.

Belknap, Bill, and Belknap, Buzz. *Canyonlands River Guide*. Boulder City, Nevada: Westwater Books, 1974.

Doolittle, Jerome, and the editors of Time-Life Books. *Canyons and Mesas*. New York, New York: Time-Life Books, 1974.

Larson, Peggy. *The Deserts of the Southwest*. San Francisco, California: Sierra Club Books, 1977.

MAPS

Arches National Park. Topographic map: scale 1:50,000, contour interval 80 feet. Reston, Virginia: U.S. Geological Survey, 1974.

Arches National Park. Perspective map, drawn by Jean-Claude Gal. Moab, Utah: Lin Ottinger's Tours, 1973.

Red Window

ACKNOWLEDGMENTS

John Donne, English poet and theologian, wrote aptly in 1623: "No man is an island, entire of itself; every man is a piece of the continent, a part of the main. . . ." So it is with this book. Many sources were consulted and used in its preparation, though any and all errors are, of course, the author's sole responsibility. Information and assistance were obtained from a host of people, from several historical societies and museums, from various governmental agencies, from many businesses, and other organizations. The author wishes to single out and to thank in particular for their cooperation:

FIRST EDITION (1981)

Ralph and Marie Hoffman, Riverside, California (*por la fe que tuvieron en este libro y por el apoyo generoso y sincero para este fin*); Board of Trustees, Canyonlands Natural History Association, Moab, Utah: Donald P. Knowles, Jr. (chairman), E. J. Claus, Dee T. Tranter, Gwen Halls, Bates E. Wilson, Peter L. Parry, and David D. May (executive secretary); staff of Arches National Park, Moab, Utah: with special thanks to Peter L. Parry (superintendent), Larry D. Reed (unit manager), James W. Capps (park interpreter), Maxine Newell (park technician), Thomas C. Wylie (park ranger), David D. May (park ranger), and Jim Stiles (seasonal park ranger); Samuel J. Taylor and Adrien F. Taylor, Moab, Utah: publishers and editors, *The Times-Independent*; Donald L. Baars, Evergreen, Colorado; Russell L. Mahan, St. George, Utah; George

J. Andersen, Moab, Utah; Stanley W. Midgley, Jr., Flintridge, California; Roby R. ("Slim") Mabery, Moab, Utah; Susan B. Dutson, Delta, Utah: editor and publisher, *Millard County Chronicle*; Jackson C. Thode, Denver, Colorado; Harold H. Leich, Bethesda, Maryland; Alex E. Creswell, Hood River, Oregon; Mrs. Fred D. Ayres, Portland, Oregon; Miss Irene Ayres, Gainesville, Florida; Mr. and Mrs. Dallas Tanner, Moab, Utah; Lloyd Pierson, Moab, Utah; Laurence M. Gould, Tucson, Arizona; Mrs. Mary Pogue, Moab, Utah; Mrs. Anna Semisch, Crystal Lake, Illinois; Doug Travers, San Antonio, Texas; Mrs. Frank Shields, Moab, Utah; Philip S. Miner, Salt Lake City, Utah; Cecil S. Thomson, Moab, Utah; Mrs. Gilbert P. Tonne, San Angelo, Texas; Library, Arches National Park, Moab, Utah; Colorado Historical Society, Denver, Colorado; Utah State Historical Society, Salt Lake City, Utah: Melvin T. Smith (director), Jay M. Haymond (librarian), Mrs. Margaret D. Lester, and Mrs. Martha R. Stewart; Field Museum of Natural History, Chicago, Illinois; Moab Museum, Moab, Utah: Mrs. Virginia Fossey; Western History Department, Denver Public Library, Denver, Colorado; Grand County Public Library, Moab, Utah; Mrs. Gloria Denney; Salt Lake City Public Library, Salt Lake City, Utah; San Diego Public Library, San Diego, California; Malcolm A. Love Library, San Diego State University, San Diego, California; Library, Scripps Institution of Oceanography, University of California, San Diego, La Jolla, California; National Park Service, Washington, D.C.: Harry W. Pfanz (chief historian) and Barry McIntosh; National Archives and Records Service, Washington, D.C.; Photographic Library, U.S. Geological Survey, Denver, Colorado: Marjorie Dalechek (chief); Natural History Museum, San Diego, California: Reid Moran (curator of botany) and David K. Faulkner (curator of entomology); Grand County Recorder, Moab, Utah; Cabrillo National Monument, San Diego, California: Howard B. Overton (chief ranger); Reed College, Portland, Oregon: Helen Fernandez (assistant to director, information services); The American Alpine Club, New York, New York; *Desert Magazine*, Encinitas, California: Julie Brazeau (publisher); Milt's Stop-N-Eat, Moab, Utah: Milt and Audrey Galbraith; Spencers' Printing and Stationery, Moab, Utah: Juanita Spencer and Randy Spencer; Tag-A-Long Tours, Moab, Utah: Mitch Williams; Mustang Aviation, Inc., Moab, Utah: Bill Groff (pilot); Lin Ottinger's Tours, Moab, Utah: Lin and Marian Ottinger; Thompson Type, San Diego, California: Jon R. Swaim, John Pierce, and Dennis Wood; American Color Corporation, San Diego, California: Emory Brazell; Arts & Crafts Press, San Diego, California: Roy L. Hutt (vice president) and Frank Anker (superintendent); Phillips and Phillips, attorneys at law, San Diego, California: Frank S. Phillips and Susan B. Phillips; San Diego Trust & Savings Bank, San Diego, California: D. A. Raush (vice president).

SECOND EDITION (1985)

Board of Trustees, Canyonlands Natural History Association, Moab, Utah: Russ Donoghue (chairman), E. J. Claus, Gwen Halls, Sue Halliday, Donald P. Knowles, Jr., David D. May, Dee T. Tranter, Del Backus, Peter L. Parry, and Jerry Rumburg, and Eleanor Inskip, executive director; Arches National Park, Moab, Utah: Sherma Bierhaus (unit manager), Joan Swanson (chief ranger), Anna Marie Fender (chief interpreter), and Steve Swanke (park ranger); Tag-A-Long Tours, Moab, Utah: Paul Niskanen and Bob Jones; Dale J. Stevens, Brigham Young University, Provo, Utah; Hugh S. Bell, Sierra Madre, California; Mark Sakovich, Fort Worth, Texas; Dan Julien, Flagstaff, Arizona; Ron Olevsky, La Verkin, Utah; Thompson Type, San Diego, California: Ruth Dixon (typographer), Bob Dehm (quality control manager), and Joe Dunn (night foreman); Arts & Crafts Press, San Diego, California: Robert J. Salt (president), Doug Town (superintendent), Gerd Sittel (production), and Al Mason (pre-press preparation).

INDEX

Page numbers in regular type are references to the text; in italics to photographs, drawings, maps, and charts.